D0848381

ANONYMITY

Studies in Phenomenology and Existential Philosophy

ANONYMITY

A Study in the Philosophy
of Alfred Schutz

MAURICE NATANSON

INDIANA UNIVERSITY PRESS   •   BLOOMINGTON

Manufactured in the United States of America

Library of Congress Cataloging-in-Publication Data

Natanson, Maurice Alexander, 1924–
  Anonymity : a study in the philosophy of Alfred Schutz.

  (Studies in phenomenology and existential philosophy)
  Bibliography: p.
  Includes index.
  1. Schutz, Alfred, 1899–1959. I. Title.
III. Series.
B945.S354N37 1986   193   85–45989
ISBN 0–253–30746–5

1   2   3   4   5   90   89   88   87   86

LOIS

CONTENTS

ACKNOWLEDGMENT

.

Schutz has been my guide to Schutz.
Where I have been misguided, I alone
led the way.

PREFACE

> In older languages there was often no verb
> and survivals of this older type of sentence
> are still common: *Nobody here? Everybody
> gone?*
>
> —George O. Curme, *A Grammer of the
> English Language*, Vol. II: *Syntax*, 2.

> A large and appreciative gathering of
> friends and acquaintances from the
> metropolis and greater Dublin assembled
> in their thousands to bid farewell to
> Nagyaságos uram Lipóti Virag, late of
> Messrs Alexander Thom's, printers to His
> Majesty, on the occasion of his departure
> for the distant clime of
> Százharminczbrojúgulyás-Dugulás (Meadow
> of Murmuring Waters). The ceremony
> which went off with great *éclat* was
> characterised by the most affecting
> cordiality. An illuminated scroll of ancient
> vellum, the work of Irish artists, was
> presented to the distinguished
> phenomenologist on behalf of a large
> section of the community and was
> accompanied by the gift of a silver casket,
> tastefully executed in the style of ancient
> Celtic ornament, a work which reflects
> every credit on the makers, Messrs Jacob
> *agus* Jacob.
>
> —James Joyce, *Ulysses*, 336–337.

"For whom does one write?" asked Jean-Paul Sartre. Damned if I know. But I do know for whom I have written this book: for myself! And for my sodality: actors, artists, writers, and other pickpockets. Admit as well the laity of old blurbs: philosophers, sociologists, psychologists, and bell ringers. I exclude only those who would remind me that, under certain circumstances, the United States Post Office *will* accept personal checks. No rush to these pages is anticipated; but there will be a fire: philosophy is incandescent.

Here is the way in which I came to write this book. I first heard of

Alfred Schutz about 1949 from Professor William H. Werkmeister. In a graduate seminar on the philosophy of the social sciences, directed by Dr. Werkmeister, I was asked to present an account of Schutz's essay "On Multiple Realities" (originally published in *Philosophy and Phenomenological Research* in 1945). Werkmeister was one of the first philosophers to cite "On Multiple Realities."[1] A little later, I made use of Schutz's essay "Sartre's Theory of the Alter Ego" in other work I was doing. A year after receiving my Ph.D., I went to New York City—a native son returning—to study with Alfred Schutz at the Graduate Faculty of the New School for Social Research. In addition to taking all the courses I could with him and auditing what he offered during the period of my stay at the New School—1951–1953—I enrolled in a tutorial with Dr. Schutz in which we discussed the phenomenology of Edmund Husserl. In effect (after the credit disappeared from my transcript), that tutorial lasted for two years. More important to me, it lasted until Schutz died—lasted by occasional visits on my part to New York (after I had taken a position far away), correspondence, telephone conversations, reading and doing some work on his manuscripts, and receiving his response and criticism to the papers I wrote and always sent to him. He was an appreciative, sympathetic but quite demanding critic.

From time to time, for about thirty-five years, I have been writing articles having to do with the thought of Alfred Schutz, philosophy of the social sciences, and subjects such as anonymity, social role, and death. In preparing for my work on the present book, I have avoided rereading my earlier essays. It has not been my intention to stitch together already published pieces of work but rather to think through afresh themes which have occupied me for a long time. I know, from memory, that I have repeated a number of quotations which I have previously used; that was inevitable. I also know that I have retold a story or two. I may have repeated some of the same sentences or expressions. Such repetitions do not concern me. This is a new venture; as far as my earlier work goes, I can only hope for overall consistency. In any case, this book must stand on its own.

Perhaps every book should come with a bill of lading. The first declaration to be made is that both my title and my subtitle are misnomers. The subject of "anonymity" is vast; I have taken up a

1. W. H. Werkmeister, *The Basis and Structure of Knowledge*, New York: Harper, 1948, Bibliography for Ch. III: "The World About Us," p. 423.

small but, I am convinced, significant aspect of that theme. I look forward someday to reading a magnificent treatise by a magisterial thinker whose examination of "anonymity" includes the place of that subject not only in philosophy and in the social sciences, but in world literature, history, art, comparative religion, and many other realms. I wish that author well. My own efforts, by contrast, are small fry. But even in philosophy, I have modest pretentions. A book such as mine might very well profit from the inclusion of detailed studies of relevant problems in Kierkegaard, Heidegger, and Sartre—thinkers I have referred to but have hardly investigated thoroughly. Some of the writers to whom I have referred in passing have had interesting things to say about anonymity but I have not gone into their views. Merleau-Ponty, for example, speaks of a "double anonymity"[2]—I have put his views to the side, largely. I remain content that I have done what I wanted to do. But—and here one might least expect it—the subtitle I have employed does not tell the truth: the "philosophy" of Alfred Schutz, strictly speaking, was never formulated. Of course, "philosophy" might pass as a general term of reference to Schutz's thought. The reader will find out that I am concerned with "philosophy" in a much more rigorous sense in Schutz's work. Yet I am satisfied that my title makes a large, if unfulfilled, gesture and that my subtitle limits my theme in a paradoxical manner.

Another declaration is in order: In the consideration of Schutz's thought, there are a number of quite central concepts to which I pay but minimum or no attention. It is not my view that "anonymity" is Schutz's leading idea or that it is more significant in its interpretive power than "relevance" or "typification" or still other Schutzian concepts. I rest my case, for the moment, by contending that "anonymity" *is* a most productive notion and that it is well worth the reader's effort to meditate on its implications. It should also be pointed out that I have not given equal emphasis to all of Schutz's writings, that I have given the greatest weight to those works which were published during his lifetime, and that his unpublished papers have not provided me with material for this book. Furthermore, this is not the kind of book in which the author reviews the secondary literature in the field, establishes a hierarchy of value for—in this case—Schutz's critics, points out errors, corrects misconceptions, leads wayward

2. Maurice Merleau-Ponty, *Phenomenology of Perception* (trans. by Colin Smith), New York: Humanities Press, 1962, p. 448.

authors back on the right track, immobolizes wretched thinkers with devastating thunderbolts, and, altogether, sets the Schutzian world aright. With one exception (and even that exception I do not regard as a true departure from my rule), I have pretty much set aside the literature on Schutz, his commentators and his critics. It is important for someone to sift through the large secondary literature devoted to his work. I choose not to be that someone. I choose to follow my own towpath, urging on the elements in Schutz's work which form my subject matter. Periodically, the reader will hear a shout or a moan as I move along, but he should ignore such cries. Part of my equanimity in pursuing a solitary bent is that I do not think of myself as in competition with other writers on Schutz. He always spoke of "common work." And that brings me to a particular point.

At times in these pages I quote or refer to something which Schutz said to me. I would prefer not to be misunderstood. My reason for writing "as Schutz once said to me" is simply to put on record statements which I remember with complete clarity and which I think deserve recording. It hardly follows that I am the only person to whom Schutz said most of these things, but I consider them valuable and have not seen them reported elsewhere. I have no wish to give the reader the impression that Schutz and I were on such close terms that he said special things to me which this book alone reveals. I take a straightforward view of the matter: here are some statements which I think interesting at least to those who are interested in Schutz. I remember them clearly and I have preserved them. Nothing else. A story which Schutz told me says it all: "In my twenties," Schutz said, "it was me and Mozart. In my thirties, it was Mozart and me. Now in my fifties, it is only Mozart."

I refuse to end with the pious formula. "I shall be satisfied if my efforts lead the reader to my author's books." Bosh! I want the reader for my own; read *me*! But can anyone do so and not find Schutz?

ANONYMITY

I

INTRODUCTION

To speak of the phenomenology of the social world is to speak of Alfred Schutz. He, more than anyone else, carried the authentic impulse of Husserl's thought to the realm of daily life, its essential structure, the order of its building—its constitution—and the modes of its unfolding as our world. In a reading of the works of Schutz, the first and lasting impression which is given is that traditional boundaries between philosophy and social science have been not so much transcended as undercut: the phenomena which the sociologist has customarily considered part of his bailiwick have been reapproached in more originary terms, have been intellectually seized in a more nearly neutral manner. The result is not a tug of war between academic antagonists but a recovery on all sides of questions which the strife of disciplines has tended to obscure or predetermine in divisive and often perverse ways. The embarrassment of common work replaces the inherited circumstance of being watchers and warders. The embarrassment is over the propriety of questions.

The matter of questions might be considered in this way: In scientific inquiry, what will count as a positive result will be determined by the criterion of evidence which, whether overtly or tacitly, has been accepted by the investigator. If the kind of result needed as well as desired is something intersubjectively verifiable, then the questions posed must be preshaped to locate those results which conform to the criterion; other findings may not be totally discarded but they will, at best, be set aside for further scrutiny, for reconsideration if more refined methods of procedure are developed. In sum, if one insists on certain kinds of results, then certain kinds of questions will be fashioned so that suitable methods may be used to try to reach appropriate conclusions or give adequate placement in the corpus of knowledge to states of affairs which stand in need of explanation. The work of the scientific-minded social scientist is not radically different. The horizon of questioning is quite open for all scientists; the choices made by the inquirer as to which questions are of decisive importance in the course of his work—those choices are part of a philosophical confession.

In philosophy, both results and questions are placed under house arrest. Directives come from obscure quarters; it is not always—if ever—possible to distinguish between the accusers and the accused. This unsettlement is akin to alienation in the psychiatric sense: academic philosophy may be the last stronghold of subsidized madness. What remains clear in philosophy is that questioning is not limitable, that part of philosophy consists and must consist of reflection on what is meant by nonlimitability. What is already known, not only by scientific analysis but in the splendid case of the individual's grasp of his own experience, comes by an interior recursion to be illuminated by philosophy. In the elegant formulation of Michael Oakeshott, "Philosophical reflection is recognized here as the adventure of one who seeks to understand in other terms what he already understands and in which the understanding sought (itself unavoidably conditional) is a disclosure of the conditions of the understanding enjoyed and not a substitute for it."[1]

The most searching of Schutz's questions concern the taken-for-granted world of daily life—"taken-for-granted," in Schutz's terminology, because the existence of everyday reality is the tacit condition for there being the differentiated world each of us experiences: the world of persons, events, and meanings. "The term 'taken for granted,'" Schutz writes, ". . . means to accept until further notice our knowledge of certain states of affairs as unquestionably plausible. Of course, at any time that which seemed to be hitherto unquestionable might be put in question. Common-sense thinking simply takes for granted, until counterevidence appears, not only the world of physical objects but also the sociocultural world into which we are born and in which we grow up. This world of everyday life is indeed the unquestioned but always questionable matrix within which all our inquiries start and end."[2] The term "taken for granted" is not a casual

1. Michael Oakeshott, *On Human Conduct*, Oxford: The Clarendon Press, 1975, p. vii.

2. Alfred Schutz, *Collected Papers*, Vol. I: *The Problem of Social Reality* (edited and introduced by Maurice Natanson with a preface by H. L. Van Breda), The Hague: Martinus Nijhoff, 1962, pp. 326–327. Note: Hereafter abbreviated as CPI.

usage in Schutz's writings; in fact, he told me that he once planned to write a book entitled "The World as Taken for Granted." That plan remained unrealized but the idea of the taken-for-granted (which I think of as hyphenated) saturates Schutz's work. Accepting the world as "unquestionably plausible" implies the rootage of the individual in a reality which is at once his and ours. "World" and "reality" are tacitly held to be integral: what is valid for me, in common-sense thinking, is—other things being equal—valid for you and for "them," the Others in our world of daily life. "Other things being equal"—that deeply satisfying and reassuring murmur which breathes through *caeteris paribus*—means that *typically* similar states of affairs will retain their *typically* stable proportions and characteristics, that nothing is expected to intervene which will upset typicality's apple cart.

Of course, other things are frequently not equal: our plans are tampered with or blocked by unexpected circumstances, what worked well in the past proves no longer reliable, the typified "Other," so staunch a companion of our everyday adventures, suddenly becomes treacherous. The taken-for-granted, however, is not easily dismayed, let alone defeated. If one course of action comes to be untrustworthy, another course of action will replace it. But then, "other things being equal" will still apply to the replacement. The sentiment of typicality is unavoidable. The root of the taken-for-granted is what Husserl called "the general thesis of the natural standpoint."[3] In a familiar passage in his book *Ideas*, Husserl displays the essential feature of the "general thesis." I will present the quotation in Professor Frederick Kersten's translation (which gives a new intonation to older language). Husserl writes:

> . . . in the following propositions we single out something most important. As what confronts me, I continually find the one spatiotemporal actuality to which I belong like all other beings who are to be found in it and who are related to it as I am. I find the "actuality," the word already says it, as a *factually existent actuality and also accept it as it presents*

3. Edmund Husserl, *Ideas: General Introduction to Pure Phenomenology* (trans. by W. R. Boyce Gibson), New York: Macmillan, 1931, p. 105. Note: The original is "Die Generalthesis der natürlichen Einstellung" in *Ideen zu einer reinen Phänomenologie und phänomenologischen Philosophie* (*Jahrbuch für Philosophie und phänomenologische Forschung*), Erster Band, Teil I (Zweiter unveränderter Abdruck), Halle: Max Niemeyer, 1922, p. 52ff. Note: Cf. the new translation by F. Kersten: *Ideas Pertaining to a Pure Phenomenology and to a Phenomenological Philosophy*, First Book: *General Introduction to a Pure Phenomenology*, The Hague: Martinus Nijhoff, 1982. Kersten's version: "The General Positing Which Characterizes the Natural Attitude" (p. 56).

itself to me as factually existing. No doubt about or rejection of data belonging to the natural world alters in any respect the *general positing
which characterizes the natural attitude.* "The" world is always there as an
actuality; here and there it is at most "otherwise" than I supposed; this
or that is, so to speak, to be struck *out of it* and given such titles as
"illusion" and "hallucination," and the like; it is to be struck out of "the"
world which—according to the general positing—is always factually
existent. To cognize "the" world more comprehensively, more reliably,
more perfectly in every respect than naive experiential cognizance can,
to solve all the problems of scientific cognition which offer themselves
within the realm of the world, that is the aim of the *sciences belonging
to the natural attitude.*[4]

The "actuality" is "factually existent" in an oblique sense: nothing
has been demonstrated or tested which might lead one to say, "Yes,
this is actual." By the same token, when one says, "No, this is illusory,"
the "factually existent" over and against which the illusory is discovered is not authenticated by something other than itself. The "actuality" with which we are concerned here is naively available to any
perceiver as the *current* of his perception rather than an objectivity
like any other—a something "cut-outable" from experience. To say
that actuality is "factually existent" is to express the manner in which
the actual is seized *through* perception (understood in the broadest
sense) rather than to make claims about what is *given* as though it
were still an object among others in the world. The sense of actuality
as factually existent is not equivalent to a claim about the reality status
of the given. "Actuality," for Husserl, is the primordial presence of
what is given to the perceiver—to each of us in the world—as the
taken-for-granted ground of our believing in mundane reality. The
reflective ascription of "actuality" to the "factually existent" would
phenomenologically presuppose the "general thesis of the natural attitude."

The essential source of the taken-for-granted, then, is embodied in
the immanent claim of individual existence that that existence is part
of actuality, part of an on-going world "out there" whose reality is
incontestable. Surely, it is rarely the case that the individual whose
existence we are discussing stops in the midst of his daily routine and
says: "Hark! Is that not the hum of mundanity?" If anything, it is
more like someone going about humming without being aware of
humming until interrupted with "Doctor, do you usually hum while

4. Ibid., pp. 56–57 (Kersten translation).

doing root canal procedures?" If the patient undergoing treatment is not in a position to ask that question, the phenomenologist is. Rather than turning to a psychological theory of the unconscious to explain the nonreflective sense of the real, I think it more interesting, let alone philosophically prudent, to look more closely at the structure of consciousness at work in nonreflective modes. For Schutz, the central way in which the individual grasps the actuality of mundane life is through the typification of daily, taken-for-granted being with Others. "Typification" is fundamental to Schutz's vocabulary; his language is incomprehensible without it. Most of Schutz's discussions of typification are introduced by or presuppose a reference to Husserl's theory of pre-predicative experience. "The world, as has been shown by Husserl, is from the outset experienced in the pre-scientific thinking of everyday life in the mode of typicality. The unique objects and events given to us in a unique aspect are unique within a horizon of typical familiarity and pre-acquaintanceship."[5] More fully:

> The factual world of our experience . . . is experienced from the outset as a typical one. Objects are experienced as trees, animals, and the like, and more specifically as oaks, firs, maples, or rattlesnakes, sparrows, dogs. This table I am now perceiving is characterized as something recognized, as something foreknown and, nevertheless, novel. What is newly experienced is already known in the sense that it recalls similar or equal things formerly perceived. But what has been grasped once in its typicality carries with it a horizon of possible experience with corresponding references to familiarity, that is, a series of typical characteristics still not actually experienced but expected to be potentially experienced."[6]

In addition to referring to types, typification, as Schutz uses the term, is a conceptual transaction which results in types. "Typification" then, means both constituting and constituted. The ambiguity which enriches the term will provide satisfactions. For the moment, let us say that the social world, according to Schutz, is a tissue of constructs. And that is certainly not to suggest that social reality is a web spun out of the filament of consciousness. It is incomparably right to say that the world in which common-sense understanding finds itself is "really real." Nothing will diminish the sense of urgency the individual feels in coming to terms with the implications and consequences of here-and-now emergencies. Philosophy was never meant to negate

5. CPI, p. 59.
6. CPI, p. 281.

life. Neither was it intended to strip life of its transcendental yearning, that is, to shun the very questions which are hidden in the sense of the "actual," questions which are generated not only by reflection but by the possibility of reflection. I am proposing nothing esoteric; to the contrary, I am saying that a "doubleness" constantly attends the taking-for-granted of the world: The social world precedes my being born into it—it is "already there"—*and* that precedence is intrinsically problematic. To whom? The expected response "To the philosopher" carries with it at least the hint that man in the "natural attitude" does not find anything about daily life which is intrinsically problematic. Rather than assuming that the issue lies between the philosopher and the ordinary person, I think it attractive to consider an alternative way of viewing matters. The issue may be approached quite differently: the "doubleness" of mundane existence may consist in the twofold givenness of the sense of the real. The raw assurance of "taking-for-granted" may be distinguished from the undeniable force of what is "taken-for-granted."

Schutz did not make the distinction about "doubleness"; I did. Before continuing the discussion, it is just as well to introduce an aside—a procedural caution. This study is neither an exposition nor a critique of the work of Alfred Schutz. I have already contributed a number of essays to Schutzian exegesis, and others have done still more in monographs and books as well as in a great many articles. As to criticism, I am ill suited for that task; my personal and intellectual allegiance to Schutz is undiminished from the time I first met him in 1951 to the present. The traditional phrase "debt of gratitude" has long ceased to do its linguistic duty. The other piece of academic claptrap is that "there is no higher tribute to a colleague than to criticize his arguments." I don't believe it! "What do you want, then, eulogies?" is the reply sometimes tendered to those who remain dissatisfied with received criticism. Not eulogies but the doing of one's own work. It is said in the Talmud that it is "better to build than to destroy." Convinced of that truth, I offer what I do as part of that "common work" which Schutz initiated. I am convinced that my reader will not cry in exasperation: "Why doesn't the man say what belongs to Schutz and what belongs to Natanson?" Where the demarcation line between us is significant, I will tell the reader what's what and what's whose regarding Schutz's ideas and my own. The time of pure exposition of Schutz's thought is largely over; the time of serious

criticism of his work is upon us, but it should be carried out by someone with different philosophical commitments than my own. What
remains is the task of reconstructing Schutz's philosophical life by
carrying forward what he began and by assessing his accomplishment
in immanent but not subservient terms. That reconstruction is my
intent in this essay; but I must follow—try to advance—in my own
way.

To return to the "doubleness" of mundane existence: "Taking-for-
granted" may be understood as the activity of the General Thesis of
the Natural Attitude—the originary process through which the individual *has* a reliable world; the "taken-for-granted" are those states
of affairs in ordinary life which the General Thesis posits: that the
world is real, that the world has a history, that the world is composed
of Others as well as ourselves, that we can communicate with Others,
that language is a normal as well as necessary feature of the social
world. Schutz, in his lectures, used to speak of "metaphysical constants" of human experience: that we are born, that we grow older,
that we must die—but also that everywhere it is normal for children
to play, that we must wait for certain things to happen—for sugar to
dissolve in our tea, for our wounds to heal—and that we do not just
throw out the dead but bury them. All the differences between cultures
and between historical periods leave standing a core of what is essentially human. These constants are taken-for-granted; the manner in
which they are appropriated by us is what makes up the taking-for-
granted at issue. Although I cannot here undertake a phenomenology
of pre-predicative experience, I hope to explore, in the course of this
essay, some of the structural aspects of "taking" and "taken" for grant-
edness and to place them in the still larger context of Schutz's phenomenology of the social world—his anatomy of the mundane. Before
any Schutzian business can be conducted, a preliminary question must
be raised and answered: What is Schutz's conception of social reality?

Once more: the social world is a tissue of constructs. For Schutz,
the individual actor on the social scene stands at the "null point," the
intersection of temporal and spatial coordinates which frame a life.
Underlying the "now" and "here" placement of the individual in the
observer's world is the phenomenological location of the person in
the "life-world." Schutz grounds his conception of mundane existence
in Husserl's theory of Man and Nature. Schutz's account of Husserl's
doctrine illuminates his own conception:

> The constitution of the world of culture, similar to the constitution of
> any "world," including the world of one's own stream of experience,
> has the lawful structure of a constitution, oriented with respect to a
> "null point" (*Nullglied*), i.e., to a personality. Here am I and my culture;
> it is accessible to me and to my cultural companions as a kind of ex-
> perience of Others. Other cultural humanity and other culture can
> become accessible only by a complicated process of understanding,
> namely, on the basic level of the common Nature, which, in its specific
> spatio-temporal structure, constitutes the horizon of being for the ac-
> cessibility to all the manifold cultural phenomena. As Nature is thus
> concretely and uniformly constituted, so human existence itself is re-
> ferred to an existent life-world as a realm of practical activity, which,
> from the first, is endowed with human significations.[7]

Egologically put, I am at the center of the world; "here" is where
my body is and "there" is the place occupied by the Other; "now" is
the present in which I find myself; "the world" is experienced by me
as an intersubjective reality; the aperture through which I glimpse
"the world" is a feature of my "biographical situation," as Schutz calls
it; my biographical situation includes the particular "stock of knowledge"— in Schutz's language—which I have at hand at any time; what
I presuppose, how I am motivated, and my action in the social world
depend upon an interconnected system of "relevances" which guide
me in my human career; the social world includes predecessors, contemporaries, "consociates" (those contemporaries, according to
Schutz, with whom I share space and time), and successors; I rely on
the future to be more or less like the past; my "projects of action" are
based on formulas which have worked so far; I typify the world.

This staccato account of Schutz's view of social reality should be
relieved by a more patient definition of "social reality." The phrase is
used deliberately by Schutz; the meaning of it matters. "By the term
'social reality,' " he writes, "I wish to be understood the sum total of
objects and occurrences within the social cultural world as experienced
by the common-sense thinking of men living their daily lives among
their fellow-men, connected with them in manifold relations of interaction."[8] The reality which Schutz explores is the structure of the
everyday world as experienced, i.e., as understood or as interpreted,
by human beings, living their lives as ordinary people in the midst of
the ordinary world. The first distinction to be drawn here is between

7. CPI, p. 127.
8. CPI, p. 53.

"ordinary" people and "scientific observers." As an ordinary man in ordinary life I tacitly assume that not only am I a real being in a real world which I share with other real human beings but that the meaning of "real" in this case is of no interest to myself or to my fellowmen. Under ordinary circumstances, real is real. Unless there is a question of hallucination or some quite remarkable set of circumstances, there is no need to seek clarification or confirmation regarding what is real. The placement of quotation marks around the word "real" usually means that a philosopher or scientist is at work. There was once a professor of philosophy—a neo-Hegelian idealist—who used to ask in class: "The table, is it real?"; "the chair, is it real?" His chant was persistent and became his trademark. At a faculty-student softball game, he was struck in the stomach by a line drive, and when he doubled up in pain, the students in the stands cried in unison: "Is it real, professor, is it real?"

As a philosopher, the meaning of "real" is part of my business. The social scientist is also concerned with what is meant by "real." There are significant differences between the ways in which philosophers and social scientists approach the meaning of "real." Rather than discuss those differences now, I think that it is more pressing to distinguish between the individual as an actor on the social scene and the individual as a formal, "science-bound" observer. Most simply, the actor interprets an event in his world naively, that is, as something which means whatever it means to *him*, whereas the observer must place the meaning of the event in the system of interpretation whose rules are defined by the science he represents. What limits the actor in his interpretations is the common-sense reality whose "rules" are largely unformulated and frequently inconsistent and whose logic remains opaque to the individual. The formal observer must answer to his scientific discipline, to the demands made upon him by scientific discourse with his colleagues, to professional strictures. But there is a deeper difference between the two kinds of interpreters and their interpretations. Constructs of different levels are involved. Schutz writes:

> The thought objects constructed by the social scientist, in order to grasp . . . social reality, have to be founded upon the thought objects constructed by the common-sense thinking of men, living their daily life within their social world. Thus, the constructs of the social sciences

are, so to speak, constructs of the constructs made by the actors on the
social scene, whose behavior the social scientist has to observe and to
explain in accordance with the procedural rules of his science.[9]

One possible misunderstanding can be disposed of quickly. It is
obviously the case that in ordinary life the actor is also, at times, an
observer. And, of course, the formal observer is also an individual in
the ordinary world. But the common-sense observer has his center in
daily life; his observation presupposes the taken-for-granted world
and is also a part of that world. The formal observer departs from
and returns to the everyday world, a perennial commuter. Not only
an "outside" interruption—a knock on his office door, a telephone
call—will "return" him to everydayness but "inside" interferences are
common: worry about his bank balance, a bad review, the sudden
memory of someone glimpsed many years ago, a seemingly inexpli-
cable fantasy. Matters here are not difficult to set right. The ordinary
actor may have an area of expertise; the scientific observer does not
cease to be a human being. Unlike objects in nature—stones and cab-
bages—human beings are, in Schutz terms, "preinterpreted" realities,
microcosms who bear their own historical being as the condition of
their humanity. In coming across a stone, I confront something *in* the
world; in meeting a fellow human being I encounter a world.

"Social reality," then, may be understood from two quite distinct
vantage points: that of the individual in the life-world and that of the
social scientist in the role of disinterested observer. Properly conceived, according to Schutz, it is the scientist's task to establish and
rank "second-order" constructs which are faithful not only to what
the actor *does* but to what the actor means by what he does, to how
the actor interprets the meaning of his own act. Here we come to a
fundamental source of Schutz's conception of subjectivity and the
nature of social action. It is to Max Weber's methodology that Schutz
turns for the paradigm concept of action. According to Weber:

> In "action" is included all human behaviour when and in so far as the
> acting individual attaches a subjective meaning to it. Action in this sense
> may be either overt or purely inward or subjective; it may consist of
> positive intervention in a situation, or of deliberately refraining from
> such intervention or passively acquiescing in the situation. Action is
> social in so far as, by virtue of the subjective meaning attached to it by

9. CPI, p. 59.

the acting individual (or individuals), it takes account of the behaviour of others and is thereby oriented in its course.[10]

Weber's statement is presented by him under the heading "The Definition of Sociology and of Social Action." His concern is with determining the basic terms of discourse for social science. Although it is evident that "action" and "meaning" are philosophical themes of the greatest complexity, Weber is concerned with science primarily, not with philosophy. He stops short of questioning the philosophical presuppositions of his definitions not because he does not recognize that there are such presuppositions but because his work lies elsewhere. As Schutz puts it:

> . . . imposing as Weber's concept of "interpretive sociology" is, it is based on a series of tacit presuppositions. It is a matter of urgent necessity to identify these presuppositions and to state them clearly, for only a radical analysis of the genuine and basic elements of social action can provide a reliable foundation for the future progress of the social sciences. It was only when this necessity became clear to him, and then with apparent reluctance, that Max Weber concerned himself with the theoretical foundations of sociology, since he greatly preferred to work with concrete problems. He was interested in epistemological problems only insofar as they bore directly on specialized research or provided tools for its pursuit. Once these tools were at his disposal, he lost interest in the more fundamental problems.[11]

In his first book (the only one which appeared during his lifetime), *Der sinnhafte Aufbau der sozialen Welt* (posthumously published in English under the title *The Phenomenology of the Social World*), Schutz turned to Husserl and Bergson for access to a philosophical means of providing the epistemological grounding absent in Weber's theory of meaning and action. Although both Bergson and Husserl are, for Schutz, sources for a conception of inner time which is of decisive importance to Weber's ideas, still more fundamental for Schutz was Husserl's view of meaning. In his *Logical Investigations*, Husserl distinguishes between the act of intention and what is intended. *What* is intended may be intended by variant acts; the acts may be different

10. Max Weber, *The Theory of Social and Economic Organization* (trans. by A. M. Henderson and Talcott Parsons), edited with an introduction by Talcott Parsons, New York: Oxford University Press, 1947, p. 88.

11. Alfred Schutz, *The Phenomenology of the Social World* (trans. by George Walsh and Frederick Lehnert with an introduction by George Walsh), Evanston: Northwestern University Press, 1967, p. 7. Note: Hereafter abbreviated as PSW.

yet what is intended by them is the same. In the natural attitude, the individual "lives in his acts," according to Husserl; that is, the individual is immersed in a "meaning-world" whose "act-history" remains unexamined, unconsidered, immanent.[12] Within daily life, the individual does not make the distinction just made between the act of intention and what is intended; it is the phenomenologist who wrenches attention away from what is taken-for-granted and renders it an object for scrutiny. Husserl, remarking on "how complex is the correct description of a phenomenological situation," writes:

> Such complexity appears inevitable once we clearly see that all objects and relations among objects only are what they are for us, through acts of thought essentially different from them, in which they become present to us, in which they stand before us as unitary items that we *mean*. Where not the phenomenological, but the naïvely objective interest dominates, where we live in intentional acts without reflecting upon them, all talk of course becomes plain sailing and clear and devoid of circumlocution. One then, in our case, simply speaks of "expression" and of "what is expressed," of name and thing named, of the steering of attention from one to the other etc. But where the phenomenological interest dominates, we endure the hardship of having to describe phenomenological relationships which we may have experienced on countless occasions, but of which we were not normally conscious as objects, and we have also to do our describing with expressions framed to deal with objects whose appearance lies in the sphere of our mutual interests.[13]

Schutz's discussion of Husserl's theory of meaning moves from the logical sphere to that of the social. The distinction between the act of intention and what is intended gives way to an analysis of the difference between the subjective interpretation of meaning and the objective meaning-content intended. When I understand my fellow passenger on the bus, who says that the recent increase in the fare has not brought with it a comparable increase in the quality of bus service, I grasp what it is he means as well as why such a comment from a stranger falls well within the range of topics of common concern. I assume that my fellow passenger thinks that his comment is socially acceptable and that he expects an answer in kind: "Everything's going up these days." An immediate impasse would be reached

12. "Living in one's acts" is Husserl's language but I am responsible for "meaning-world" and "act-history."

13. Edmund Husserl, *Logical Investigations* (trans. by J. N. Findlay), London: Routledge and Kegan Paul, 1970, Vol. I, pp. 283–284.

if I instead replied: "Why don't you keep your filthy little thoughts to yourself?" Or: "If you don't like your Uncle Sammy, then go back to your home o'er the sea." Most often, the exchange of banalities is secured by veering away from potentially harmful shoals—politics, sex, religion, race, nationality are subjects that are broached only when it is thought safe or relatively safe to do so. In the initial moment of his speech, however, these considerations have not yet arisen; I "take in" what the Other says without pausing to analyze his subjective intentions in the sense of what this concrete human being means by his particular statement. In fact, Schutz maintains, I cannot know what the Other means by his act; I can only approximate a true understanding. That approximation stops at the point at which it "works" for the situation at hand. In fine, my knowledge of the Other is typified. Yet I may comprehend the subjective meaning intended by the Other in the sense of what is *typically* intended. Schutz writes:

> Now in the social world the question can in principle be posed . . . as to what the subjective meaning is of any datum of objective meaning-content which we attribute to another mind. Furthermore, it can be asserted that it is possible to comprehend the meaning-content with a maximum degree of clarity. We can fulfill this claim if, by "subjective meaning," we mean nothing more than the referral of constituted objectivities (*Gegenständlichkeiten*) to the consciousness of others. On the other hand, we shall be unsuccessful if, by "subjective meaning," we mean the "intended meaning" of other persons. The latter remains a limiting concept even under optimum conditions of interpretation.[14]

The subjective interpretation of meaning in Weber's terms is provided by Schutz with a philosophical grounding which comes chiefly from Husserl and—though I will not give him his just due here—Bergson. Most often, Schutz's work (especially in *The Phenomenology of the Social World*) is summarized by saying that he attempted to bring together Weber and Husserl. Without being false, this summary is really not true. It is not even fully correct to say that Schutz used Husserl as a philosophical corrective to Weber. There are two levels to the discussion of the use Schutz made of Husserl in connection with Weber. We have already noticed that, according to Schutz, Weber's theory of social action needed a philosophical foundation which, again according to Schutz, Husserl's theories of inner-time consciousness and meaning could suitably provide. Here there is in-

14. PSW, pp. 37–38.

deed a meeting brought about between the two thinkers. However, the enriched ideas generated by the confrontation of Weber with Husserl cannot of themselves yield a distinctive advance either in sociology or epistemology. The mediation of Schutz in this affair must be understood at a level other than that of "confrontation manager" if we are to see what Schutz was doing in *The Phenomenology of the Social World*—the development of his own phenomenological sociology, his constitutive phenomenology of the natural attitude. Although I disagree with his assertion that Schutz's concept of the "we-relationship" owes something to Heidegger, Ricoeur is most insightful when he says: "Schutz did not, in fact, limit himself to reconciling Husserl and Weber. He integrated their concepts of intersubjectivity and social action with a concept of the we-relationship borrowed from Heidegger, without losing the force of the first two thinkers' analyses, and without limiting himself to a convenient eclecticism combining all these masters."[15]

There is a qualitative philosophical difference between a concrete we-relationship and a pure we-relationship. In face-to-face encounter with a fellow-man, I experience his presence from the outset as that of a real existent. "From the outset," phenomenologically speaking, means that I have a prepredicative experience of the Other. The pure we-relationship is a limiting concept. The phenomenological starting point for the comprehension of the we-relationship lies in what Schutz

15. Paul Ricoeur, *Time and Narrative*, Vol. I (trans. by Kathleen McLaughlin and David Pellauer), Chicago: University of Chicago Press, 1984, p. 261. Further: On Schutz's response to Heidegger's *Sein und Zeit*, see Helmut R. Wagner, *Alfred Schutz: An Intellectual Biography*, Chicago: University of Chicago Press, 1983, pp. 156–157. As to the larger relationship between "circles," between the group around Weber and those who followed Husserl, Honigsheim gives the following report, starting with Max Scheler: "The Weber circle . . . was never much influenced by Scheler . . . the influence of Husserl, Scheler's temporary mentor, was incomparably greater. There were three reasons for this. Husserl wrote for *Logos*, which was the journal for philosophy at Heidelberg. Rickert, Weber, and Troeltsch supported it and published there. The second reason was that in 1912 and 1913 Husserl's name occurred, if vaguely, in connection with the question of a successor to Windelband; at that time Husserl was only a *persönlicher Ordinarius* at Göttingen. The third reason was that at that time Helmuth Plessner began to exert an influence in Heidelberg. He came from the discipline of biology but he belonged to the Weber circle, and even as a student he was thought to be a literary type. He wrote me later during the first World War to say that he rejected the rather phenomenological position he had taken as a young man. In any case, at that time he was familiar with Husserl's and Scheler's phenomenology as few of the young men were, and he kept bringing the conversation around to this subject" (Paul Honigsheim, *On Max Weber* [trans. by Joan Rytina], New York: The Free Press, 1968, 22–23. Cf. W. G. Runciman, *A Critique of Max Weber's Philosophy of Social Science*, Cambridge: Cambridge University Press, 1972, footnote 128, pp. 80–81).

calls the "Thou-orientation" of the individual who meets another individual face-to-face. He writes:

> The Thou-orientation is the general form in which any particular fellow-man is experienced in person. The very fact that I recognize something within the reach of my direct experience as a living, conscious human being constitutes the Thou-orientation. In order to preclude misunderstandings, it must be emphasized that the Thou-orientation is not a judgment by analogy. Becoming aware of a human being confronting me does not depend upon an imputation of life and consciousness to an object in my surroundings by an act of reflective thought. The Thou-orientation is a prepredicative experience of a fellow being.[16]

The concrete we-relationship is lived through in the synchronization of my inner time with that of the Other, my partner in a face-to-face relationship. And we share not only time but space. In the immediacy of encountering the Other, the Thou-orientation arises. However, the structural origin of concrete we-relations is founded on the pure we-relationship. In Schutz's words:

> ... we may say that concrete social relations in face-to-face situations are founded upon the pure We-relation. Not only is the latter logically prior to the former in the sense that it contains the essential features of any such social relation; the grasp of the specific traits of the partner which is an element of concrete social relations presupposes the community of space and time which characterizes the pure We-relation. The pure We-relation may be thus also considered as a formal concept designating the structure of concrete social relations in the face-to-face situation.
>
> This point becomes clear if one considers the fact that no specific *"pure"* experiences correspond to the pure We-relation. The participant in an ongoing We-relation apprehends this relation only in the shared experiences which refer, by necessity, to the specific partner confronting him. The essential features of the pure We-relation can be seen in reflection, after the concrete We-relation has come to an end; they are experienced only in the variety of its actualizations.[17]

If the Thou-orientation is tied to particular human beings who are encountered in concrete situations, the Thou-orientation may also be understood in its generality as referring to the pure experience of

16. Alfred Schutz, *Collected Papers*, Vol. II: *Studies in Social Theory* (edited with an introduction by Arvid Brodersen), The Hague: Martinus Nijhoff, 1964, p. 24. Note: Hereafter abbreviated as CPII. Further note: The passage quoted from CPII is an adaptation into English by Professor Thomas Luckmann of Section IV of Schutz's *Der sinnhafte Aufbau der sozialen Welt*.
17. CPII, p. 28.

the Other. That experience must be taken as a limiting concept. Schutz
is quite explicit:

> The essential feature of the Thou-orientation is the recognition that a
> fellow-man *is* before me; the orientation does not presuppose that I
> know what are precisely the particular characteristics of that fellow-
> man. The formal concept of the Thou-orientation refers to the "pure"
> experience of another Self as a human being, alive and conscious, while
> the specific content of that consciousness remains undefined. Of course,
> I never have such a "pure" experience of another Self. I always confront
> a particular fellow-man, living his particular life and having his own
> particular thoughts. The Thou-orientation is therefore not "pure" in
> fact but is always actualized in different degrees of concreteness and
> specificity.[18]

Although Schutz does not have anything to say in his works about
Martin Buber, I believe that he read Buber sympathetically. "Buber
is right on the Thou," Schutz once said to me. *Some* influence of Buber
does show itself in Schutz's treatment of the Thou-orientation. It is
not necessary to say too much. Had the views of Buber been of decisive
importance to Schutz, there would have been direct credit given; even
if the influence had been indirect, Schutz would have taken notice.
He was scrupulous and generous in his acknowledgments and in his
references. I mention Buber because I think that he and Schutz em-
phasized the ontological weight of concrete encounter with Others.
"Buber is right on the Thou" would mean, for Schutz, that the concrete Other—the person with whom I share a face-to-face relationship—is ontologically prior to the Other as *a* partner in social relations.
In *I and Thou*, Buber's concerns are directed toward the integral reality
which comes to life in I-Thou relationships; Schutz is interested in
the phenomenological foundations of the we-relationship. Still, the
question of ontological priority is central to the thought of both men.
Most specifically: For Schutz the ontological givenness of the Other
in concrete we-relations cannot be spun out of a pure, a priori, or
transcendental "We." Nor can the "We" be *created* out of the ego,
however primordial or powerful that ego may be in its transcendental
character. That the concrete person who is my Other in a face-to-face
relationship is indeed an individual means that individuation is bitterly
ambiguous, for "an individual" is what every individual is and is not.
The pure we-relationship accommodates "an individual" who is, typi-

18. CPII, p. 24.

cally, perceived as "someone encountered." Ontologically speaking, however, the concreteness of the individual is unsubstitutable, the encounter is unrepeatable, the person and the moment are absolute.

We are brought in this discussion, then, to a portrait—if only a miniature—of Schutz's view of social reality in the "meaning-consti-tution" of the social world. Some qualifications are necessary. It is important to note that a fundamental reversal in epistemology is un-dertaken in Schutz's work: no longer is the traditional emphasis on perception accepted; *action* is the operative notion. At surface glance, this alteration would seem to be at odds with Husserl's stress on *seeing* as the organon of phenomenology. But "seeing" for Husserl is always intentional, is always seeing-of-something. To say this is not to conflate methodology with intentionality; rather, I suggest that phenomeno-logical "seeing"—intuition, in the broadest Husserlian sense—was never meant to be restricted to what is commonly taken to be the paradigm example, the grand metaphor, of vision. Husserl refers to "evidence," that which originarily presents itself "in person," the bed-rock of the perceptual stream of consciousness, as (". . . in an ex-tremely broad sense . . ."[19]) an " 'experiencing,' of something that is, and is thus, it is precisely a mental seeing of something itself."[20] "A mental seeing" is not a retinal moment but rather the controlled play of reflective consciousness attending with utmost caution to the flow of its fictive capacities. If "seeing" be tied to the neurophysiology of vision, then "a mental seeing" is out of place—a misnomer. In these terms, Husserl's utilization of the language of "vision" is misappre-hended if it is taken to mean an emphasis on the *faculty* of vision. If it is at all correct to speak of a "metaphor" of vision as dominant in phenomenology, the metaphor should be understood as a nuanced indication of intuition, not as feeling but as "a mental seeing." Ac-cordingly, action is as central to Husserlian *seeing* as any other aspect of the spectrum of perception. It is the narrowing of perception which Schutz rejects; it is the enlargement of perception which he advances. In this matter, Schutz is thoroughly phenomenological.

The work of Schutz presents us with another caution. The tradi-tional emphasis on perception in epistemology tends to bring with it a concentration of philosophical concern on the present. In seeking

19. Edmund Husserl, *Cartesian Meditations: An Introduction to Phenomenology* (trans. by Dorion Cairns), The Hague: Martinus Nijhoff, 1960, p. 12.
20. Ibid.

to understand the social world, the analyst turns to the "now-world" as the domain of urgent attention. To be sure, the past, the historical realm, and the near and distant future are of pressing concern. But in the interpretation of, say, face-to-face relationships, of the concrete situations in which human beings act, the present tense almost naturally tends to dominate discussion. The metaphor of vision proves to be a temporal figure, rhetorically speaking. Recall the distinctions which Schutz draws between predecessors, contemporaries, consociates, and successors. For him, social action involves all of these temporally bound fellow-men, not just our consociates or even our contemporaries. The social world has been interpreted by Others before our birth; that preinterpretation is of decisive importance for anyone—actor or observer—who needs or wishes to understand what is going on around him. The traces of preinterpretation are to be found not only in the memories of contemporaries or in the chronicles of predecessors but in the "sedimentation of meaning"—to use Husserl's phrase—indirectly provided by the artifacts of our civilization. Still more deeply: apart from artifacts, the sedimentation of meaning may be located in the typifying medium par excellence, in Schutz's judgment—language. What applies in this fashion to the preinterpreted past has different but correlative application to the understanding of those Others who will be born after we die, our successors. We will stop short of any consideration of that domain.

Another caution: The entire discussion of daily life requires a placement of "the world of working as paramount reality."[21] A careful and sympathetic reader of William James, Schutz was especially attuned to the chapter "The Perception of Reality" in the second volume of *The Principles of Psychology*. There James has a section headed "The Paramount Reality of Sensations."[22] Indebted to James's language, but adapting it to his own philosophical purposes, Schutz's "world of working as paramount reality" becomes the cardinal "sub-universe of reality." Schutz writes:

> The world of working as a whole stands out as paramount over against the many other sub-universes of reality. It is the world of physical things, including my body; it is the realm of my locomotions and bodily operations; it offers resistances which require effort to overcome; it

21. CPI, p. 226.
22. William James, *The Principles of Psychology*, New York: Henry Holt, 1893, vol. II, p. 299.

places tasks before me, permits me to carry through my plans, and enables me to succeed or to fail in my attempt to attain my purposes. By my working acts I gear into the outer world, I change it; and these changes, although provoked by my working, can be experienced and tested both by myself and others, as occurrences within this world independently of my working acts in which they originated. I share this world and its objects with Others; with Others, I have ends and means in common; I work with them in manifold social acts and relationships, checking the Others and checked by them. And the world of working is the reality within which communication and the interplay of mutual motivation becomes effective.[23]

The paramount reality is the first among other sub-universes of reality. James lists: "The world of sense, or of physical 'things' as we instinctively apprehend them . . ."; "The world of science, or of physical things, as the learned conceive them . . ."; "The world of relations, or abstract truths believed or believable by all . . ."; "The world of 'idols of the tribe,' illusions or prejudices common to the race"; "The various supernatural worlds, the Christian heaven and hell, the world of Hindoo mythology . . ."; "The various worlds of individual opinion, as numerous as men are"; "The worlds of sheer madness and vagary, also indefinitely numerous."[24] To move, as Schutz does, from the world of sense to the working world as primary in the range of "multiple realities," is to effect a shift from perception to action. The other sub-universes are no less "real," but their reality is grounded in an intersubjective matrix of meaning which, according to Schutz, presupposes the "paramount reality." It is the emphasis on meaning which distinguishes James's discussion of the sub-universes from that of Schutz. The question is that of how James's treatment of the "sense of reality" is to be taken, whether James's primarily psychologistic approach to "reality" will serve the purposes of a phenomenology of the social world. Schutz makes clear where it is he differs from James: "We speak of provinces of *meaning* and not of sub-universes because it is the meaning of our experiences and not the ontological structure of the objects which constitutes reality."[25] As Schutz would have said: So Schutz.

The different provinces of meaning present a "storied" picture of the social world—not so much levels as spirals in which the sense of

23. CPI, pp. 226–227.
24. *The Principles of Psychology*, Vol. II, pp. 292–293.
25. CPI, p. 230.

the real displays its character. And just as the different provinces have "borders" which are crossed or at least recognized, so what I (not Schutz) would term "province-crossing" implies the "transcendences" of Nature and Society. Throughout the movement of the individual in the "storied" world, there are limits imposed upon action. The transcendences of Nature and Society are experienced, Schutz maintains, ". . . as being imposed upon me in a double sense: on the one hand, I find myself at any moment of my existence as being within nature and within society; both are permanently coconstitutive elements of my biographical situation and are, therefore, experienced as inescapably belonging to it. On the other hand, they constitute the framework within which alone I have the freedom of my potentialities, and this means they prescribe the scope of all possibilities for defining my situation. In this sense, they are not elements of my situation, but determinations of it. In the first sense, I may—even more, I have to— take them for granted. In the second sense, I have to come to terms with them. But in either sense, I have to understand the natural and the social world in spite of their transcendences, in terms of an order of things and events."[26]

The transcendences of Nature and Society are demands made upon me: I find myself in a world in which the knowledge that I did not "make" it is part of mundane experience and part of my "biographical situation."[27] In recognizing the limits of my world, I honor its transcendence; in the act of such recognition, I transcend the epistemic "submission" of the natural attitude. Transcendence, then, pulls in two directions: limits are imposed upon me and yet I traverse those limits in the response I make to them. For Schutz, "coming to terms" with transcendence has an even stronger sense. The transcendent may irrupt in "the world of everyday life" and transform its significance. Symbolization is empowered to achieve such transfigurations. "Jacob," Schutz writes, "awakened from his dream of the ladder in which God revealed himself to him (Genesis, 28, 10–25), took the stone that he had put for his pillow and set it up for a pillar and poured oil upon the top of it, vowing that this stone shall be God's house."[28] What starts with the recognition of the large transcendences of Nature and Society

26. CPI, p. 330.
27. See CPI, p. 329.
28. CPI, p. 337.

ends with the acknowledgment of the source of the "metaphysical constants"—the ultimacy of transcendence.

Finally: The social world is the home of anonymity and of anonymization. At last we are in a position to use these terms with the inflections which Schutz gave them. Some condensation is inescapable for the moment. "Anonymity" refers primarily (but not exclusively) to the typified structures of the "objective" aspect of the social world, that is, to the social world viewed as an interlocking complex of meanings which enable any actor to manage his affairs in the world of working and to find his way in the other provinces of meaning. To post a letter successfully, Schutz tells us, the individual must follow certain rules and requirements whose rationale he may grasp in the most general or vague ways. All that is needed for the task to be accomplished is that the letterposter stick to a certain "recipe": addressing the envelope in an acceptable manner, affixing sufficient postage, dropping the letter in a mailbox. It is not necessary for the average person—someone who is not, for purposes of this example, an employee of the mail service—to understand the intricacies of the postal system, how it works, who does what in processing the mail, how mail is transported and delivered. If the letter reaches the addressee in a reasonable period of time, that is all that is wanted. The details of postal service are typified into "what they do with the mail," and the particular individuals who are involved with the mail are and remain almost entirely anonymous. Their identities are irrelevant to the act of mailing a letter. Here a serious turn is taken in the understanding of "objective" and "subjective" meaning with respect to the social world. Schutz writes:

> When we make the transition to the social sphere, there accrues, in fact, to the pair of concepts "objective and subjective meaning" a new and sociologically relevant significance. I can, on the one hand, attend to and interpret in themselves the phenomena of the external world which present themselves to me as indications of the consciousness of other people. When I do this, I say of them that they have objective meaning. But I can, on the other hand, look over and through these external indications into the constituting process within the living consciousness of another rational being. What I am then concerned with is subjective meaning. What we call the world of objective meaning is, therefore, abstracted in the social sphere from the constituting processes of a meaning-endowing consciousness, be this one's own or an-

other's. This results in the anonymous character of the meaning-content predicated of it and also its invariance with respect to every consciousness which has given it meaning through its own intentionality. In contrast to this, when we speak of subjective meaning in the social world, we are referring to the constituting processes in the consciousness of the person who produced that which is objectively meaningful. We are therefore referring to his "intended meaning," whether he himself is aware of these constituting processes or not. The world of subjective meaning is therefore never anonymous, for it is essentially only something dependent upon and still within the operating intentionality of an Ego-consciousness, my own or someone else's.[29]

If anonymity is a feature of objectified meaning in the social world, "anonymization" is on the side of consciousness understood as an abstractive activity. The anonymous, I suggest, may be thought of as both constituted and constituting. Schutz's conception of social reality, his theory of the meaning-constitution of the social world, his analyses of constructs, types, and projects of action, his view of multiple realities, his insights into language and symbolization, and what he has to say about transcendence—all include the fundamental notion of anonymity. But "inclusion" is a weak and a potentially misleading word here. I consider anonymity to be a central philosophical no less than methodological term in Schutz's discourse. Without trying to claim too much, I am convinced that anonymity provides what Husserl called "a transcendental clue" to the understanding of Schutz's philosophy of the social world. Our task is the tracing of that clue.

29. PSW, p. 37.

II

ANONYMITY

The answer "anonymity" to those who have asked me what I was "working on" has sometimes produced puzzlement. More detailed explanation has not always satisfied or relieved the inquirer. The subject, I have decided, is so obvious that it is dark. Occasionally, my explanations have been met by a clairvoyant response: "I know what you are going to do; you are going to show that. . . ." Philosophers' minds are busy bodies. They are frequently up to no good. What I am now writing is the only answer which I can provide to those who wish to know what I have been "doing." But there should be no reason for surprise about the obscurity of my theme. The last time I looked, there was no entry for "anonymity" in the subject-card catalog of Yale's Sterling Memorial Library. The closest thing was "anonyms." "Anonymity" has some place in the literature of sociology and psychiatry, but it is closer to such notions as "alienation" and "depersonalization." "Anon" may be a commonly cited source in certain reference books; "anonymity" seems to be an instance of what it names. In literal terms, being anonymous is being nameless. Anonymity, in general parlance, means the state of being unknown, without identity, a kind of hiddenness. For the most part, anonymity is not considered by most of us in daily life to be a desirable condition or circumstance. Who "most of us" are is one of the philosophical aspects of the problem of anonymity. For the moment, let us say that if the "man on the street" were asked by one of those roving photographer-questioners who work for the tabloids, "Would you rather be anonymous?", the reply, very likely, would be "My feet are killing me. *That's* what I'd rather be." Here, as Charles Dickens knew, is a philosopher. Dickens later.

Anonymity has its place in the round of daily life. Of the host of my contemporaries on earth, I know only a few. Franklin D. Roosevelt's Postmaster General, James A. Farley, was reputed to know thousands of people. At some critical moment in the politics of his day, he would win a crucial vote for the administration he served by coming up with the name of a grandchild of a South Dakota United States Senator—Had Timothy's colic abated? But Farley is long dead and Timothy is probably a grandfather himself by now. Most of us must settle for knowing a much smaller number of people, for knowing *about* a larger circle of fellow-men, and for being aware of multitudes who are and who will remain anonymous. This is the normal state of affairs. And if it is "normal" that most individuals are anonymous to most other individuals, then it is evident that anonymity is a standard feature of everyday life; anonymity is part of the structure of the social world. Before any predications of value are made about anonymity, it should be understood that anonymity is an invariant feature of an existence lived in the taken-for-granted terms of ordinary life. What is implied by this taken-for-grantedness is the reciprocity of anonymity: I am anonymous to most Others just as most Others are anonymous to me. What seems compellingly obvious about this reciprocity is qualified by the essentially egological standpoint of the person who is quick to acknowledge that *Others* are largely anonymous to him. To paraphrase Tolstoi's Ivan Ilych, it seems *right* that Others (at large) should be anonymous, but as for *me*, that would be too terrible. Yet in the most neutral terms, I—as an ordinary person—recognize that the reciprocity of anonymity in the social world cannot be gainsaid.

In the natural attitude of daily life, "anonymity" is not a commonly used word. We recognize the language of typical encounters, the bits of verbal barter we offer up and receive in the name of decency:

> "Cold enough for 'ya?"
> "Goes right through you."
> "Ain't that the living truth!"

It is difficult to think up a similar exchange for "anonymity."

> "Anonymous enough for you?"
> "They say there's a lot of it going around."
> "You can't be too careful."

Somehow, it doesn't work. In any case, there is no difficulty in understanding what it means for someone to be treated as a number by the bureaucracy, to be looked at as though you weren't there, to have nobody interested in you, to be a perpetual stranger, not to belong—anywhere. The *experience* of anonymity is widespread, if not commonplace; the concern with that experience—its thematization, in phenomenological terms—is not an integral part of daily life. That is not to say that daily life is unreflective. We are speaking, of course, of the individuals who comprise our world. Ultimately, there must be an appeal to what, as men and women, we *know* about our lives—what we know that is not part of a retrieval system but the "tensed" awareness of our own unmediated surprise and disappointment with the yield of existence. In fine, the ordinary person does not need a phenomenologist to tell him about anonymity; but he does. Professor Dorion Cairns once told me that Edmund Husserl often found non-philosophers to be better readers of his books than many colleagues and students of philosophy. Those in or aspiring to the profession of philosopher—professor of philosophy—had, most often, accumulated too much conceptual material to be able to take a fresh look at radical ideas; their philosophical commitments were barricades against admitting the emissaries of a new conceptual delegation; their very training made it difficult for them not to distort proposals by translating them swiftly into the language of their education. Husserl was almost a slave of rigor in philosophical work, but he was unimpressed by those who would not or could not see for themselves. There is a credential of daily life.

For Schutz, typification is the medium through which man in daily life finds his way through the anonymous structure of his everyday world. That letter safely posted, I turn to a consideration of its probable results. In my letter, I tried to explain to an acquaintance why his proposal to have his entourage stay at my home during their two-week visit to Seattle would not be possible: not enough room to begin with, besides another acquaintance would be sleeping on the living room couch while *his* friends were occupying the living room floor with their sleeping bags, *and* my son-in-law was storing his sample cases in the foyer. . . . Simply the wrong time for a visit. Would he understand? Had I not asked him to drop in at any time? Did my explanation—truthful as it in fact was—sound phony? Should I have made up an excuse which sounded more credible? And how would he interpret my suggestion that a hotel suite would be more comfortable? Had I made a mistake in saying that? Perhaps I should telephone him to explain more fully. And what about that time he went out of his way to do me a favor? Here is a Schutzian reconstruction of this situation:

Let us set aside the assumptions involved in the mailing of a letter. Something about that has already been said. Instead, we turn directly to the letter writer. When I received my acquaintance's inquiry about coming to Seattle, I already had a common-sense grasp not only of what might be called the "etiquette" of visits but a more specific "picture" of my correspondent: his age, occupation, interests, general "style" as a person, and perhaps some of his idiosyncrasies. Let us also set aside the more complicated question of how well I know him or think I know him. What remains is this: someone I know fairly well has asked for something which I am not in a position to provide. On the asker's side—so my assumption goes—there is a reasonable basis for the request (he knows me, has done something for me in the past, is making what might seem like a plausible request). I assume that he assumes that I will respond to his letter, that my response will be rational, that I will—other things being equal!—try to accommodate him. But on the receiver's side, other things are not equal. Not only do circumstances compel me to say "no," but it is also necessary to make it clear that even without his companions, I am unable to offer him a place to stay in my apartment. "There is simply no room," I say aloud—and it is true. Yet the moment those words are uttered, I am unsettled. What do I really know about Burndell Slidemoor? I try to form an image of him; it has been three years since we met. He was drunk on that occasion, I think; "yes," says the voice of Bad Faith, "and you were a little damp." The more I think over the matter of the letters (received and sent), the more I am troubled by the "picture" I have of my acquaintance.

The trouble is that the "picture" of Slidemoor upon which I have relied is rather vague. What I know about him is based on a relatively brief association, and that association is characterized by artificial conditions. He seems a decent fellow, we seemed to hit it off, he did go out of his way to be of help that time; still, I don't know him well enough to say whether my letter will offend him or at least dissatisfy him. At this point, I relinquish my efforts to fill out the "picture" and think in the silence of my reflection, "Well, after all, it was a bit pushy of him to send that letter. Four people! Why didn't he ask to bring his Boy Scout troop? What does he think I am, the army barracks? To hell with Slidemoor and his cousins; I should have told him off!" The "picture" now lies in shards, splintered by my vehemence. "Imagine the nerve of the guy! That bastard!" My choleric self is now in sway: "I've wasted enough time on that nonsense!" With a convulsive movement, I shoot my cuffs.

What I know of my acquaintance, in Schutz's terms, is the result of the formation of ". . . a construct of a typical way of behavior, a typical pattern of underlying motives, of typical attitudes of a personality type, of which the Other and his conduct under scrutiny, both outside of my observational reach, are just instances or exemplars."[1] The "picture" to which I have referred is, in Schutz's formulation, a common-sense version of an "ideal type." Indeed, Max Weber's theory of ideal types is a central influence on Schutz's thinking. But rather than having here a purely methodological construction formulated by the theorist (a "second-order construct"), we are confronted by a naive "first-order" schema of an acquaintance who writes a letter asking a favor. There is also a "self-typification" constructed by the recipient of the request. A bit of that has already been intimated: "I'm a reasonable person; I can see that he's due a decent answer; I'm also nobody's fool and if he thinks I'm going to. . . ." The issue before us, however, is the common-sense construction of ideal types. Schutz is unequivocal about the grounding of first-order constructs: ". . . in the common-sense thinking of everyday life" is to be found "the origin of . . . constructive or ideal types. . . ."[2] The understanding of common-sense constructs presupposes the meaning of Schutz's notion of the "biographical situation" of the actor in social life. We have mentioned the "biographical situation"; now it is time to define it. Schutz writes:

> Man finds himself at any moment of his daily life in a biographically determined situation, that is, in a physical and sociocultural environment as defined by him, within which he has his position, not merely his position in terms of physical space and outer time or of his status and role within the social system but also his moral and ideological position. To say that this definition of the situation is biographically determined is to say that it has its history; it is the sedimentation of all man's previous experiences, organized in the habitual possessions of

1. CPI, p. 17.
2. CPI, p. 61.

his stock of knowledge at hand, and as such his unique possession, given to him and to him alone.[3]

It is in terms of his biographical situation that the individual in daily life orders his constructions, his "ideal types"—writ small—of human action in the social world. Language, history, the events of the time and of a concrete life—these are some of the conditions with regard to which the individual forms his sense of how the social world "works," how to go about getting plans enacted, how to organize one's activities, how to cope with Others, how to make one's way in a world which is not the individual's private enterprise but instead a public domain, affected as well as controlled by the Law, the State, the "powers that be." The individual's conception of any segment of experience is derived socially, that is, from his parents, his family, his teachers, his employers, his fellow employees, his friends and acquaintances, and the large range of other persons and associations which make knowledge, in Schutz's view, a socially structured achievement. He writes:

> Only a very small part of my knowledge of the world originates within my personal experience. The greater part is socially derived, handed down to me by my friends, my parents, my teachers and the teachers of my teachers. I am taught not only how to define the environment . . . but also how typical constructs have to be formed in accordance with the system of relevances accepted from the anonymous unified point of view of the in-group. This includes ways of life, methods of coming to terms with the environment, efficient recipes for the use of typical means for bringing about typical ends in typical situations.[4]

A certain important aspect of my biographical situation is included under the heading of "recipes" for social action. Schutz is concerned with what he also calls "cook-book" knowledge—formulas for getting things done—which provide the ingredients and procedures needed for securing typical results. Not laws but rather "typical sequences and relations" are at issue here:

> This kind of knowledge and its organization I should like to call "cookbook knowledge." The cook-book has recipes, lists of ingredients, formulae for mixing them, and directions for finishing off. This is all we need to make an apple pie, and also all we need to deal with the routine matters of daily life. If we enjoy the apple pie so prepared, we do not

3. CPI, p. 9.
4. CPI, pp. 13–14.

ask whether the manner of preparing it as indicated by the recipe is the most appropriate from the hygienic or alimentary point of view, or whether it is the shortest, the most economical, or the most efficient. We just eat and enjoy it. Most of our daily activities from rising to going to bed are of this kind. They are performed by following recipes reduced to automatic habits or unquestioned platitudes.[5]

Such "platitudes" are, in many cases, condensed "recipes" whose ingredients and instructions for mixing and preparation can be set aside in favor of what is deemed a typical result. The platitude becomes an instant recipe.[6] It is typicality, however, which emerges as the dominant term of discourse in this discussion. Whether the recipe for action in the social world is precisely mastered by the actor is not a decisive consideration; most recipes are themselves typified, so that the individual "more or less" understands how to utilize them effectively. In fine, typicality is itself typified. The urgent consideration, for Schutz, is that the intersubjectivity of the social world does not depend on the individual's knowing his fellow-man's subjective meanings in their uniqueness; it is enough to grasp them in their exemplification. We begin to see anonymity as the great signifier. Schutz gives us a summation:

> . . . the world of everyday life is from the outset also a social cultural world in which I am interrelated in manifold ways of interaction with fellow-men known to me in varying degrees of intimacy and anonymity. To a certain extent, sufficient for many practical purposes, I understand their behavior, if I understand their motives, goals, choices, and plans originating in *their* biographically determined circumstances. Yet only in particular situations, and then only fragmentarily, can I experience the Others' motives, goals, etc.—briefly, the subjective meanings they bestow upon their actions, in their uniqueness. I can, however, experience them in their typicality. In order to do so I construct typical patterns of the actors' motives and ends, even of their attitudes and personalities, of which their actual conduct is just an instance or example. These typified patterns of the Others' behavior become in turn motives of my own actions, and this leads to the phenomenon of self-typification. . . . Here, I submit, in the common-sense thinking of everyday life, is the origin of the so-called constructive or ideal types. . . .[7]

The types upon which the individual relies form much of the mother-wit upon which he depends for getting on with the affairs of daily

5. CPII, pp. 73–74.
6. Cf. Anton C. Zijderveld, *On Clichés: The Supersedure of Meaning by Function in Modernity*, London: Routledge and Kegan Paul, 1979, p. 58.
7. CPI, pp. 60–61.

life. What a particular person knows about any subject or procedure turns, in the first instance, on his "stock of knowledge at hand," in Schutz's terminology, that is, an inventory of facts, techniques, and information about a wide range of states of affairs in the social world. The "stock" obviously varies from person to person, with regard to its scope and mastery of detail as well as to its richness and the acuity of the mind which holds it. For the normal, "wide-awake" adult, as Schutz says, it is taken for granted that there is a "right" or "proper" or at least "proven" way of acting in order to achieve certain goals. We leave aside what is manifest: the relativity of time, place, language, and culture. We attend instead to the invariance of structure. As long as my biographical situation and my stock of knowledge at hand are reliable grounds for applying my "recipes" to a situation, I continue to believe in myself as someone capable of managing his affairs. Exaggerated claims comprise no part of typification; to the contrary, the edifice of types is founded, in Schutz's view, on a principle of limitation:

> The outstanding feature of a man's life in the modern world is his conviction that his life-world as a whole is neither fully understood by himself nor fully understandable to any of his fellow-men. There is a stock of knowledge theoretically available to everyone, built up by practical experience, science, and technology as warranted insights. But this stock of knowledge is not integrated. It consists of a mere juxtaposition of more or less coherent systems of knowledge which themselves are neither coherent nor even compatible with one another. On the contrary, the abysses between the various attitudes involved in the approach to the specialized systems are themselves a condition of the success of the specialized inquiry.[8]

My confidence in "cook-book" knowledge, my expectation that my typical constructs will enable me to act competently in the world, and the reassurance that my past action has largely been successful in steering me through the traffic of the social world—all shore up my belief that what has worked will continue to work, that what has proved trustworthy will not let me down. The principle of limitation still holds: it is essentially a pragmatic motive that guides my action. I do not claim to know everything about the world; I do maintain that keeping faith with what has typically worked in the past is plausible, is "good common sense." Furthermore, the principle of limitation

8. CPII, p. 120.

concerns itself with probabilities, not certainties. It is more than merely useful to understand that, for Schutz, the word "probable" is indispensable to the vocabulary of typification. The "knowledge" in "cookbook knowledge" refers to probabilities, not necessities. In his book on *Relevance*, Schutz writes:

> Knowledge, as used in this study, has to be conceived in the *broadest possible sense*; not as the result of ratiocination, nor in the sense of clarified and distinct knowledge, nor clear perceptions of truth. The term rather includes all kinds of beliefs: from the unfounded, blind belief to the well-founded conviction, from the assumption of mere chance or likelihood to the confidence of empirical certainty. Thus, *knowledge may refer to the possible*, conceivable, imaginable, to what is feasible or practicable, workable or achievable, accessible or obtainable, what can be hoped for and what has to be dreaded.[9]

Earlier in the same book, Schutz discusses the concept of "the probable" in the doctrine of Carneades. What emerges from Schutz's analysis of the treatment of "the probable" and related notions in Husserl and Bergson (among others) is the contention that what is deemed "plausible" is the clue to the meaning of "knowledge" in common-sense matters. The actor's decisions in ordinary life are not governed by scientific laws but by "plausibilities." Thus Schutz maintains: "The ideal of everyday knowledge is not certainty, nor even probability in a mathematical sense, but just likelihood."[10] Some methodological clarification is necessary. The typifications which Schutz has described—the very process of typification—are the interpretations (and the process of interpretation) which actors in daily life employ in "coming to terms" with the demands of an intersubjective world. The common-sense actor is not a theorist of action; he simply acts. However, his acts are structured and coherent in their structure. Schutz, as a theorist, has attempted to describe and to illuminate that structure. Mundane life is essentially unreflective life, despite the great factor of reflection which takes place within its bounds. "Unreflective" here means that in the course of thinking about many matters of social action, the ordinary actor does not examine the question of how it is possible that there *is* such a thing as "mundane life"—a current of existence which is revelatory of "the natural attitude" and which re-

9. Alfred Schutz, *Reflections on the Problem of Relevance* (edited by Richard M. Zaner and introduced and annotated by him), New Haven: Yale University Press, 1970; p. 153. Note: Hereafter abbreviated as RPR.

10. CPII, p. 73.

flection on reflection uncovers by philosophical if not phenomenological thematization. Genuine reflection has its place in mundane life:
choice, decision, acting as well as refraining from acting are all possible
occasions for earnest reflection. What lies beyond the limits of common sense is that transcendental turn which requires the inquirer to
look to the conditions of inquiry—in Kantian language, "the conditions *a priori* necessary for the possibility" of inquiry. Here we have a
matter of quality, not degree. Earlier, it was noted that Schutz distinguishes between "first"- and "second"-order constructs; now it may be
added that he builds his work on a distinction which is less overtly
presented but nevertheless methodologically important—that between the constructs of mundanity and their theoretical interpretation.

As a theorist of likelihood, Schutz is concerned with what is taken-
for-granted by the actor, whether what is taken-for-granted is reflectively recognized or intended or whether it is "unconsciously" at work
in his course of action. And if there *is* reflection on the actor's part,
we shall now understand that, for Schutz, such understanding is itself
part of the pattern of mundane life. At the moment when the actor
probes the meaning of action itself as part of the life-world (the *Lebenswelt*, as Husserl calls it)—the domain of daily life as interpreted by
ordinary people—and comprehends the life-world *as* life-world, then
at that moment the actor has become a philosopher. As long as the
actor goes his taken-for-granted way in daily life, philosophy is tacitly
held at bay; philosophy remains a "possibility" of mundane existence.
But the relationship between self-reflective and tacit knowledge at the
common-sense level is, I would say, not altogether clear. Consider
once again Schultz's claim: "The outstanding feature of a man's
life in the modern world is his conviction that his life-world as a
whole is neither fully understood by himself nor fully understandable
to any of his fellow-men."[11] What is "understood" and "understandable" here is embedded in the matrix of everydayness rather than
in the framework of a rational system of knowledge. Not "knowledge"
but "conviction" is the operative word in Schutz's statement. My conviction that daily life has its irrevocable opaqueness, that daily life
will never yield up its full meaning either to me or to my fellow men,
is not a truth-claim in the stock of truth-claims but a certitude which
is based on my life's experience. Such certitudes may be called "gen-

11. CPII, p. 120.

eralizations" by some; I think differently. We are not concerned with conclusions that are derived from piecemeal evidence but with an apperception in which one's self-awareness is awareness of oneself in the thick of the mundane—a being in everyday reality.

That the life-world is neither understood nor understandable fully is a view expressed by Schutz, the theorist. Perhaps it is tempting to call his view an aperçu or a visionary insight. If such a temptation presents itself to the reader, I suggest that it be resisted. For it is precisely at this point that the status of philosophy and the claims of the philosopher are in the balance. Who is to decide what are the right questions to ask about Schutz's statement? If I were to intercept a "life-worlder" hurrying on his way to an appointment and cry, "Are you convinced that the outstanding feature of man's life in the modern world is that the life-world is not fully understandable?", what would his response signify? Suppose he said, "Right on target, amigo!" or "Nourishment, man, nourishment; don't give me that metaphysical anorexia!" or "Put me down as undecided!" What, in principle, would validate or invalidate Schutz's assertion? More importantly, what kind of statement are we concerned with here? "Checking up" on the legitimacy of Schutz's thesis presupposes that a "checking up" procedure is the only alternative to labeling his claim as a purely personal, private, idiosyncratic pronouncement, at best a bit of "wisdom," at worst a crotchet. But if it is Schutz the theorist who is speaking to us, then it would appear that other theorists should evaluate his claim. By what standards? Is there a matter of fact in question, which the scientific expert might settle? Is there a logical or mathematical problem to be solved? Or is the issue to be tossed into that wastebasket of deviant questions: the arms of the philosopher? And if the last, what difference is there then between the theorist and the philosopher? Some further distinctions, at least, are possible.

The actor in life, according to Schutz, builds constructs which form patterns—miniature ideal types, I have called them—through which the individual manages his affairs, presumably with some reasonable degree of appropriateness and success. Underground men and lunatics also have their "first-order" constructs; the results of their action may strike their consociates as bizarre or outrageous; indeed, they may themselves find their actions to be unacceptable to themselves—and *still* they persist in those actions. Ordinarily, however, typified action is "normal" action, that is, action which is "by and large" what most people in a society at a given time take to be rational, reasonable, acceptable behavior. "By and large" is another one of those linguistic freeloaders: give him a toehold in a sentence and he will seize a paragraph; allow him a word and he will claim the language. Thus, other things being equal, normal action is, by and large, what most people accept as agreeable or at least satisfactory or at the very least understandable behavior. The typifier is rooted in his biographical situation and operates with his stock of knowledge at hand. That location differentiates the mundane actor from the theoretical analyst. The last has his methodological, scientific, or philosophical commitments; his rootage is in the "scientific situation" of the formal observer or theorist, whose professional allegiance takes precedence over his personal concerns in so far as scientific inquiry is going on. Schutz writes:

> . . . the social scientist *qua* theoretician has to follow a system of relevances entirely different from that which determines his conduct as an actor on the social scene. The scientific situation, that is, the context of scientific problems, supersedes his situation as man among his fellowmen within the social world. The problems of the theoretician originate in his theoretical interest, and many elements of the social world that are scientifically relevant are irrelevant from the viewpoint of the actor on the social scene, and *vice versa*.[12]

The difference between the biographical situation of the ordinary individual and the scientific situation of the theorist is not restricted to orders of typification. Schutz points out, in some detail, the significance of my body as *I* am aware of it in the run of my ordinary experience, my body as being the ". . . center *O* of the system of coordinates in terms of which I organize the objects surrounding me. . . ."[13] From the placement of my body at any time, objects (including Others' bodies) are *there* from the standpoint of my *here*. Furthermore, what Schutz terms "topological organization" involves the "world within my reach" and that, in turn, implies ". . . my possibilities, my ability to move, and thus . . . the practicability of the projects of my future action."[14] And finally, the ordinary actor is subject to the strictures of time—the time of inner life, of "growing older," and of being death-bound. The recognition of my death as a presage of inner time is, for Schutz, an aspect of ". . . the ontological structure of things."[15] These remarks bring us to the conclusion that, apart from

12. CPII, p. 248.
13. RPR, p. 173.
14. RPR, see pp. 176–177.
15. RPR, p. 178.

orders of typification, what distinguishes the actor from the theorist is that the actor has a "center *O*," a body situated "here," a "world within reach," possibilities for future action, and a temporal reality within which growing older and dying are distinctively related to and defined by the *actor*, that is, by the concrete person whose world is *his*. The theorist *qua* theorist has none of this. *As theorist*, he has no "center *O*," no "here," no temporal reality. Compressed: when the actor says, "speaking as a common-sense person . . ." and when the theorist says, "speaking purely as a theorist . . .," what appears to be a parallel formulation is not.

We have been discussing—that is what it comes to—the relationship between philosophy and life. It would seem that the primary recognition of a philosophy of common sense would be the qualitative distance between the two. Implied in such a recognition is the ice of theory and the fire of life. We will refrain from quoting Goethe but we cannot withstand the temptation to move in quite a different direction than that which seems to be indicated. There are, as Schutz has pointed out, fundamental differences between actors and theorists, but I would say that his distinctions leave open the possibility of understanding "philosophy" in other ways, chiefly because he has nowhere presented his conception of what philosophy is. If philosophy be equated with theory (and this is what I have done in the present context), then philosophy remains hidden within mundane experience as a transcendental possibility. I think that this is the case and I believe that Schutz would not disagree with this formulation, though he would have developed the theme in a different way. But Schutz took the word "philosophy" most seriously; in his conversation that word was freighted with responsibility; he did not use it casually, and when I once said ". . . but in your philosophy . . ." he treated me to a Viennese interruption of appalled glee from which I still have not recovered. "My *what?*," he cried. How was it, I was left to ask myself, that after all those years of study, I had never made the acquaintance of that word, that word of the most severe reckoning? For Schutz, philosophy was a rare, an ultimate possibility. If he did not present his idea of philosophy, he left open a variety of options.

In what other particular way, then, can philosophy as theory be understood? As—and here I speak for myself alone—the gist of practice. The experience of the everyday world for the actor in the midst of its turnings is typified, to be sure, but it is at the same time the

essential residue of a recalcitrant oppositeness, an abrasive otherness
which is at variance from the comforts of the life-world but which
hardly "balance out" that injustice which lies in the nature of things.
When ordinary people speak of "philosophy," we know what is coming; we know the embarrassment which remains after they have done
speaking—like the stir in the water where someone has gone down.
But there is a tougher meaning of "philosophy" which also belongs
to common sense and of which no one need be ashamed. That meaning is philosophy as the hardness, the adversity of existence, the creak-
ing of the life-world, its hernias and hemorrhages. We promised to
return to Dickens; let his Mr. Squeers say what philosophy is:

> Measles, rheumatics, hooping-cough, fevers, and lumbagers . . . is all
> philosophy together, that's what it is. The heavenly bodies is philoso-
> phy, and the earthly bodies is philosophy. If there's a screw loose in a
> heavenly body, that's philosophy, and if there's a screw loose in a earthly
> body that's philosophy too; or it may be that sometimes there's a little
> metaphysics in it, but that's not often. Philosophy's the chap for me.[16]

Whatever the relationship between philosophy and life may be, it
is Schutz's contention that the "picture" which the actor has of the
social world has its foundation in common-sense experience; "life" in
this sense is no stranger to philosophy. If there is a weakness in what
has been said so far, however, it is the notion of "picture." Inevitably,
a visual connotation follows at the heels of the word, like a well-trained
dog trotting beside its master. But "picture" is not the equivalent of
"image." To the contrary, a "picture" of the Other's course of action
may be a matter of a purely conceptual kind, a question of rules which
govern conduct, an "ideal type" only in the sense of a construction.
There *is* an aspect of the notion of "picture" which is akin to the sense
of a portrait. Indeed, my own discussion has played upon that
"portrait-sense," though I intended to be helpful to the reader. The
equivocation in the meaning of "picture" as ideal type can be overcome, I think, by presenting and considering Schutz's distinction between the "personal ideal type" and the "course-of-action type" (also
called the "course-of-action pattern"). For Schutz:

> The concept "ideal type of human behavior," can be taken in two ways.
> It can mean first of all the ideal type of another person who is ex-

16. Charles Dickens, *Nicholas Nickleby* (edited with an introduction and notes by Michael Slater and original illustrations by Hablet K. Browne ["Phiz"]), New York: Penguin
Books, 1978, Chapter 57, pp. 849–850.

pressing himself or has expressed himself in a certain way. Or it may mean, second, the ideal type of the expressive process itself, or even of the outward results which we interpret as the signs of the expressive process. Let us call the first the "personal ideal type" and the second the "material" or "course-of-action *type*." Certainly an inner relation exists between these two. I cannot, for instance, define the ideal type of a postal clerk without first having in mind a definition of his job. The latter is a course-of-action type, which is, of course, an objective context of meaning. Once I am clear as to the course-of-action type, I can construct the personal ideal type, that is "the person who performs this job." And, in doing so, I imagine the corresponding subjective meaning-contexts which would be in his mind, the subjective contexts that would have to be adequate to the objective contexts already defined. The personal ideal type is therefore *derivative*, and the course-of-action type can be considered quite independently as a purely objective context of meaning.[17]

The "objective" world, then, has the purity of constructions understood in their generality, apart from the concrete individuals who take up their "roles" in acting in the social world. It must be recalled that what we may now term, following Schutz, course-of-action types or patterns are based not only on the paradigm of the conduct of "consociates"—those fellow human beings with whom we share space and time—but also include "contemporaries," "predecessors," and "successors." Nor is it precise to say, as I have, that course-of-action types are *based* on consociates or any order of fellow-men; rather, it is personal types which derive from course-of-action types. Still, personal types are formed without benefit of or recourse to concrete individuals. The point is that methodological priority must not be *arbitrarily* assigned to face-to-face encounters. Both personal and course-of-action types are constructed in common-sense experience without the aid of a "picture" of this or that individual. How then does it come about that I have a "picture" of a friend, an acquaintance, a colleague or associate, my physician or my spiritual adviser? And do I have a "picture" of my wife or of my child? A vast qualifier must be introduced right now: Ideal types in their purity are necessarily limiting cases; they cannot be grasped in the actuality of experience. Approximations, methodologically contaminated specimens of human action, are what is grasped by the actor no less than by the theorist. The latter may posit pure types—but they remain "posits." The actor *lives* those "posits" in the indeterminacy of the social world. But the relationship

17. PSW, pp. 187–188.

of personal types to individuals we actually know still awaits clarification.

From the course-of-action type, we are able, according to Schutz, to develop or generate a personal type: knowing the details of the job requirements of a postal clerk brings us to the personal type, "postal clerk." Now, I have known Alicia Cornsweet, the postal clerk at my neighborhood post office, for a number of years. I knew Alicia's father—gone these many years—when he plied (if that is the proper word) the trade of dental mechanic. And I knew Alicia's younger sister, Ceil (is that short for "Celia"?; anyway, the name rhymes with "seal"). For a very long time, Alicia has called me "Grove" (she may think my name is "Grosvenor"; actually, it *is* "Grove"—one of those family names used as a first name) and I have called her "Alicia." When I think of Alicia, the picture I have of her varies with what aspect of Alicia's life is at issue. As a postal clerk, she is better than run of the mill, efficient, easy to deal with, generally O.K. But as a person, Alicia is outstanding; always bright, always remembers to ask after my cousin Theodore (institutionalized for over eighteen years; his promise as a clarinetist starkly ruined) and never fails to send her best to Mr. Trentstaven, our long-time boarder, who was crippled by a stroke and lives on a pension provided by some organization to the descendants of veterans of the Spanish-American War. Now the following scene:

> "Alicia, I have to pay for these stamps with a check."
> "A personal check?"
> "That's right."
> "The Post Office won't accept personal checks. You're going to have to pay cash."
> "Come on, Alicia."
> "It's no use, Grove, it won't work; the Government wants cash."
> "You mean I'm not good for ten dollars?"
> "Make out the check to me; I'll give you the ten dollars and you can use that to buy the stamps."
> "Sweetheart!"
> "Don't 'sweetheart' me, Grove Enters, I haven't forgotten what you said to Ceil that time in the movies."
> "That was almost twenty years ago!"
> "Never mind."
> "And anyway, Ceil started the whole thing. Actually it was a sort of joke."
> "Some joke; they had to call the manager!"

"I thought we were friends."

"So we are. NEXT!"

The intersection between postal clerk and person, the division between job requirements—the rules—and friendship (or acquaintanceship)—what one will do for a chum, the point of separation between the strict demands of "office" and the leeway in how a role is played, are here put to the test. Alicia cannot accept Grove's personal check as a postal clerk but she can take it as an individual. Grove may feel or pretend to feel insulted or hurt by Alicia's refusal to accept his check in exchange for the stamps, but he must recognize that in certain cases the rules cannot be bent to suit cases—at least not without risking one's job, let alone breaking the law. How, then, does Grove view Alicia? She is doing her duty as a postal clerk *and* she is a person who will not be induced not to do her duty. Or: On the side of the postal clerk, *cash*; but on the side of the person, more than duty-commitment. Grove did not realize that Alicia was still that sensitive to the old embarrassment regarding Ceil. It *was* a joke. And after all those years! Anyway, a reverie overcomes Grove: Why is "Ceil" no longer a common name? How common had it ever been? What *did* a dental mechanic do? Did technology overtake the job? Are there still dental mechanics about? What organization was it that sent Mr. Trentstaven his pension? Did the officers of that organization also have to be descendants of veterans of the Spanish-American War? Is there still a survivor of that War? Suppose he was a twelve-year-old drummer boy in 1898—possible but unlikely. And poor Theodore. How kind of Alicia to think of him. Perhaps she had a soft spot for failed clarinetists. Not failed but utterly, utterly desolate.

The "picture" one has of a personal type is composed not only of a knowledge of the job requirements but also of a set of expectations of how a "postal clerk" will act in various circumstances which are related to his job. But the requirements, as far as the post office patron is concerned, need not be spelled out in manual form—as they somewhere are printed in a code governing the United States Post Office, its employees, services, rates. All the patron knows or even wishes to know, for the most part, is what the typical duties of the clerk are. He wants to know what can be reasonably expected and what is prohibited, what falls within the province of "postal information" and what is confidential. And beyond the duties of a clerk, what are the services which the post office provides? Is it reasonable to call the post office in the United States if I wish to secure information about how to get a passport? Yes, it is. Is it appropriate to call "Customer Services" to find out how General O. O. Howard lost his right arm? No. For details about the Civil War, one might try the reference desk at the municipal library. Is it sensible to consult *Who's Who* to learn about the decorations and medals of a famous person? They might be listed. How about the war wounds of a famous judge? Unlikely. Yet Justice Oliver Wendell Holmes included the wounds he had received in battles of the Civil War in his entry for *Who's Who*. Lines of demarcation are worrisome to draw in these examples; the provisos which would have to be attached to instructions about what is probable or improbable would so far outstrip the demands for decision in daily life as to render any recommendations practically useless. How then does the actor distinguish between the personal type and the concrete individual in a typified role? And what is the difference between consulting an employee in a government office and a reference work—what difference once the surface differences have been set aside?

I suggest—and here I speak for myself alone—that a "schematism" of sorts operates in the relationship between type and individual. Although my use of the term "schematism" may be indebted to Kant, I wish to free the word from its philosophical trappings and to use it in my own way. The schematism operative in the case I am describing may be understood as a mediating notion: social role mediates between the typifications through which a personal type is understood and the ways in which a particular individual is understood, comprehended, perceived—"pictured." When Grove asks Alicia whether she will accept his check, let us say that he is addressing Alicia as—in the role of—postal clerk but hoping that his old acquaintance will do him a favor. A typology of possible interpretations of this situation will serve no good purpose here. For the moment, we are interested in the contrast between the clerk and the individual. The Alicia who is employed by the government may be understood without recourse to her sister or the Spanish-American War; Grove's Alicia is someone tied to his past, someone whose good will he values. If the line of those awaiting service in the post office is momentarily held up by Alicia's inquiries about Theodore, there has been no radical breach in the schema of the type; if Alicia chooses to go on and on about old times, there may be some muttering or protest from irritated customers still to be served; if Alicia turns her conversation with Grove into a prolonged engagement, she will very likely be reproved by her supervisor. "Say hello for me to Mr. Trentstaven" is type-acceptable despite the fact that it is, strictly speaking, not part of the clerk's job. What happens is that if what is not "type-acceptable" is inconsequential to the type, trivial to the job, then the type-aspect of the schema is retained in italics, as it were, while the personal reference remains in ordinary print for the duration of its brief exposure. The bounds of toleration in this context are typified. If Alicia has not a single personal word to say to Grove, he may wonder whether she is fully "herself" today, whether he has unknowingly offended her, whether—at very long last—she is weary of asking to be remembered to anyone.

The schematism which I have introduced mediates between the personal type and the actual individual. However, the weight of Schutz's contribution to the discussion of ideal types rests elsewhere. I have followed a digression, though I think it is an interesting one. For Schutz, the central issue concerning the constitution of types has far more to do with the anonymity of all constructs than it does with the particularities of a biographical situation or a stock of knowledge at hand or a set of relevances. The particularities—the singular affairs of one life—are at the existential core of human existence but are peripheral to the "meaning-construction of the social world." We are not interested in whether sociology must necessarily describe and ana- lyze types rather than individuals. That old but not venerable for- mulation has little to recommend it; instead it has a history of largely unchallenged repetition. The digression which I have pursued in dis- cussing personal types and real individuals through the notion of a schematism is thematically close, in my judgment, to the problems with which Schutz is concerned in his theory of typification. Among those problems are two major issues in his work which we will examine before long: the way in which an individual enters into a role and the significance of transcendence for becoming truly a human being. Hu- man fragmentation and human fulfillment cannot be made a footnote to the discussion of types. Alicia and Grove may be my fictions but they are not phantoms in these pages—irrelevant to the theory of types because they are not pure constructions and because if they were real people they would not qualify as subjects for sociological inquiry. Before these matters can be explored more carefully, we must return to Schutz's own voice in his discussion of course-of-action and personal types:

> . . . when I seek to understand another's behavior in ideal-typical fash-
> ion, a twofold method is available to me. I can begin with the finished
> act, then determine the type of action that produced it, and finally
> settle upon the type of person who must have acted in this way. Or I
> can reverse the process and, knowing the personal ideal type, deduce
> the corresponding act. We have, therefore, to deal with two different
> problems. One problem concerns which aspects of a finished act are
> selected as typical and how we deduce the personal type from the
> course-of-action type. The other problem concerns how we deduce
> specific actions from a given personal ideal type.[18]

The "picture" we have, then, of both the course-of-action type and
the personal type is based on a selective process; only certain aspects
of these types are relevant for the process of typification in a given
circumstance. "Banks cash checks" is a typified description of a course-
of-action type. I expect the teller at one of the windows at the bank
to cash my check; that expectation is part of the personal type I have
of "bank teller." But before I can complete the banking transaction,
a number of qualifications must be considered: Is the check drawn
on my account at *this* bank? If so, am I known at the bank? Am I
known to this particular teller? Do I need identification in order for
the check to be honored? And if another person's check is made out
to me, can I simply endorse it and receive payment or will I be required
to deposit the check and make out my own in order to get what I
want? If I am a local businessman who makes frequent deposits and
withdrawals and if the teller has known me for years as a depositor,
then I may get immediate action. If, on the other hand. . . . A seemingly simple engagement with types proves to be freighted with a
variety of possibilities. Atypical practices sometimes occur. I once fre-
quented a bank which cashed my checks swiftly, without the slightest
question; but they claimed never to have heard of me when I went
in to make a deposit! If I am an experienced bank customer, I will
have mastered quite a number of variations on the theme of checking
accounts and I will know my way about. I will quickly recognize
whether a visit to the bank promises complications or whether it will
in all likelihood be routine. I come with my typifications ready.

There is a further aspect to course-of-action and personal types.
Schutz asks us to consider the difference between types which are
understood by way of their temporal progression—types in the making—and types which are temporally completed, finished, done. Language reveals the typifying mechanism involved. Schutz writes: "By

18. PSW, p. 188.

looking at language we can see the personal ideal type in the very process of construction. I am referring to those nouns which are merely verbs erected into substantives. Thus every present participle is the personal typification of an act in progress, and every past participle is the ideal type of a completed act."[19] The broader implication of the distinction between course-of-action and personal types concerns the nature of human action altogether. It is central to Schutz's theory of meaning to distinguish between two different aspects of the word "action":

> This word can, first of all, mean the already constituted act (*Handlung*) considered as a completed unit, a finished product, an Objectivity. But second, it can mean the action in the very course of being constituted, and, as such, a flow, an ongoing sequence of events, a process of bringing something forth, an accomplishing. Every action, whether it be my own or that of another person, can appear to me under both these aspects.[20]

Meaning, then, is a function of a reflective glance back at action which has been completed and not something which experiences "have." Course-of-action types are already "fixed" in their typical structure; they are the inheritance, largely, of what our predecessors have passed on to us. Since personal types arise out of course-of-action types and are, in that sense, derivative, it is possible to say that the actor generates personal types in a more nearly (though far from completely) autonomous manner. Both kinds of types may be understood as "fixed"; both course-of-action and personal types have some spontaneity attaching to them. Between course-of-action and personal types there is a distinction but not a qualitative difference to be noted in accounting for their constitution. More fundamental still to their understanding is the recognition of the sphere within which these types operate. Common-sense constructs, Schutz maintains, have two points of reference: as naive, taken-for-granted features of daily life, types are rooted (I would say constitutively *formed*) in what Husserl called "prepredicative" experience. The ordinary person who typifies his experience into "course-of-action" and "personal types" is not self-consciously aware that this is what he is doing. Obviously, the language of typification may be foreign to him. Here we have "first-order constructs." But the social scientist or theorist in his professional role *does* use these types reflectively, not pre-predicatively. Here we have "second-order constructs." Common-sense human beings are first of all

19. Ibid.
20. PSW, p. 39.

actors in the social world; even as observers they are primarily actors. Theorists are model-creators; theorists are individuals who are paid to be observers. More than that, theorists are tinkerers of the imagination. The models of human actors and action which are built by the theorist are stripped of their concrete, life-historical biographies and endowed by their creators with no rights save those ascribed to them by their authors. In his discussion of course-of-action and personal types, Schutz is chiefly concerned with the theorist's model of the social world; at the same time, he is deeply engaged in the exploration of daily life. What Schutz offers us is an architectonic of common sense.

In retrospect, it might appear as if we were concerned with anonymity as a cardinal feature of an "objectified" world—the world at distance, which is presented to us by the theorist. Human beings seem to have been translated into their typified functions. In these terms, the anonymity which we have been examining would seem to be counterbalanced by the specificity of "life"—the actuality of a more fragile life-world. There is a more pressing balance to be established, and it might be presented in this way: The anonymity of theoretical distance has as its primordial alternative not the concreteness of life but the anonymity of pre-predicative sources. At this moment, what needs clarification is the logic of typification. That logic entails a theory of abstraction, and it is to that theory that we must attend. Here Schutz's work comes closest to that of his teacher (as he used to call him), Edmund Husserl. It might be worth saying that although Schutz was invested with phenomenology, he was also a close reader of Bergson, a profound student of Leibniz, and—though it is not manifest in his writings—knowledgeable about St. Thomas Aquinas (Schutz told me that had he time he would have liked to devote an essay or monograph to St. Thomas's angelology). Schutz did not write out of one book! And so, though I restrict myself to Schutz, he brings along with him— What is it? A gaggle of geese, a pride of lions?—a quarrel of philosophers.

Note: Quite some time after writing that Grove Enters wonders whether there is still a survivor of the Spanish-American War, I came across an obituary, headed "Veteran of 1898 War is Dead": "Tacoma, Wash., July 24 (AP)—Albert Tanner, the last surviving Spanish-American War veteran in the state of Washington and the nation's fourth-oldest veteran, has died at a hospital here. Mr. Tanner, who was 105 years old, served in the Army from 1898 to 1902, and later fought in World War I. Mr. Tanner's death leaves only 14 Spanish-American War veterans still living out of 392,000 Americans who fought in that war" (*The New York Times*, July 25, 1985, p. B5).

III

ABSTRACTION

To typify is to repeat and to go on repeating. With regard to the typical, to repeat is to intend the same unity of meaning again. *What* is intended is typified when the act of repeating—its actual occasion—is set aside in favor of what Husserl would call the "intended object." Mere repetition, however, is not typification. Continuing a regular drum beat is not typifying. The repetition we are interested in is selective: what is repeated which marks the typical is, as phenomenological language has it, what is *meant*. Language itself may serve as a straightforward example. Imagine the primal birdwatcher's cry: "archaeopteryx!" The first sighting! Set aside complications. *We* may say that how that astonishing word is pronounced, how it is *said*, does not affect what is designated, what is referred to: that no less astonishing creature which once flapped about chaotic skies. The word may be pronounced or mispronounced in an anarchy of accents; that Jurassic bird-snake (at least in my bestiary) remains itself. The meaning intended is distinct from the acts which intend it. This comes to: Typification is essentially an abstracting of meaning from the occasions of designation. For Schutz, typification is a form of abstraction which concerns mundane life. And language is a fundamental illustration. "Typification," Schutz writes, "is indeed that form of abstraction which leads to the more or less standardized yet more or less vague, conceptualization of common-sense thinking and to the necessary ambiguity of the terms of the ordinary vernacular."[1]

The "standardized" conceptualizations of common-sense thinking to which Schutz refers are the ways by which "unities of meaning" are experienced and utilized in daily life. Let there be an evolutionary falling off: let archaeopteryx give way to sparrow. In common-sense terms, sparrow means bird. Refinements of meaning here depend on

1. CPI, p. 323.

situations. Without ever having seen a sparrow, I know from many sources that a sparrow is a small bird. The precise size is of no great consequence unless exactitude is required by the situation in which I find myself discussing sparrows or birds of different sizes. The "standardized" conceptualization of "sparrow" is "more or less vague," in common-sense thinking and discourse, depending on the demands of the occasion. In similar fashion, the shape, color, and other characteristics of the sparrow may well be irrelevant to my use of the word "sparrow" when all I need to say to make my point is "No bigger than a sparrow." Something small, something tiny, a wee creature is all I mean; and that meaning is grasped immediately by Others, who are equivalently placed in ordinary life. Those Others may also understand by "sparrow" nothing more exact than a diminutive bird. What is "standard" between speaker and listeners is something at once distinct and uncertain; the "standard" *is* standard in common-sense terms because what is standard tolerates a considerable range of what is vague. "Surely, not as small as a sparrow!" "Oh, well, perhaps a bit larger—but pretty dinky." "Let's call it a sparrow and some." More sophisticated calibration is not only unnecessary for these conversants, it is or would be distracting. "Standard" conceptualization does not mean universally accepted or even generally acknowledged usage. What is standard is workable, works. If one word won't do, another can be used; if a more subtle shading of meaning is required, a lively image may serve the purpose. The linguistic motto might be: If you've got it, use it; if you don't, improvise.

"Working" language includes language which sometimes doesn't work. Occasionally an individual, in the course of an otherwise "standard" conversation may use a word which is not understood by the Other. Imagine:

> "And so the problem takes on a new Gestalt."
> "How's that?"
> "A new Gestalt, a new Gestalt altogether."
> "Quite so, but are you saying that of me?"
> "Why would you think that?"
> "Oh, I don't, but there's some that might."
> "No it's an entirely new Gestalt."
> "I can see that."
> "Are we agreed, then?"
> "Well, it's six of one and half-dozen of the other, isn't it?"

There may, of course, be language purposely used to impress:

stilted, purple, technical. Rhetorical strategy has its occasions. But in the dense hive of mundane chatter, in the argot of everyday banter and barter, language hurtles or traces its own laconic arc. "Standard" language is empowered by its very capacity to absorb contrary indicators without canceling out their claims and to relinquish discriminatory ground without giving up the right to make a multitude of effective distinctions. The elasticity of the idiom of daily discourse, the vernacular, the colloquial, empowers conceptualization in common-sense thinking. Nor is the correct word always the empowering word. Here ordinary language shares something with poetry: the direct, effective, word—the word which *works*—is not always chosen for use; the oblique or stray word may give to the casual scene, the offhand encounter, an auditory flush of sudden awareness. "Personally, I like words to sound wrong," Wallace Stevens once wrote.[2]

The "wrong-sounding" word may not even be wrong. At least, we arc sometimes aware of an unusual or perhaps dated word, perhaps a word which may once have been fairly commonly used among a certain group or even class but whose original meaning has been obscured. Around 1935, at least where I grew up, it was not uncommon to hear people saying "Dasn't"—"She dasn't marry him; what a rage there would be!" "Dasn't" was, I suppose, a contractual form or derivative of "dare not." I have not heard anyone say "dasn't" in a good many years, but what I think is surely a related word appears in Arthur Miller's *Death of a Salesman*. In the Requiem scene—a famous scene of a famous play—there is a speech which is so familiar to those interested in drama that it may no longer be heard. Biff says of his father: "He never knew who he was." And Charley, Willy Loman's friend, says to Biff:

> "Nobody dast blame this man. You don't understand: Willy was a salesman. And for a salesman, there is no rock bottom to the life. He don't put a bolt to a nut, he don't tell you the law or give you medicine. He's a man way out there in the blue, riding on a smile and a shoeshine. And when they start not smiling back—that's an earthquake. And then you get yourself a couple of spots on your hat, and you're finished. Nobody dast blame this man. A salesman is got to dream, boy. It comes with the territory."[3]

"No one dare blame this man" or "Let nobody blame this man" are

2. (Wallace Stevens), *Letters of Wallace Stevens* (selected and edited by Holly Stevens), New York: Alfred A. Knopf, 1966, p. 340.
3. Arthur Miller, *Death of a Salesman: Certain Private Conversations in Two Acts and a Requiem*, New York: Penguin Books, 1984, p. 138. Note: originally published in 1949.

reasonable translations of "Nobody dast blame this man," but the
translations are unfaithful to every character in the play. What is
reasonable is, in this instance, unworkable. I think that "dast" is the
most illuminating single word in the play. We are told, just before the
start of Act One that "The action takes place in Willy Loman's house
and yard and in various places he visits in the New York and Boston
of today." The play was first presented in New York in 1949. But the
"today" of the playwright's preliminary statement is a persistent "now."
Within "today" there is included the speech-root of Charley, a world
which hums with the inflections of American language surging
through both World Wars—the "dast" of 1914 already faded by 1941.
Not only old-fashioned but not quite grammatical in his speech, Charley is, in virtue of language which is neither cultivated nor up-to-date,
a *truth* of speaking which binds the characters of the play in their
irresolvable grief. Had Arthur Miller had Charley say, "Let no one
blame this man," I cannot imagine that *Death of a Salesman* would have
folded; I do think that had he used the optative mood, the character
of Charley (and through him the rest of the cast) would have disen-
gaged itself from Charley's childhood, that the historicity of the play
would have been impoverished, that the "standard" language which
strikes through Charley's speech would have failed to find its voice.
In that case, a summary of the dialogue would do just as well; there
would be no need for the play.

If it appears that I have made too much of "dast," consider the
reverberations of the word in the life of the play's protagonist. Had
Willy gone to Alaska with his brother Ben—had he dared—Willy
would have made his fortune. To dare is the passion of the Dream,
its lure and its lament. "Be daring!" we might fancy Willy crying out
in Bad Faith; "Nobody dast!" Charley admonishes the son who would
judge his father. But for the play's audience—for the one who attends
the theatrical performance or the one who reads the script—Charley's
speech is quite clear and piercing: the precise meaning and etymology
of "dast" are almost irrelevant to what is grasped *through* the force of
the language, through the weight of the entire play, sustained now
by a curious and wonderful eulogy. *Death of a Salesman*, however, also
bears a descriptive subtitle: "Certain Private Conversations in Two
Acts and a Requiem." It is largely in those "conversations" that the
poetry of the drama appropriates the vernacular, seizes its wrong-
sounding words, and, in what I would call subjunctive reality, realizes
the possibilities of "standard" speech. In *Death of a Salesman*, "con-

versations" become those dialogues which transcend time and place, communication with the dead as well as those who are about, interruptions of interrupted action, misalliances and evasions. What is "standard" in the vernacular is abstracted from the entire range of communication without there being any detailed or comprehensive sense of what that range includes. Instead of abstraction being a selection, it is a selective process. Here language proves to be a "transcendental clue" to abstraction as the primordial ground of social reality.

Now we are at a rendezvous with the formative elements of a phenomenology of abstraction. Husserl speaks of certain "idealizations"—*a priori* forms which are constitutive of meaning and of the capacity of consciousness to grasp identity in the flow of experience and to return to that identity again and again. Of "the *fundamental form* 'and so forth' " [*und so weiter*], Husserl goes on to say that it is "the form of *reiterational* 'infinity'; never stressed by logicians, it has its subjective correlate in 'one can always again' [*man kann immer wieder*]. This is plainly an idealization, since de facto no one can always again. Still this form plays its sense-determining rôle everywhere in logic. One can *always return* to an ideal significational unity or to any other ideal unity. . . ."[4] Although Husserl's immediate concern in these formulations is the logic of predication and mathematics as "the realm of infinite constructions,"[5] the significance of the idealizations which he discusses go beyond problems of formal relations. For Schutz, the idealizations apply to the entire realm of social action. He writes:

> Any action refers by its being projected to pre-experiences organized in what may be called the stock of knowledge actually at hand, which is, thus, the sedimentation of previous experiencing acts together with their generalizations, formalizations, and idealizations. It is at hand, actually or potentially recollected or retained, and as such the ground of all of our pretentions and anticipations. These, in turn, are subject to the basic idealizations of "and so forth and so on" ("*und so weiter*") and "I can do it again" ("*Ich kann immer wieder*") described by Husserl.[6]

4. Edmund Husserl, *Formal and Transcendental Logic* (trans. by Dorion Cairns), The Hague: Martinus Nijhoff, 1969, pp. 188–189 (section 74); cf. the original: *Formale und transzendentale Logik* (*Jahrbuch für Philosophie und phänomenologische Forschung*, zehnter Band, Halle: Max Niemeyer, 1929, p. 167 [section 74]). Also see Suzanne Bachelard, *A Study of Husserl's "Formal and Transcendental Logic"* (trans. by Lester E. Embree), Evanston: Northwestern University Press, 1968, p. 122ff.

5. *Formal and Transcendental Logic*, p. 189 (section 74).
6. CPI, p. 146.

Of particular importance to Schutz is the application of Husserl's idealizations to the individual's placement in the world as being *here* (*hic*) and the Other as being *there* (*illic*). And beyond spatial placement, the individual's experience of temporal reality is also affected by these subtle *a priori* forms. Schutz writes:

> We may say that the world within my actual reach belongs essentially to the present tense. The world within my potential reach, however, shows a more complicated time structure. At least two zones of potentiality have to be distinguished. To the first, which refers to the past, belongs what was formerly within my actual reach and what, so I assume, can be brought back into my actual reach again (*world within restorable reach*). The assumption involved is based upon the idealizations, governing all conduct in the natural sphere, namely, that I may continue to act as I have acted so far and that I may again and again recommence the same action under the same conditions. Dealing with the universal role of these idealizations for the foundation of logic and especially pure analytic, Husserl calls them the idealizations of the "and so on" and of the "I can do it again," the latter being the subjective correlate of the former. To give an example: By an act of locomotion there came out of my reach what was formerly "world within my reach." The shifting of the center *O* of my system of coordinates has turned my former world in the *hic* into a world now in the *illic*. But under the idealization of the "I can do it again" I assume that I can retransform the actual *illic* into a new *hic*. My past world within my reach has under this idealization the character of a world which can be brought back again within my reach. Thus, for instance, my past manipulatory area continues to function in my present as a potential manipulatory area in the mode of *illic* and has now the character of a specific chance of restoration.[7]

There are several ways in which the "idealizations" of "and so forth" and "I can again" can be understood. As *a priori* forms through which consciousness grasps the real, the conceptualizations are, in the Kantian sense, conditions necessary for the possibility of experience. Rather than being teased out of the logic of conceptualization, the idealizations are requirements which must be met if experience is to be coherent. In the phenomenological sense, however, the *a prioris* are instrumentalities of consciousness, mobile features of intentionality understood as an essentially abstractive force. The arrow of intentionality, in Husserl's sense, is in flight toward its target before it can be fitted into time's bow; the arrow, as it were, is comprehensible

7. CPI, pp. 224–225.

only as already-in-flight; it lives through its movement. Identities of meaning are the work of "and so forth" and "I can again": the selfsame unity of meaning may be continued or repeated. Without the intended meaning, however, there is nothing to cognize as "continuable" or "repeatable." We are left in a quandary—an ancient one: if the arrow must be understood as "already-in-flight," then what is its source? How could the arrow ever have been propelled? Or does it somehow—when it comes to intentional consciousness—contain its own engine which is brought to life by its own energy? Are we left with the image of someone glancing up to the sky to notice, for a bare and lucid moment, a flight of birds soaring and vanishing in their self-created darkness? Husserl releases us from Zeno's spell.

The arrow moves along what Husserl calls a "horizon"—a complex concept which means that "already-in-flight" is an image of openness, a moving along a coherent trajectory toward what may be an indeterminate but nevertheless integral goal. "Consciousness-of," Husserl's arrow, is intentional in a far more fundamental sense than what is ordinarily termed "awareness" or "reflection" or "purposing." Whether or not an individual is self-consciously thinking "about" something, that thinking is *about*. The idealizations of "and so forth" and "I can again" *lean* toward continuity in a particular manner: they are "horizonal" in their ideality. Husserl writes:

> . . . every substrate of determination is originally always already passively pregiven as something determinable, as something with a horizon of indeterminate determinability and known in conformity with a most general type. In the course of the explication, this prescription is increasingly fulfilled, but there still constantly remains a *horizon* beyond the succession of actually constituted determinations and *open to new properties which must be expected*. Every mental process with several members, progressing in an orderly manner, carries with it such an open horizon. It is not *one* next unique member which is prescribed but the continuance of the process itself, which thus always has the intentional character of an *open process*.[8]

The horizonal matrix in which Alfred Schutz places Husserl's ideal-

8. Edmund Husserl, *Experience and Judgment: Investigations in a Genealogy of Logic* (revised and edited by Ludwig Landgrebe and trans. by James S. Churchill and Karl Ameriks, with an introduction by James S. Churchill and an afterword by Lothar Eley), Evanston: Northwestern University Press, 1973, pp. 217–218 (section 51b). See Helmut Kuhn, "The Phenomenological Concept of 'Horizon'," in *Philosophical Essays in Memory of Edmund Husserl* (edited by Marvin Farber), Cambridge: Harvard University Press, 1940, pp. 106–123.

izations is the social world as it is given to the actor in his experience of everyday life through taken-for-granted acts of typification. The phenomenology of abstraction becomes the organon of common sense. In a passage of decisive importance to his work, Schutz reveals the anatomy of typification:

> All projects of my forthcoming acts are based upon my knowledge at hand at the time of projecting. To this knowledge belongs my experience of previously performed acts which are typically similar to the projected one. Consequently all projecting involves a particular idealization, called by Husserl the idealization of "I-can-do-it-again," i.e., the assumption that I may under typically similar circumstances act in a way typically similar to that in which I acted before in order to bring about a typically similar state of affairs. It is clear that this idealization involves a construction of a specific kind. My knowledge at hand at the time of projecting must, strictly speaking, be different from my knowledge at hand after having performed the projected act, if for no other reason than because I "grew older" and at least the experiences I had while carrying out my project have modified my biographical circumstances and enlarged my stock of experience. Thus, the "repeated" action will be something else than a mere re-performance. The first action A' started within a set of circumstances C' and indeed brought about the state of affairs S'; the repeated action A" starts in a set of circumstances C" and is expected to bring about the state of affairs S". By necessity C" will differ from C' because the experience that A' succeeded in bringing about S' belongs to my stock of knowledge, which is an element of C", whereas to my stock of knowledge, which was an element of C', belonged merely the empty anticipation that this would be the case. Similarly S" will differ from S' as A" will from A'. This is so because all the terms—C', C", A', A", S', S"—are as such unique and irretrievable events. Yet exactly those features which make them unique and irretrievable in the strict sense are—to my common-sense thinking—eliminated as being irrelevant for my purpose at hand. When making the idealization of "I-can-do-it-again" I am merely interested in the typicality of A, C, and S, all of them without primes. The construction consists, figuratively speaking, in the suppression of the primes as being irrelevant, and this, incidentally, is characteristic of typifications of all kinds.[9]

To say that suppression of the primes is characteristic of typifications of all kinds is to hold that the "miniature" ideal types of common-sense thinking and the "second-order" constructs of scientific thought share, in strikingly different ways, the same ground of abstraction. In

9. CPI, pp. 20–21.

common-sense experience, the individual relies on "personal" and "course-of-action" types as more or less well-proved recipes of action. Those recipes have worked in the past and they are therefore used in the present as well as held in reserve for future application, as the circumstances warrant. The current of daily life is moved not only by the efficacy of the utility of recipes but by the assurance that the "and so on"—the strong likelihood that the recipes are repeatable in typically efficacious terms—is deeply reliable. Within Weber's "subjective interpretation of meaning," Schutz finds a "subjective interpretation" which is expressed through patterns of action. The actor on the social scene has his own sense of what "things mean," of how events in "his" world affect him as well as other individuals, of how things get done, of how to go about arranging his affairs, of what to say and of what to do. A quite vague conception of the banking system, far from deterring the "average man" from making out and depositing checks, may very well make it easier for him to proceed with his payment of a bill. "Easier" in the sense that he need only repeat a formula which he has repeatedly followed in the past with satisfactory results. On special occasions, the recipe must be changed. Transacting some unfamiliar business at the bank, the "average man" will ask, "To whom should this check be made out?" "Just write 'On Sight'," he is told. Now the asker of that question may never have made out a check in that way, may never have heard of such a thing as "On Sight," may have no idea of what the expression means. But he follows instructions because he has confidence in the senior officer of the bank who is handling his business, because the "average man" knows that his understanding of banking language is limited, because he takes it for granted that the payee will find the check in order, because his concern is with getting his business accomplished quickly, and because the explanation of "On Sight" does not matter to him really; what matters is getting his banking *done*. A plethora of primes is suppressed.

The "purer" the type, the greater the suppression. From the standpoint of common sense, bureaucracy represents the "typing" of human beings and of human action in distant, often arbitrary ways. To be treated as a "petitioner" before the courts is to be stripped of one's ownness. The individual has not lost his name; his name has been transformed into any name; the petitioner is a variable, a slot into which anyone may be placed. "Abandon Your Name" is the legend above this gate. Rather than retrace steps along this path which have already been luminously marked, it might be useful to reverse the traditional relationship between officials and their clients, between "the system" and the individual. The extremes of coldness, arrogance, indifference, impatience, and disdain which seem to be inherent in bureaucracy and its functionaries might be fancifully transposed—however improbably—so that the "courts" petition and the "petitioner" judges. Suppose that a three-year-old child has strayed from his parent in a major airport, that a preliminary search has failed to locate the child, that a full-scale effort has been made to find him and has met with no success, that after four hours of hunting, inquiries, announcements, and advisories, it appears that the child has vanished. After all this:

"I want to assure you that everything we can do is being done."

"Oh I'm already convinced of that."

"Yes, the airport security people, the city police department, the highway patrol—we've even alerted the FBI."

"Do you think he might have been kidnapped?"

"We can't ignore that possibility."

"I don't see why anyone would want to take Jonathan."

"There is a lot of pathology at airports."

"I can't credit kidnapping. I imagine he'll turn up somewhere. Jonathan always loved movement; perhaps he's on one of those luggage-conveyer belts."

"You mean he might be hiding in the baggage?"

"Something like Freight on Board."

"That's a terrifying thought!"

"Not especially. Jonathan is a survivor; he doesn't need much oxygen and he likes to amuse himself."

"He could be crushed!"

"I doubt it. More likely, he'll turn up in Houston or L.A.—pop right out of those little doors onto a carousel."

"We're in touch with our people everywhere."

"Yes, well my flight has just been called."

"Surely you're not leaving?"

"What's the point of hanging around?"

"You're leaving your child?"

"Oh, I'll be in touch. Meanwhile, you have my home and office numbers. You can always leave a message with my answering service."

"This is unbelievable!"

"It's all part of parenting."

"I simply cannot grasp it!"

"There's the final call for boarding."

"Isn't your heart wrung?"

"I'm not into anguish."

Our typified expectations in daily life presuppose the range of what is "more or less" standardized action; the "range" itself is defined by what Schutz has called the "relevancies" of both the taken-for-granted and the unfamiliar as well as of the incredible. For the moment, we may say of the "range" that it accommodates considerable differences because of the gravity of common sense, that is, the tug of the ordinary toward simple acceptance of what there is because it is. It is I who speak of "gravity," not Schutz. One may feel frustrated, annoyed, irritated, disgusted—what there is may occasion all of these responses and still "hold" the individual, bind him to a recognition of reality, a recognition which is more fundamental than acceptance or revulsion. Acceptance and revulsion are "about" some state of affairs; "what there is" exerts an ancient compulsion, which I have noted but not described. A primordial "belief" in "what there is" is an act of "animal faith" (to appropriate Santayana's phrase for my own friendly but perhaps subversive purposes), not a self-conscious positing of belief but rather an uninhibited reliance on immediacy with no more "evidence" than "nature" provides. The "pull" of daily life is toward reliance on what has always supported the individual: enough order, sequence, consequentiality, and predictability to assure success in finding one's way in the world. We cannot be given absolute certitude by the precepts of common sense, but it is enough if we are guided with a reasonable degree of probability, of likelihood. As common-sense human beings, we do not ask for infallibility; reassurance suffices.

Abstraction is the instrument of suppression. The primes which are suppressed are, in effect, deemed superfluous or distractive to the type. But in assessing the type, one may move from the course-of-action back to the personal or, confronted with a "picture" of the individual, move to the kind of action through which such an individual may, in Schutz's terms, "gear into" the social world. In either case, it is requisite that a distinction be made between the individual steps through which a type is formed and the formed type, taken as a unity. *Given* the formed type, one may move back in order to trace out its order of constitution. Husserl has prepared the phenomenological foundation for a theory of the constitution of types by distinguishing between "polythetic" and "monothetic" acts. Take the simplest—though remarkable—example: In learning to read, a child may be taught the phonetic elements and so come to understand words as units. Most adults have little if any recollection of being taught to read; the individual steps involved in mastering the elements have faded from memory, but the results vividly remain. Even in childhood, the struggle over the elements gives way to ease in reading comparatively advanced texts. Monothetic synthesis supersedes polythetic activity: a *formed* meaning-unity may be grasped without going through each of the polythetic acts which was involved in its constitution. Schutz offers an especially lucid illustration of how this occurs in youth:

> As high school students we all learned to derive the Pythagorean theorem $a^2 + b^2 = c^2$ from certain other geometrical propositions by developing step by step certain conclusions from certain assured premises. This performance of many separate although interconnected mental operations disclosed to us the meaning of the theorem in question, and this meaning has since become our permanent possession. It is not necessary now for us to repeat this mental process of deriving the theorem, in order to understand its meaning. On the contrary, although some of us might have some difficulty if we had to prove why the sum of the squares of the sides of a right triangle must always be equal to the square of the hypotenuse, we do understand the meaning of this proposition, which we find ready at hand within the stock of our experience.[10]

Our experience of the world, understood in mundane terms, is that of both polythetic and monothetic activity. As I come to know the social world more definitively, I also come to recognize that the ingredients of my recipes for action must be modified and even changed. The steps involved in a pattern of action may require alternation or substitution; their timing may have to be varied. But the more I can repeat a typical procedure and get typical results, the less noteworthy the individual steps in the procedure become. It is only when something "goes wrong," when the recipe which has worked in the past does not "turn out right," that I need to retrace my path and reflect on my "cooking" or indeed on the recipe itself. Monothetic acts must be regarded in a somewhat different way. Finding a formed result is

10. CPI, p. 111. Note: Husserl's own formulations of the "polythetic" and "monothetic" are more forbidding. In *Ideas*, he writes: "Every . . . many-rayed (polythetic) constitution of synthetic objectivities—which are essentially such that '*originally*' we can be aware of them *only* synthetically—possesses the essential law-conforming possibility of *transforming the many-rayed object of awareness into one that is simply one-rayed*, of '*rendering objective*' *in the specific sense* and in a *monothetic* act what is synthetically constituted in the many-rayed object" (Boyce Gibson translation, p. 336 [section 119]. Cf. Husserl's *Experience and Judgment*, p. 112ff., p. 208ff. [sections 24 and 50]). Cf. Aron Gurwitsch, *Studies in Phenomenology and Psychology*, Evanston: Northwestern University Press, 1966, p. 250. Also see Robert Sokolowski, *The Formation of Husserl's Concept of Constitution*, The Hague: Martinus Nijhoff, 1964.

like coming upon a hieroglyph: it signifies. The likeness, however, is not complete. The hieroglyph, for the observer who does not understand it, signifies *that* something meaningful has been presented. The monothetic act signifies, in strong measure, by what is *not* presented, by meaning which is "sedimented" (to adopt Husserl's word) in the act.

The phenomenological concept of the "sedimentation" of meaning operates at a number of quite different levels. The Pythagorean theorem, in Schutz's example, is retained as a monothetic result after its polythetic demonstration has been forgotten. In geometry, it is always possible to return to those steps in the proof which lead to the theorem. Nonmathematical monothetic results must be traced back in other ways. Consider a trivial rule in the regulation of ordinary street traffic: Stop at a red light. An automobile driver who has been a daily commuter for thirty years may have forgotten when he first learned of this precept. Certainly, all manuals for driving include this information. In most instances, knowing what to do when the light is red is a bit of common-sense lore which is absorbed in childhood. Reminders about always waiting until the light turns green before crossing the street are heard by the city child long before he is old enough to operate a car. But it is difficult—and ordinarily unnecessary—to recapture the exact history of instruction in such a matter. When one reads about red lights in official booklets prepared for those who are planning to secure a driver's license or when one is told by a driving instructor always to remember to stop for a red light, the information or advice is redundant. Police officers—who are said to have heard all excuses—can hardly have many drivers who, when stopped for running a red light, say in all seriousness: "I never knew you couldn't go through red lights." Even people who do not drive know that. Children know that. It is something which "everybody knows." The steps by which the individual comes to learn the rule are lost except for their generality. That there were instructions given and probably repeated is accepted as true, though a more precise reconstruction of how one came to learn the rule is unavailable. The "steps" at issue prove to be easily dispensable; they are either ignored or treated in their typicality: "How did I learn? In the usual way, I expect." In an odd manner, the way back leads to anonymity.

More accessible to retracing is the experience of "character." It may be said truly of the Tolliver twins, Deirdre and Duncan, that they are delightful: high-spirited, vibrant, adventuresome, loyally unpredict-able. Our particular encounters with them can be rehearsed, incidents described, tales. From a richness of memorable events, certain espe-cially instructive and revealing moments may be selected. Some notion of "character" emerges which explains why the term "delightful" is apposite in describing the twins. The particular traits which are, as we say, characteristic of Deirdre and Duncan may be revealed quite indirectly and in fragmentary form. Duncan celebrates the birth of Alaric the Visigoth with a blast of the shofar; Deirdre completes all short-answer questions with "*Der Einzige und sein Eigentum.*" College officials are unhappy. The twins have given their food stamps to the less fortunate; their friends continue to rally round them. The mono-thetic "delightful" has been formed by circumstances of inventiveness, fresh deeds, bizarre announcements. The polythetic moments of the synthesis can be tagged but—more important—each delight-yielding expression of the effervescent twins points insistently toward the promise of renewal, toward still more maggoty pranks. In the shower of their delight, Deirdre and Duncan cast a band of color which dis-arms those who might discount them as self-conscious and pretentious zanies. Even the recollection of their capers creates an after-flow of laughter in the twins' friends. It is no longer possible for one who is familiar with the Tolliver twins to view their latest antic on its own terms; the traces have overpowered the result.

There is also a pathology of sedimentation (but here I speak not for Husserl or for Schutz but for myself alone). In the course of synthesis, some of the polythetic acts (and *their* sedimented meaning) may be condensed into an acceptable forgetfulness, so that the mono-thetic result varnishes over or conceals what formed the result.

> "What times, what times we had in the old gang!"
> "Oh, we mostly just hung around."
> "Do you remember when we set fire to that bum?"
> "No. I remember just hanging around."

The condensation or at least slighting of certain formative acts may be considered a normal part of synthesis, but the shading of selectivity hardly accounts for an act of mayhem.

> "We really made a torch of that geezer!"
> "No, it was just his clothes."
> "Did he ever howl!"
> "Shook him up a bit. He wasn't hurt."
> "Then why did we run?"

The sedimented memory of cruelty and shame may be transformed in alternative, more subtle ways: the heroism of evil may be fused into abiding images of youth, service, and the "good innocence" of a cryptic vision.[11] In the landscape of historical decay, a rat crouches, turns to stare at us, sways—a rat with a stained tail.

In Husserl's terms, "historical" sedimentation of meaning has to do with the "reactivation" of passively "dormant" meaning-structures—"ideal objects," in the present context—which once were "originarily" given, that is, present in utter immediacy, "in person."[12] A strong example is given in Husserl's manuscript "The Origin of Geometry."[13] There is a transference from the originary presentation of ideal structures to their reproduction in documentary form. Husserl writes:

> The important function of written, documenting linguistic expression is that it makes communications possible without immediate or mediate personal address; it is, so to speak, communication become virtual. Through this, the communalization of man is lifted to a new level. Written signs are, when considered from a purely corporeal point of view, straightforwardly, sensibly experienceable; and it is always possible that they be intersubjectively experienceable in common. But as linguistic signs they awaken, as do linguistic sounds, their familiar significations. The awakening is something passive; the awakened signification is thus given passively, similarly to the way in which any other activity which has sunk into obscurity, once associatively awakened, emerges at first *passively* as a more or less clear memory. In the passivity in question here, as in the case of memory, what is passively awakened can be transformed back, so to speak, into the corresponding activity: this is the capacity for reactivation that belongs originally to every human being as a speaking being. Accordingly, then, the writing-down effects a transformation of the original mode of being of the meaning-structure, e.g., within the geometrical sphere of self-evidence, of the

11. See Saul Friedländer, *Reflections of Nazism: An Essay on Kitsch and Death* (trans. by Thomas Weyr), New York: Harper and Row, 1984.

12. What is "originarily given" is "it-itself" (*Selbstgebung*). The phrase "in person" was used by Dorion Cairns over fifty years ago (Dorion Cairns, *The Philosophy of Edmund Husserl* [unpublished Ph.D. dissertation, Department of Philosophy, Harvard University, 1933]). Also see Dorion Cairns, "Phenomenology," in *A History of Philosophical Systems* (edited by Vergelius Ferm), New York: Philosophical Library, 1950, pp. 353–364. Cf. Dorion Cairns, *Guide for Translating Husserl*, The Hague: Martinus Nijhoff, 1973. Note: Husserl writes: "In the broadest sense, evidence denotes a universal primal phenomenon of intentional life, namely . . . the quite pre-eminent mode of consciousness that consists in the *self-appearance*, the *self-exhibiting*, the *self-giving* of an affair, an affair-complex (or state of affairs), a universality, a value, or other objectivity, in the final mode: 'itself-there,' 'immediately intuited,' 'given originaliter' " (*Cartesian Meditations*, p. 57 [section 24]).

13. Included (as an Appendix) in Edmund Husserl, *The Crisis of European Sciences and Transcendental Philosophy* (trans. with an introduction by David Carr), Evanston: Northwestern University Press, 1970, pp. 353–378.

geometrical structure which is put into words. It becomes sedimented,
so to speak. But the reader can make it self-evident again, can reactivate
the self-evidence.[14]

Phenomenology, for Husserl, demands an essential search for "originary" presentations. Moving from monothetic results to their polythetic sources requires a "reenactment" of the "history" of the
constitution of meaning. The primordial "evidence" of the originary
is sedimented in the experience of the individual, however hidden
the trace of the originary may be. In a nontemporal and nonpsy-
chological sense, the phenomenologist seeks to return to the originary
world. Husserl has given a new placement to the concept of "history"
as well as to the station of "science." What emerges from this new
placement is an understanding of the world of everyday experience—
the *Lebenswelt*—as the ultimate ground from which all "higher level"
abstraction derives.[15]

The "sedimented" world of daily life is, for Schutz, a "pre-interpreted" reality, defined by the actors in society—the "cast" of the
immense spectacle of intersubjectivity. The social world, then, is not
given to me simply as "to-be-interpreted." Rather, I am confronted
with the pre-interpretations of Others, including my "predecessors."
For Schutz, ". . . Social reality . . . has a specific meaning and relevance
structure for the human beings living, acting, and thinking within it.
By a series of common-sense constructs they have pre-selected and

14. Ibid., pp. 360–361. Also see Jacques Derrida, *Edmund Husserl's "Origin of Ge-
ometry": An Introduction* (trans. with a preface by John P. Leavey and edited by David
B. Allison), New York: Nicolas Hays, 1978. Note: David Carr's translation of Husserl's
"The Origin of Geometry" is included as an Appendix. Cf. Maurice Merleau-Ponty,
Themes from the Lectures at the Collège de France 1952–1960 (trans. with a preface by John
O'Neill), Evanston: Northwestern University Press, 1970, Ch. 11: "Husserl at the Limits
of Phenomenology," pp. 113–123.

15. Jacob Klein writes: "To inquire into an object means, according to Husserl, first
to 'bracket' its 'objectivity' and then to seek for its 'constitutive origins,' to reproduce
its 'intentional genesis.' Any object, as a 'significant' or 'intentional' unity, contains the
'sedimented history' of its 'constitution.' That 'history,' of course, did not take place
within 'natural time.' Yet it can be understood as a 'history' because the intentional
genesis belongs to the 'life of consciousness,' and consciousness itself is primarily constituted as an 'absolute stream' determined by the 'internal temporality.' 'Internal temporality' is thus the universal eidetic 'form' of the intentional genesis. In any inner
experience of an intentional object, that object is given originally in the mode of
immediate 'presence'; this immediate 'presentation' is followed, of necessity, by a 'retention' of the object, in which the object appears in the mode of 'just-having-been-
experienced'; through all the successive modes of retentional consciousness—that is to
say, through a continuous 'modification'—the object is constituted as persisting, as one
and the same (identical, 'invariant') object. But just as there is a 'limit' which the continuous modification of the retentional consciousness approaches and beyond which

pre-interpreted this world which they experience as the reality of their daily lives."[16] Except for the wish to avoid terminological confusion, I would suggest that instead of the "first"- and "second"-order constructs (those of the actor and the social scientist) which Schutz has detailed, an additional "order" construct be introduced to describe the actor's construal of the pre-interpretation of experience made by his alter ego. Not only do I interpret the Other's action, but I interpret the Other as an interpreting creature. I would say that Schutz condenses but does not conflate the primary constructs instituted by the common-sense human being in all of his intricate naiveté. The "meaning-construction of the social world" is borne by mundane man, the Atlas of common sense. The symbolic force of this insight was best stated by Eric Voegelin:

> Human society is not merely a fact, or an event, in the external world to be studied by an observer like a natural phenomenon. Though it has externality as one of its important components, it is as a whole a little world, a cosmion, illuminated with meaning from within by the human beings who continuously create and bear it as the mode and condition of their self-realization.[17]

The "externality" of human society is a problem not only for the individual but also—and centrally—for the theoretical observer. The nature of sedimentation of meaning as well as of abstraction must be reapproached from the standpoint of scientific procedure. The sci-

---

the 'prominence' of the object flows away into the general substratum of consciousness, there is the 'past history' of the original 'presentation' of the object, which is the proper domain of transcendental phenomenology. It is here that the 'evidence' experienced in the immediate presentation assumes the character of a transcendental problem of constitution. It is here that the intrinsic 'possibility' of the identity of an object is revealed out of its categorical constituents, that the 'intentional genesis' leads back to the 'constitutive origins,' that the 'sedimented history' is reactivated into the 'intentional history'. Moreover, such a transcendental inquiry into an object may reveal the essential necessity of a historical development within natural time" ("Phenomenology and the History of Science," in *Philosophical Essays in Memory of Edmund Husserl* [edited by Marvin Farber], pp. 150–151). See Herbert Marcuse, "On Science and Phenomenology," in *Boston Studies in the Philosophy of Science*, Vol. II: *In Honor of Philipp Frank* (edited by Robert S. Cohen and Marx W. Wartofsky), New York: Humanities Press, 1965, pp. 279–290 and the response to this paper by Aron Gurwitsch, "Comment on the Paper by H. Marcuse," Ibid., pp. 291–306. Also see Ludwig Landgrebe, *The Phenomenology of Edmund Husserl: Six Essays* (edited with an introduction by Donn Welton), Ithaca: Cornell University Press, 1981 (Ch. 6: "The Problem of a Transcendental Science of the A Priori of the Life-World").

16. CPI, p. 59.

17. Eric Voegelin, *The New Science of Politics: An Introduction*, Chicago: University of Chicago Press, 1952, p. 27. Note: Schutz quotes this passage (and its continuation) in CPI, p. 336.

entific observer—and here we shall speak of him not as a "private
party" but strictly as a scientist—is responsible to the professional
stance which he has assumed: he is defined (and self-defined) by the
theoretical framework of his discipline, by the methodological procedures demanded of him as a "privileged" observer, by the setting
aside of his personal inclinations, private interests, particular loyalties,
and intimate involvements. I am not presently concerned with the
usual questions of whether or to what extent such "setting aside" is
possible. It is the matter of an "ideal observer" which needs attention.
Such an observer, according to Schutz, enters into a role in which his
concrete biographical situation is "put out of action." A special set of
relevances governs his conduct. The common-sense individual's interaction with other common-sense individuals is qualitatively different from the scientist's interaction with his fellow scientists. Schutz
writes:

> We have . . . to characterize the special case of the observer who is not
> a partner in the interaction patterns. His motives are not interlocked
> with those of the observed person or persons; he is "tuned in" upon
> them but not they upon him. In other words, the observer does not
> participate in the complicated mirror-reflexes involved by which in the
> interaction pattern among contemporaries, the actor's in-order-to mo-
> tives become understandable to the partner as his own because motives
> and vice versa. Precisely this fact constitutes the so-called "disinterest-
> edness" or detachment of the observer.[18]

By "in-order-to" motives, Schutz means ". . . the orientation of the
action to a future event . . ."[19] and by "because" motives he means the
relation of the action to "a past lived experience."[20] "I joined the navy

18. CPI, p. 26. Schutz goes on to say that the observer ". . . is not involved in the
actor's hopes and fears whether or not they will understand one another and achieve
their end by the interlocking of motives. Thus, his system of relevances differs from
that of the interested parties and permits him to see at the same time more and less
than what is seen by them. But under all circumstances, it is merely the manifested
fragments of the actions of *both* partners that are accessible to his observation. In order
to understand them the observer has to avail himself of his knowledge of typically
similar patterns of interaction in typically similar situational settings and has to construct
the motives of the actors from that sector of the course of action which is patent to his
observation. The constructs of the observer are, therefore, different ones than those
used by the participants in the interaction, if for no other reason than the fact that the
purpose of the observer is different from that of the interactors and therewith the
system of relevances attached to such purposes are also different" (CPI, pp. 26–27).
Cf. Alfred Schutz, "Choice and the Social Sciences" (edited by Lester E. Embree), in
Life-World and Consciousness: Essays for Aron Gurwitsch (edited by Lester E. Embree),
Evanston: Northwestern University Press, 1972, p. 580 ff.
19. PSW, p. 87.
20. Ibid.

in order to see the world" and "I joined the navy because I wanted to see the world" is an ordinary language translation—two ways of saying the same thing—which veils the distinction that Schutz makes between "genuine" and nongenuine because motives. A genuine because motive cannot be translated into an in-order-to motive. "I was expelled from Harvard because I was found guilty of witchcraft" does not translate into an in-order-to variant. For Schutz, the interlocking of because and in-order-to motives binds the social order. More terminology: The "tuning-in relationship"—being "tuned in"—refers to a prereflective mode of sociation which makes "association" possible. Schutz:

> . . . the concrete researches of many sociologists and philosophers have aimed at certain forms of social intercourse which necessarily precede all communication. Wiese's "contact-situations," Scheler's perceptual theory of the alter ego, to a certain extent Cooley's concept of the face-to-face relationship, Malinowski's interpretation of speech as originating within the situation determined by social interaction, Sartre's basic concept of "looking at the Other and being looked at by the Other" (*le regard*), all these are just a few examples of the endeavor to investigate what might be called the "mutual tuning-in relationship" upon which alone all communication is founded.[21]

These distinctions made, we can understand why the scientific observer stands outside of lived experience: postulates circulate through the observer's veins; the ventricles of his heart pump not blood but doctrine. But it is not only the scientific observer who stands outside of everyday life; the models which the observer constructs of mundane human beings in social action also stand apart from living beings. In setting himself methodologically apart from actuality, the observer substitutes fictions for his fellow-men. He creates, Schutz says, "puppets or homunculi":[22]

> He [the social scientist] begins to construct typical course-of-action patterns corresponding to the observed events. Thereupon he co-ordinates to these typical course-of-action patterns a personal type, a model of an actor whom he imagines as being gifted with consciousness. Yet it is a consciousness restricted to containing nothing but all the elements relevant to the performance of the course-of-action patterns under observation and relevant, therewith, to the scientist's problem under scrutiny. He ascribes, thus, to this fictitious consciousness a set of typical in-order-to motives corresponding to the goals of the observed course-

21. CPII, p. 161.
22. CPI, p. 41.

of-action patterns and typical because-motives upon which the in-order-to motives are founded. Both types of motives are assumed to be invariant in the mind of the imaginary actor-model.[23]

Both the observer and the observed abstract: the social scientist self-consciously and with rigor constructs a model in place of the concrete individual; the living person enters the social world in the naive anticipation that its typicality may continue to support his everyday existence. Again, there is a "doubling" effect. By practicing scientific abstraction, the observer also constructs a self-typification; he knows himself to be an observer rather than an actor. To the extent that becoming a formal observer involves a mode of social intervention (the anthropologist in the field, living with the individuals he observes), the scientist attempts to move within the limits of his self-typification. There is no assurance provided by methodological techniques that the observer may not transcend his formal limits. It has not been said that the observer ceases to be a human being because he assumes a professional role. We are concerned with the "ideal observer." On the side of the actor, there is also a "doubleness." The common-sense person is *in* the everyday world. At any moment, I find myself in the thick of on-going "everydayness." Acting in that taken-for-granted world, however, has its demands: the actor must confront not only intimate "consociates" but also consider unknown contemporaries, not to mention predecessors and successors. All of

23. CPI, p. 40. Schutz continues (p. 41): "Yet these models of actors are not human beings living within their biographical situation in the social world of everyday life. Strictly speaking, they do not have any biography or any history, and the situation into which they are placed is not a situation defined by them but defined by their creator, the social scientist. He has created these puppets or homunculi to manipulate them for his purpose. A merely specious consciousness is imputed to them by the scientist, which is constructed in such a way that its presupposed stock of knowledge at hand (including the ascribed set of invariant motives) would make actions originating from it subjectively understandable, provided that these actions were performed by real actors within the social world. But the puppet and his artificial consciousness is not subjected to the ontological conditions of human beings. The homunculus was not born, he does not grow up, and he will not die. He has no hopes and no fears; he does not know anxiety as the chief motive of all his deeds. He is not free in the sense that his acting could transgress the limits his creator, the social scientist, has predetermined. He cannot err, if to err is not his typical destiny. He cannot choose, except among the alternatives the social scientist has put before him as standing to his choice. Whereas man, as Simmel has clearly seen, enters any social relationship merely with a part of his self and is, at the same time, always within and outside of such a relationship, the homunculus, placed into a social relationship is involved therein in his totality. He is nothing else but the originator of his typical function because the artificial consciousness imputed to him contains merely those elements which are necessary to make such functions subjectively meaningful."

the illustrations which we have utilized come to bear upon the way in which the individual acts in situations which require varying degrees of abstraction from spiky particulars. For the most part, mundane action is unreflective action: the ordinary individual engages in a typical course-of-action pattern without ratiocination. When reflection is needed as to how, for example, a request should be framed, what is called for is not an epistemology of solicitation. Most often, "wording" is all that needs attention. Yet the actor also has a typification of himself. That self-typification is at once tacit and picturable.

"Practicing scientific abstraction" sounds vague and would be vague were it not for the specific meaning that has been given that phrase in our discussion: We are speaking of the activity of the social scientist who purposely turns away from what he methodologically judges to be superfluous to his description or explanatory task. What characterizes "abstraction" in this sense is a self-conscious and deliberate, controlled effort on the part of the observer to refrain from giving free rein to what is ordinarily taken for granted about the reality of straightforwardly grasped experience—the world of daily life as we unquestioningly accept it and "live" it. Husserl calls such methodological restraint "epoché." Rather than turn to the phenomenological procedure which Husserl presents, I prefer to turn to a more neutral and accessible account of the gist of "epoché." "When by a difficult suspension of judgement," Santayana writes, "I have deprived a given image of all adventitious significance, when it is taken neither for the manifestation of a substance nor for an idea in a mind nor for an event in a world, but simply if a colour for that colour and if music for that music, and if a face for that face, then an immense cognitive certitude comes to compensate me for so much cognitive abstention."[24] The philosophical inquirer—the social scientist as observer—practices *epoché* by placing in doubt (or, more precisely, by abstaining from believing in) all the "certitudes" of perception, history, causation, and value which typify common sense. But, says Schutz, there is also an "epoché" of mundane life:

> Phenomenology has taught us the concept of phenomenological *epoché*, the suspension of our belief in the reality of the world as a device to overcome the natural attitude by radicalizing the Cartesian method of philosophical doubt. The suggestion may be ventured that man within

24. George Santayana, *Scepticism and Animal Faith: Introduction to A System of Philosophy*, New York: Dover Publications, 1955, p. 74.

the natural attitude also uses a specific *epoché*, of course quite another one than the phenomenologist. He does not suspend belief in the outer world and its objects, but on the contrary, he suspends doubt in its existence. What he puts in brackets is the doubt that the world and its objects might be otherwise than it appears to him. We propose to call this *epoché* the *epoché of the natural attitude*.[25]

A phenomenology of anonymity and abstraction leads me to the conclusion that the "doubling" effect is a way of talking about these states of affairs: The social world as a matrix of types precedes its "construction" by the individual; without the construction of the typified world by the individual, there can be no common-sense reality. The "precedence" of the social world is of a logical order; the individual's construction of common sense has a genetic history but no chronology. In sum: that which the abstractive instrumentality of consciousness—"intentional consciousness," for the phenomenologist—abstracts from is already a tissue of constructions. There is no "before" or "after," properly speaking, in the realm of abstraction. And the "doubling" of anonymity is the recognition of the anonymous and of anonymization. I would suggest (though Schutz never expressed himself in this way) that the "suppression of the primes" has taken place pre-predicatively in a passive mode *a priori* to the naive expression of abstraction in common-sense terms or the sophisticated enactment of *epoché*. It is neither reality which is "double" nor the construction of reality which is double; the "doubling" is a recognition of the integrity of social reality as it is "for itself" as well as "for us." Writing of Husserl, Merleau-Ponty maintains:

> As far as the social is concerned . . . the problem is to know how it can be both a "thing" to be acquainted with without prejudices, and a "signification" which the societies we acquaint ourselves with only provide an occasion for—how, that is, the social can exist both in itself and in us.[26]

Although I have invoked "a phenomenology of anonymity and abstraction," I cannot claim to have carried out such an investigation. A

25. CPI, p. 229.
26. Maurice Merleau-Ponty, *Signs* (trans. with an introduction by Richard C. McCleary), Evanston: Northwestern University Press, 1964, p. 102. Peter L. Berger and Thomas Luckmann put the matter this way: "Society does indeed possess objective facticity. And society is indeed built up by activity that expresses subjective meaning. . . . It is precisely the dual character of society in terms of objective facticity *and* subjective meaning that makes its 'reality *sui generis*' . . ." (*The Social Construction of Reality: A Treatise in the Sociology of Knowledge*, New York: Doubleday, 1966, pp. 16–17).

less grandiose contention is in order. Understood as a form of abstraction, anonymity is indeed the "transcendental clue" to the philosophy of Alfred Schutz. As surely as "social reality" is his theme, so Schutz's analysis of the meaning-construction of the social world generates a new question: Does "reality" have a phenomenological plural? We must be wary of simple answers, despite Schutz's reliance on William James and in the face of Schutz's prominent use of "realities." His essay "On Multiple Realities" would seem to make nonsense of my question. But my question remains: Does "reality" have a phenomenological plural? Schutz poses what I think is a similar question regarding Husserl's doctrine of the "transcendental ego":

> is it conceivable and meaningful to speak of a plurality of transcendental egos? Is not the concept of the transcendental ego conceivable only in the singular? Can it also be "declined" in the plural, or is it, as the Latin grammarians call it, a *singulare tantum*?[27]

To return to primordial questions: Is reality One or Many?

---

27. Alfred Schutz, *Collected Papers*, Vol. III: *Studies in Phenomenological Philosophy* (edited by I. Schutz with an introduction by Aron Gurwitsch), The Hague: Martinus Nijhoff, 1966, p. 77. Note: Hereafter abbreviated as CPIII.

IV

REALITIES

Unannounced, we dropped in earlier on William James's account of "the various orders of reality"; now we will linger as a self-appointed guest. Schutz, we know, sets himself off from James by asserting that ". . . it is the meaning of our experiences and not the ontological structure of the objects which constitutes reality."[1] But a good deal may be said of James's orders of reality this side of ontology. Under the "various supernatural worlds,"[2] James lists, in addition to the "Christian heaven and hell" and the "Hindoo mythology," classical mythology and "the various worlds of deliberate fable . . . —the world of the *Iliad*, that of *King Lear*, of the *Pickwick Papers*, etc."[3] It might be thought that James simply lumps together supernatural belief and fiction. The claim that he does not discriminate between the supernatural worlds of religious belief and the fictional worlds of the novel and play is far too quick to be satisfying. In a footnote to the passage just quoted, James writes:

> It thus comes about that we can say such things as that Ivanhoe did not *really* marry Rebecca, as Thackeray *falsely* makes him do. The real Ivanhoe-world is the one which Scott wrote down for us. *In that world* Ivanhoe does *not* marry Rebecca. The objects within that world are knit together by perfectly definite relations, which can be affirmed or denied. Whilst absorbed in the novel, we turn our backs on all other worlds, and, for the time, the Ivanhoe-world remains our absolute reality. When we wake from the spell, however, we find a still more real world, which reduces Ivanhoe, and all things connected with him, to the fictive status, and relegates them to one of the sub-universes grouped under [the various supernatural worlds].[4]

Can "truth" and "falsity" be ascribed to the mythological worlds?

1. CPI, p. 230.
2. James, *The Principles of Psychology*, Vol. II, p. 292.
3. Ibid.
4. Ibid., footnote, pp. 292–293.

The believing Christian says that it is true that Jesus rose from the dead and Shakespeare's reader says that it is true that Cordelia died. But an argument ensues between Christian and reader if it be asserted that the term "true" means the same thing in both statements. For the believer, Jesus is not a fiction; even if His resurrection is understood "symbolically," the symbolism stands outside of the Jamesian world in which belief holds good. Lear's "never, never, never, never, never" does not interfere with Cordelia's curtain call. Applause cannot bring back Jesus; there is at least a chance that if sustained applause will not do it, stomping will persuade Cordelia to return for a final bow. But, we say, it is not Cordelia but the actress who portrays Cordelia who can take a curtain call. We are not simply concerned with the historical Jesus or with the historicity of Christianity. Religious belief in James's supernatural world is taken as a fiction without the epistemological status of fiction ever being considered. Nor will it do to say that of course there are differences between fictions of various sorts. James has homogenized the supernatural. His believer becomes a fiction. Robert Fitzgerald says of Flannery O'Connor:

> Among the writing people who were our friends Flannery, as a devout Catholic, was something of a curiosity (they were curiosities to her, too). She could make things fiercely plain, as in her comment, now legendary, on an interesting discussion of the Eucharistic Symbol: "If it were only a symbol, I'd say to hell with it."[5]

5. Flannery O'Connor, *Everything That Rises Must Converge* (with an introduction by Robert Fitzgerald), New York: Farrar, Straus and Giroux, 1978, p. xiii. What would Flannery O'Connor have made of Charles Peirce's remarks on the doctrine of transsubstantiation? Peirce writes in "How To Make Our Ideas Clear": "The Protestant churches generally hold that the elements of the sacrament are flesh and blood only in a tropical sense; they nourish our souls as meat and the juice of it would our bodies. But the Catholics maintain that they are literally just meat and blood; although they possess all the sensible qualities of wafer-cakes and diluted wine. But we can have no conception of wine except what may enter into a belief, either

1. That this, that, or the other is wine; or
2. That wine possesses certain properties.

Such beliefs are nothing but self-notifications that we should, upon occasion, act in regard to such things as we believe to be wine according to the qualities which we believe wine to possess. The occasion of such action would be some sensible perception, the motive of it to produce some sensible result. Thus our action has exclusive reference to what affects the senses, our habit has the same bearing as our action, our belief the same as our habit, our conception the same as our belief; and we can consequently mean nothing by wine but what has certain effects, direct or indirect, upon our senses; and to talk of something as having all the sensible characters of wine, yet being in reality blood, is senseless jargon" (Charles Peirce), *The Philosophy of Peirce: Selected Writings* (edited by Justus Buchler), New York: Harcourt, Brace, 1940, pp. 30–31.

At the time of writing *The Principles of Psychology*, or at least having assumed a distinctively psychological stance, James seems to have slighted the importance and to have underestimated the subtlety of the religious symbol; it is simply relegated to the supernatural world. Considering the different emphasis on religion which James presents in *The Varieties of Religious Experience*, published twelve years after *The Principles*, it would appear that it is not so much religious experience as doctrine which is his concern as a psychologist and which accounts for his theory of "the various supernatural worlds." In any case, the status of the "fictive" remains philosophically obscure. When James says that "*any object which remains uncontradicted is ipso facto believed and posited as absolute reality*,"[6] he implies that "objects" of the imagination no less than objects of sensory perception may, under appropriate circumstances, be taken by their imaginers or beholders as real. But, as students of theology are wont to point out—at least those who have aspired to or taken post-Wittgensteinian cloth—there is a decisive difference in "roses" between "Jesus rose from the dead" and "Jesus rose from bed." For our purposes, which are not theological, it may be enough to say that there are privileged fictions: "objects" which unendingly confront contradiction, which may be enflamed as much as soothed by paradox, and which, nevertheless, are "posited as absolute reality." But James's point is that "contradiction" becomes insistent when the world utterly fundamental to an individual comes into conflict with another "world." When that happens, the fundamental world is reaffirmed and the "lesser" world is set aside. As James writes:

> Each thinker . . . has dominant habits of attention; and these *practically elect from among the various worlds some one to be for him the world of ultimate realities*. From this world's objects he does not appeal. Whatever positively contradicts them must get into another world or die.[7]

What James terms "the paramount reality of sensations"[8] appears, at first glance, to be the "objective" or "empirical" world—hard, resilient, recalcitrant, *there*, like the Bank of England. Another glance is needed, for the ultimate ground of reality, James thinks, is the "subjective." James:

> *The fons et origo of all reality, whether from the absolute or the practical point of view, is thus subjective, is ourselves.*[9]

6. *The Principles of Psychology*, Vol. II, p. 289.
7. Ibid., pp. 293–294.
8. Ibid., p. 299.
9. Ibid., pp. 296–297.

And he goes on to conclude that ". . . *our own reality, that sense of our own life which we at every moment possess, is the ultimate of ultimates for our belief.*"[10] Thus "our own reality" has the indubitability which Descartes ascribed to the *cogito*, but, for James, sensibility and not conception is at the root of certitude. Conceived objects must give way, ultimately, to sensible objects: "*Sensible vividness or pungency is then the vital factor in reality when once the conflict between objects, and the connecting of them together in the mind has begun.*"[11] Not what is real for "the self" as a general conception but what is real for *me*, for "my-self," is the sign of the ultimate. Despite no want of trying, no philosopher will rob me of myself. In James's formulation:

> The world of living realities as contrasted with unrealities is thus anchored in the Ego, considered as an active and emotional term. That is the hook from which the rest dangles, the absolute support. And as from a painted hook it has been said that one can only hang a painted chain, so conversely, from a real hook only a real chain can properly be hung. *Whatever things have intimate and continuous connection with my life are things of whose reality I cannot doubt.* Whatever things fail to establish this connection are things which are practically no better for me than if they existed not at all.[12]

In a footnote to this passage James warns the reader: "I use the notion of the Ego here, as common-sense uses it. Nothing is prejudged as to the results (or absence of results) of ulterior attempts to analyze the notion."[13] In the first volume of *The Principles*, James has presented his critical view of the "transcendentalist theory" of the Self.[14] James is consistent: his account of the sense of reality is one in which common sense immediately recognizes itself. It is not embarrassing to pay tribute to William James: he is an honest and robust philosopher. The affinity between James and Schutz is obvious: the difference between them concerns the nature of common sense.

Once named, the different worlds, in James's description, seem to be readily sortable; for the most part, they are viewed from the "outside." In this way, it becomes easier to understand why so sophisticated a mind as William James should unhesitatingly place in the same category such different "worlds" as religion and fiction. The "outside" view is the Peircean contribution to this aspect of James's thought.

10. Ibid., p. 297.
11. Ibid., p. 301.
12. Ibid., pp. 297–298.
13. Ibid., p. 297.
14. Ibid., Vol. I, pp. 360 ff.

What Flannery O'Connor would say "to hell with" is the symbol without inwardness. But James reserves an "inside" view for the paramount reality of common sense: within each of us, James believes, there is the beat of what is living, an impenetrable sense of concrete existence, a luxury of the sensible. It is that stress on the familiar which Schutz finds especially welcome. James's "world of sense, or of physical 'things' as we instinctively apprehend them"[15] is the world not only of sensibility but also of work and, what Schutz dotes on, the world of "action." Here the affinities and disparities between James and Schutz come into relief. For both thinkers, the "paramount" reality holds philosophical rule; for Schutz, however, mundane existence is infinitely problematic and (if I may—and who is to stop me?— vandalize Kierkegaard) an "offense" to the philosophers.[16]

"The world of working in daily life," Schutz writes, "is the archetype of our experience of reality. All the other provinces of meaning may be considered as its modifications."[17] Despite its privileged status for Schutz, the world of working has its interiority. Although each province of meaning—and here Schutz separates himself from the Jamesian implications of ontology—has its own coherence, its boundaries are epistemically formidable. What is compatible within one province may be incompatible with another province. "For this very reason," Schutz maintains, "we are entitled to talk of *finite* provinces of meaning. This finiteness implies that there is no possibility of referring one of these provinces to the other by introducing a formula of transformation. The passing from one to the other can only be performed by a 'leap,' as Kierkegaard calls it, which manifests itself in the subjective experience of a shock."[18] Ultimately, as Schutz indicates,[19] we are led to problems of "indirect communication." More immediately, we are concerned with the interiority of the world of working. This Schutz analyzes by way of a remarkable contrast: the world of Don Quixote. A detailed examination of the "inner" world of Cervantes's hero is presented in the essay "Don Quixote and the Problem of Reali-

15. Ibid., Vol. II, p. 292.
16. See Søren Kierkegaard, *Philosophical Fragments: Or A Fragment of Philosophy* (trans. with an introduction by David F. Swenson), Princeton: Princeton University Press, 1944 (Appendix: The Paradox and the Offended Consciousness—subtitled "[An Acoustic Illusion]," p. 39 ff. Cf. Alastair Hannay, *Kierkegaard*, London: Routledge and Kegan Paul, 1982, p. 110, where "affront" is used instead of "offense").
17. CPI, p. 233.
18. CPI, p. 232.
19. CPI, P. 233.

ty,"[20] but a preliminary account is offered in the essay "On Multiple Realities." There, in a condensed formulation, Schutz tells us why Don Quixote remains within the world of working: "To him who is a fantast confronted with realities (as Eulenspiegel is a realist confronted with phantasms) there are no imagined giants in the reality of his world of working but real giants."[21]

Impervious as his finite province of meaning—his world of chivalry—is to Don Quixote, it proves to be impervious only from "without," from invasion from the mundane reality of Others. The fault, the flaw in the construction of his special world, lies within; Don Quixote is vulnerable to his own strength. Here Schutz must be allowed to speak for himself at length:

> The true tragedy for Don Quixote is his discovery that even his private sub-universe, the realm of chivalry, might be just a dream and that its pleasures pass like shadows. This creates not only a conflict of consciousness which thus becomes, in Hegel's words, an "unhappy" one, but also of conscience, especially so when the Clavileño adventure proves that even Sanchos are capable of intermingling elements of dreams with their reality of everyday life. Don Quixote's insight that only mutual faith in the Other's terms of reality guarantees intercommunication, his appeal to Sancho to believe his visions if he wants his own to be believed, is a kind of declaration of bankruptcy; and the knight's final words on this occasion, "I say no more," heighten the tragedy of this unhappy consciousness and conscience. It is his bad faith which in the remaining chapters leads to his downfall and the destruction of his sub-universe. He becomes aware of the reality of everyday life, and no enchanter helps him to transform it. His capacity to interpret the common-sense reality in terms of his private universe is broken. Whereas the disenchantment of Dulcinea fails, his own succeeds completely. The great process of disillusionment consists in a piecemeal withdrawal of the accent of reality from his private sub-universe, the world of chivalry.[22]

Although the withdrawal of the accent of reality is not unrelated to the sub-universe of what is ordinarily taken to be the everyday common-sense world, what is essential to the motive which accounts for withdrawal is to be located in the inner world of the knight: Don Quixote fails from within; his vision loses its internal coherence; imagination and dream invade his solitude. Don Quixote, I would say, loses faith in his own madness. Schutz's analysis of Don Quixote's

20. CPII, pp. 135–158.
21. CPI, p. 236.
22. CPII, pp. 156–157.

reliance on the mysterious, often impenetrable activity of the "enchanters," shows that even if, for the knight, all mysteries cannot be revealed to him, there *is* a coherent and consistent explanation for them. Thus, ". . . we are sure that whatever happens, happens reasonably, that is, within the motivation of the enchanters."[23] "We might be tempted," Schutz continues most incisively, "to speak of a non-Hegelian dialectic in a similar way in which we speak of a non-Euclidian geometry."[24] If belief in the erratic dialectic of enchantment is eroded, then the accent of reality which Don Quixote places on the world of chivalry is undermined. But madness is not easily sustained; it demands niceties, talent, and courage. Nor, as Schutz indicates, is Don Quixote unaware of the subtleties of establishing what is real not only for oneself but for Others. Schutz writes:

> Don Quixote . . . knows from his own vision in the cave of Montesinos how difficult it is to establish the border line between fiction and reality. He approaches Sancho after the adventure on Clavileño and whispers in his ear: "Sancho, if you want me to believe what you saw in the sky, I wish you to accept my account of what I saw in the Cave of Montesinos. I say no more."[25]

Here, what might appear to be collusion must be understood in quite different terms. Don Quixote is not asking Sancho to strike a bargain; he is saying instead: "Let us believe in each other." Perhaps the knight's madness consists in the charity of his calling; who else believes it an honor to be the Other?[26] The everyday world, so se-

23. CPII, p. 141.
24. CPII, p. 141.
25. CPII, p. 155.
26. Schutz considers this point. He writes (CPII, p. 155): "Miguel Unamuno, in his wonderful commentary on Don Quixote, interprets this statement of the knight as the expression of the highest magnanimity of his candid soul, since Don Quixote is well convinced that what he experienced in the cave of Montesinos was true and what Sancho tells cannot be true. But another interpretation is possible. Don Quixote is convinced that only the experiencing self can judge upon which sub-universe it has bestowed the accent of reality. Intersubjective experience, communication, sharing of something in common presupposes, thus, in the last analysis faith in the Other's truthfulness, animal faith in the sense of Santayana; it presupposes that I take for granted the Other's possibility of bestowing upon one of the innumerable sub-universes the accent of reality, and on the other hand that he, the Other, takes for granted that I, too, have open possibilities for defining what is my dream, my phantasy, my real life. This is the last insight into the intersubjective dialectic of reality, it seems to me, and therefore the climax in the analysis of this problem in Cervantes' work."
    Note: In Anthony Kerrigan's translation of Miguel de Unamuno's *Our Lord Don Quixote* we find: "The rest of the adventure is terribly sad, if we judge it by worldly standards. And yet, how many people mount a Clavileño and without moving from the spot where they mounted, fly through the regions of air and of fire! The adventure is so sad that I want to reach the end of it, when Don Quixote and Sancho found

cure—it would seem—in the truth of intersubjectivity, has (and here I speak for myself alone) an unexpected fragility. The "one" reality of mundane existence is the "objective" world which is built out of the ideal types and constructs of the subjective interpretation of meaning. The "truth" of the individual can be communicated only indirectly, as Kierkegaard maintained; but that "truth" cannot be spoken by the individual even to himself. If it were appropriate to speak of indirect communication with oneself, *that* communication would have to be doubly indirect. James's Ego, the living subject, is adrift in his certitude, bereft of the gifts due one who is an absolute ground of experience. In these terms, daily life is fragile because its reality is

---

themselves saved, with only a slight toss in the air and a singeing to show for their travail: the squire, freed of his fear, gave himself over to inventing lies; when Don Quixote heard them he approached and whispered these pregnant words: '*Sancho, you want me to believe what you saw in the heavens, and I want you to believe what I saw in the cave of Montesinos*; I say no more.'

"Behold here the most comprehensive, the most all-encompassing formula for tolerance: if you want me to believe you, you believe me. The society of man is cemented with mutual credit. Your neighbor's vision is as true for him as your own vision is true for you. Provided, of course, that it is true vision, and not a lie or a hoax.

"And herein lies the difference between Don Quixote and Sancho: Don Quixote really saw what he said he saw in the cave of Montesinos—despite Cervantes' malicious insinuations to the contrary—and Sancho did not see what he said he saw in the celestial spheres as he rode Clavileño's back, for the squire lyingly invented his visions, to try to imitate his master and to get rid of his fear. We are not all of us privileged to see visions, and even less to believe in them, and by believing in them to make them true" (Princeton: Princeton University Press, 1967, pp. 220–221).

Schutz used the J. H. Cohen translation of *Don Quixote*:

"But Don Quixote went up to Sancho and whispered in his ear: 'Sancho, if you want me to believe what you saw in the sky, I wish you to accept my account of what I saw in the Cave of Montesinos. I say no more'" (Harmondsworth: Penguin Books, 1952, p. 735).

Cf. Samuel Putnam's rendition:

"Don Quixote now came up to him, to whisper in his ear. 'Sancho,' he said, 'if you want us to believe what you saw in Heaven, then you must believe me when I tell you what I saw in the Cave of Montesinos. I need say no more'" (*The Portable Cervantes* [trans. and edited with an introduction by Samuel Putnam], New York: Viking Press, 1958, p. 578—for our present purposes this edition is acceptable).

The original:

"—Sancho, pues vos queréis que se os crea lo que habéis visto en el cielo, yo quiero que vos me creáis a mí lo que vi en la cueva de Montesinos. Y no os digo más" (Miguel de Cervantes Saavedra, *Don Quijote de la Mancha*, [texto y notas de Martín de Riquer], Barcelona: Editorial Juventud, 1979, Vol. II, Part Two, Chapter XLI, p. 837).

How transcendently at home Unamuno is with author and text that he can speak so audaciously of "Cervantes' malicious insinuations." So, too, with regard to another passage in the novel, Américo Castro writes: "But neither Spain nor the *Quixote* are comprehensible if the historian cannot tie up the loose ends left undone by the flow of life" (*The Spaniards: An Introduction to Their History* [trans. by Willard F. King and Selma Margaretten], Berkeley: University of California Press, 1971, p. 552). Such scholars as Unamuno and Castro seem not only to have appropriated what is Spanish but to communicate with their authors; Cervantes is their contemporary.

neither one nor many; it is only by placing the accent of reality on one sub-universe or another that the familiarity of the everyday can be sustained. Otherwise, it is continually threatened, whether or not the individual is in a state of psychological upset. What would Cervantes have thought of Jaspers's patient who "called his whole fantastic world 'the novel'."[27]

Speaking of the "many worlds," James admonishes us that "the complete philosopher is he who seeks not only to assign to every given object of his thought its right place in one or other of these sub-worlds, but he also seeks to determine the relation of each sub-world to the others in the total world which *is*."[28] Presumably, *Don Quixote* would be assigned by James to the "various worlds of deliberate fable"; Don Quixote, however, might, taken as a "case-history," be placed in "the worlds of sheer madness and vagary."[29] But what if Don Quixote, before his madness, had learned "to sit still"? It is possible to think of him as a melancholic. James writes:

> In certain forms of melancholic perversion of the sensibilities and reactive powers, nothing touches us intimately, rouses us, or awakens natural feeling. The consequence is the complaint so often heard from melancholic patients, that nothing is believed in by them as it used to be, and that all sense of reality is fled from life. They are sheathed in india-rubber; nothing penetrates to the quick or draws blood, as it were.[30]

Yet Don Quixote recovered, Don Quixote sane, is no longer himself but, as we are told, Alonso Quixano the Good. Vaulting melancholy, the transformed Don Quixote prepares to die. There is no return to the blood of reality, unless such a return is signified by the call for a priest and a clerk to draw up a will. The numbness of melancholy which William James described becomes, for Alonso Quixana the Good, the banality of the everyday. The consolation is the book itself: " 'For me alone Don Quixote was born and I for him.' "[31]

What is original in Schutz's account of *Don Quixote* is the analysis of common sense—a fundamental term of discourse for Cervantes's commentators but one they build upon rather than dig beneath. And

27. Karl Jaspers, *General Psychopathology* (trans. by J. Hoenig and Marian W. Hamilton), Chicago: University of Chicago Press, 1963, p. 78.
28. *The Principles of Psychology*, Vol. II, p. 291.
29. Ibid., p. 293.
30. Ibid., p. 298.
31. *The Adventures of Don Quixote* (trans. by J. M. Cohen), p. 940.

this same concern with the structure of common sense defines what is distinctively phenomenological about Schutz's critique of everyday reality. For him, the paramount reality of everyday life, understood as a sub-universe or finite province of meaning, has the following essential characteristics "which constitute its specific cognitive style":

> 1) a specific tension of consciousness, namely wide-awakeness, origi-nating in full attention to life;
> 2) a specific *epoché*, namely suspension of doubt;
> 3) a prevalent form of spontaneity, namely working (a meaningful spontaneity based upon a project and characterized by the intention of bringing about the projected state of affairs by bodily movements gearing into the outer world);
> 4) a specific form of experiencing one's self (the working self as the total self);
> 5) a specific form of sociality (the common intersubjective world of communication and social action);
> 6) a specific time-perspective (the standard time originating in an in-tersection between *durée* and cosmic time as the universal temporal structure of the intersubjective world).[32]

The "specific tension of Consciousness" of which Schutz speaks comes from Bergson. Full quotation is justified. Schutz tells us:

> One of the central points in Bergson's philosophy is his theory that our conscious life shows an indefinite number of different planes, rang-ing from the plane of action on one extreme to the plane of dream at the other. Each of these planes is characterized by a specific tension of consciousness, the plane of action showing the highest, that of dream the lowest degree of tension. According to Bergson, these different degrees of tension of our consciousness are functions of our varying interest in life, action representing our highest interest in meeting reali-ty and its requirements, dream being complete lack of interest. *Attention à la vie*, attention to life, is, therefore, the basic regulative principle of our conscious life. It defines the realm of our world which is relevant to us; it articulates our continuously flowing stream of thought; it de-termines the span and function of our memory; it makes us—in our language—either live within our present experiences, directed toward their objects, or turn back in a reflective attitude to our past experiences and ask for their meaning.[33]

Schutz's "wide-awake man" is fully attentive to life; but it would be

32. CPI, pp. 230–231.
33. CPI, pp. 212–213. In a footnote to this statement, Schutz says (p. 213) that his presentation "does not strictly follow Bergson's terminology but it is hoped that it renders his important thought." Schutz goes on to cite as his sources passages in Berg-son's *Essai sur les données immédiates de la conscience*, *Matière et mémoire*, and other works.

a misreading of "wide-awakeness" to make of human action a reality confined to one subuniverse of meaning. Schutz warns against such a misunderstanding: "A word of caution seems to be needed here. The concept of finite provinces of meaning does not involve any static connotation as though we had to select one of these provinces as our home to live in, to start from or to return to. That is by no means the case. Within a single day, even within a single hour our consciousness may run through most different tensions and adopt most different attentional attitudes to life."[34] A specific shock is the condition which occasions a shift from one finite province to another and "there are as many innumerable kinds of shock experiences as there are different provinces of meaning upon which I bestow the accent of reality."[35] It might seem that the "shock" to which Schutz refers comes from a different province of meaning; it would be more precise to say that it is "founded in a different *attention à la vie*."[36] A shock is "a radical modification in the tension of our consciousness."[37] With so much of Schutz's language freshly before us, we might take a step away from his definitions, explanations, and examples of provinces of meaning and the logic of the movement between them.

Consider the current of a day: Dawn jogging, breakfast with one's family, a morning of real estate transactions at the office, lunch with cronies, thinking through a little talk ("Man's Estate: His Real Estate") for the firm's weekly inspirational coffee break, business again, visiting a relative who is hospitalized, home again, an evening of cello sawing with our neighborhood quartet, in bed for love, asleep. But this is nothing more than routine; the list is disspiriting, a revisionist's reading of Kierkegaard which turns his leap into a shuffle. O the chatter of the provinces, the engorgement of language, the minimalism of observations, the pastime of matching the expression with the profession:

In the midst of the act of love, the lover says to his beloved: "I love you, i.e. . . ."

Musil's madman-murderer, Moosbrugger, exhibits bizarre behavior

34. CPI, footnote p. 233.
35. CPI, p. 231.
36. CPI, p. 232.
37. CPI, p. 232.

in court: "During the proceedings Moosbrugger made quite unpredictable difficulties for his counsel. He sat there at huge ease on his bench, like an onlooker, calling out 'Hear! Hear!' to the public prosecutor whenever he made a point of Moosbrugger's being a public menace and did it in a way that Moosbrugger considered worthy of himself."[38]

Miss Morrow is a paid companion to Miss Doggett in *Crampton Hodnet* by Barbara Pym. Sitting with her employer, Miss Morrow has made an observation which is not to Miss Doggett's liking. Reproved by her employer, shrewd Miss Morrow confesses ignorance in the matter at issue and retreats (or advances) to a paradigmatically unexceptionable comment:
" 'I feel the sun is doing us so much good,' she ventured."[39]

"Dr. Marshall B. Katzman of St. Louis has attempted to quantify obscenity but a scientific phenomenological study has not yet been accomplished. It is to be hoped that sooner or later this will be remedied."[40]

At the end of F. L. Green's *Odd Man Out*:
" 'It's finished'," the Inspector said, addressing the priest. He removed his hat for a few seconds. His quick, tense breathing was audible as he leaned over the bodies beside which Father Tom had got to his knees.
'She got him,' he said softly. 'She took him, and herself. . . .'
The priest mumbled words and made the sign of the cross. He rose slowly to his feet.
'. . . a few seconds before us, and shot him and herself,' the Inspector said again. 'Took him. . . .'
'She loved him,' Father Tom murmured.
He moved unsteadily through the big groups of Police. Then he halted and looked about for Shell and saw him, a pallid, horrified form who shuddered as he cried out in a thin voice:
'Killed him . . . .'

38. Robert Musil, *The Man Without Qualities* (trans. with a foreword by Eithne Wilkins and Ernst Kaiser), Vol. I, London: Secker and Warburg, 1979, p. 83.
39. Barbara Pym, *Crampton Hodnet* (with a note by Hazel Holt), New York: E. P. Dutton, 1985, p. 80.
40. J. B. Lyons, *James Joyce and Medicine*, New York: Humanities Press, 1974, p. 164.

'Redeemed him!' the old priest said, resting a soothing hand on him."[41]

Finally, a cross section—a *Querschnitt*—of overheard conversations: a selection which is unrepresentative and inevitable:
   "So what's become of your nephew, Julia's boy?"
   "He's a homeopathic physician in Philadelphia."
   "With other doctors . . . ."
   "Yes, he's in group practice."
   "Thank God his mother is dead, she didn't live to see such a tragedy."
   "Mrs. Ehrlich, you don't understand—homeopathy means *very* diluted drugs."
   "Drugs too?"

The primacy which Schutz gives to the world of working—the paramount reality of the natural attitude—is attached to the system of relevances which governs the individual. Although Schutz has devoted a book (*Reflections on the Problem of Relevance*) as well as numerous passages in his essays to the subject of "relevance," it is difficult to reduce his conception of it to a quick formula. An accessible statement of what he means by relevance is included in a discussion of language in which Schutz writes:

> We turn our interest to those experiences which for one reason or another seem to us to be relevant to the sum total of our situation as experienced by us in any given present. Of course, such a present is a specious present, encompassing parts of my past and of my future, and my situation includes . . . not only my physical but also my human environment, my ideological and moral position. The system of relevance determines not only what belongs to the situation with which . . . the individual has to come to terms, but also what has to be made a substratum of the generalizing typification, what traits have to be selected as characteristically typical, and how far we have to plunge into the open, still undisclosed horizon of typicality.[42]

41. F. L. Green, *Odd Man Out*, Boston: Rowan Tree Press, 1982, p. 214.
42. CPI, pp. 283–284. Note: The essay from which this quotation is drawn is entitled "Language, Language Disturbances, and the Texture of Consciousness" and is concerned with the ideas of Kurt Goldstein and a number of other thinkers. For present purposes, in quoting Schutz, I have omitted references to Goldstein and Merleau-Ponty. On Schutz's concept of relevance, see Aron Gurwitsch, *The Field of Consciousness*, Pittsburgh: Duquesne University Press, 1964, pp. 342–343.

There Is no doubt that for Schutz relevance was a fundamental term of discourse; indeed, at times he suggested to me that it was the root-term of his entire conception of the social world. The "system" of relevances for an individual is a complexly structured, many-tiered edifice—a vast "plan"—whose moments are both presented by the world and defined by the person. Thus Schutz:

> To the experiencing subject's mind, the elements singled out of the pregiven structure of the world always stand in sense-connections, connections of orientation as well as of mastery of thought or action. The causal relations of the objective world are subjectively experienced as means and ends, as hindrances or aids, of the spontaneous activity of thought or action. They manifest themselves as complexes of interest, complexes of problems, as systems of projects, and feasibilities inherent in the systems of projects. The system of these complexes, which are interwoven in manifold ways, is subjectively experienced by the individual as a system of his plans for the hour or the day, for work and leisure; all these particular plans being integrated into one supreme system which, without being free from contradictions, encompasses all the other plans. We shall call the supreme system the "life-plan."[43]

Schutz points out that he speaks of "plan" "in an enlarged sense which does not necessarily involve the element of deliberateness" and that "there also exist plans which are imposed."[44] Indeed, as a reading of *Reflections on the Problem of Relevance* will quickly show, the term "relevance" is a simplification for a plural which Schutz analyzes in considerable detail. Here I have been making use of what Schutz calls "motivational relevancy."[45] It will not be productive for my purposes to enter into a discussion of the general theme of relevance. Rather, I am concerned with two aspects of that theme: the dynamic of an individual's existence which engenders shifts in the attention to life and the place of death in the architectonic of relevance. Both are of critical importance to the natural attitude. Schutz writes:

> . . . the whole system of relevances which governs us within the natural attitude is founded upon the basic experience of each of us: I know that I shall die and I fear to die. This basic experience we suggest calling the *fundamental anxiety*. It is the primordial anticipation from

43. CPIII, p. 122.
44. Ibid. On "life-plan" see Alfred Schutz and Thomas Luckmann, *Strukturen der Lebenswelt*, Vol. II, Frankfurt: Suhrkamp, 1984 and Helmut R. Wagner, *Alfred Schutz: An Intellectual Biography*, Chicago: University of Chicago Press, 1983.
45. CPIII, p. 123.

which all the others originate. From the fundamental anxiety spring
the many interrelated systems of hopes and fears, of wants and satisfactions, of chances and risks which incite man within the natural attitude to attempt the mastery of the world, to overcome obstacles, to
draft projects, and to realize them.[46]

On the surface, it might appear that Schutz's conception of "the
fundamental anxiety" is similar to Heidegger's views on death in *Being
and Time*. To follow appearances here would be misleading. Heidegger's view of death is integral to his conception of the temporality of
human existence (what he calls *Dasein*), the rootage of that temporality
in the inauthenticity of daily life, and the possibility—occasionally, at
least—of wresting one's *ownness* from the "publicness" of human reality into which one has been "thrown." In Heidegger's terms, what
Schutz refers to as fear of my death is quite different from "anxiety
in the face of death."[47] But apart from the distinction between "fear"
and "anxiety," what separates Schutz from Heidegger is the manner
in which each thinker poses and resolves—if only tacitly—the philosophical problem of "anonymity." Of course, Schutz explicitly utilizes
the term "anonymity"; Heidegger does not.[48] But it is evident, to me
at least, that Heidegger's treatment of "everydayness" in conjunction
with the "they" (*das Man*) is both a formulation and interpretation of
anonymity as a cardinal feature of human existence in the social world.
The "they" at issue is the "they" of "What will they think?," "What are

46. CPI, p. 228.
47. Martin Heidegger, *Being and Time* (trans. by John Macquarrie and Edward Robinson), New York: Harper, 1962 (section 50), p. 295 (English pagination). In the same
passage, Heidegger says: "Anxiety in the face of death is anxiety 'in the face of' that
potentiality-for-Being which is one's ownmost, non-relational, and not to be outstripped. That in the face of which one has anxiety is Being-in-the-world itself. That
about which one has this anxiety is simply Dasein's potentiality-for-Being. Anxiety in
the face of death must not be confused with fear in the face of one's demise. This
anxiety is not an accidental or random mood of 'weakness' in some individual; but, as
a basic state-of-mind of Dasein, it amounts to the disclosedness of the fact that Dasein
exists as thrown Being *towards* its end. Thus the existential conception of 'dying' is made
clear as thrown Being towards its ownmost potentiality-for-Being, which is non-relational and not to be outstripped. Precision is gained by distinguishing this pure dis-
appearance, and also from merely perishing, and finally from the 'Experiencing' of a
demise." For discussion of Heidegger's views on death, see James M. Demske, *Being,
Man, and Death: A Key to Heidegger*, Lexington: The University Press of Kentucky, 1970;
Adolf Sternberger, *Der verstandene Tod: eine Untersuchung zu Martin Heideggers Existenzialontologie*, Leipzig: S. Hirzel, 1934 (reprinted: New York: Garland Publishing, 1979);
Régis Jolivet, *Le Problème de la mort: chez M. Heidegger et J.-P. Sartre*, Abbaye Saint
Wandrille: Editions de Fontenelle, 1950.
48. See Hildegard Feick (Compiler), *Index zu Heideggers "Sein und Zeit,"* 3rd ed.,
Tübingen: Max Niemeyer, 1980. Note: See entry for "Man," p. 51.

they wearing this year?," and it is the "they" of "They never let go, they never give up, they never forgive." The paranoiac says that "They are after him," though his psychiatrist cannot determine who "they" are. "They never leave you alone," cries the child, even if who is at fault is indeterminable. According to Heidegger, the "they" relieves the individual of (what I would call) his unique gravity as an existing creature. The "voice" of the "they" is a summons to surrender what is individual, to join "them." Heidegger writes:

> . . . the particular Dasein in its everydayness is *disburdened* by the "they." Not only that; by thus disburdening it of its Being, the "they" accommodates Dasein . . . if Dasein has any tendency to take things easily and make them easy. And because the "they" constantly accommodates the particular Dasein by disburdening it of its Being, the "they" retains and enhances its stubborn dominion.
> Everyone is the other, and no one is himself. The "they," which supplies the answer to the question of the "*who*" of everyday Dasein, is the "*nobody*" to whom every Dasein has already surrendered itself in Being-among-one-other [Untereinandersein].[49]

"Disburdened" *Dasein* is inauthentic *Dasein*. Despite Heidegger's ontological neutrality, his conception of the "they" has a moral inflection. For Schutz, the anonymity into which human existence is thrust is neither "authentic" nor "inauthentic"; rather, anonymity is a necessary condition for there being a social world. Resolute, *Dasein* is, according to Heidegger, a "being-toward-death"; its being achieves authenticity by escaping *das Man* and coming into a luminous recognition of the meaning of its *own* death. In egological terms: *my* temporality arises from the ashes of time—time as the measure of "anyone's" life. Schutz had little use for Heidegger on death; he told me that Heidegger's fundamental conception of death was "perfectly phony." That is not the language which Schutz would have used had he written out his views, nor is it the language which he employs in speaking of Heidegger in *The Phenomenology of the Social World*, but I think it proper to be blunt at present. Schutz is not concerned with the life-world from the vantage point of a "fundamental ontology." The "wide-awake" man, at work in the paramount reality of everyday life, does not ponder the meaning of death with each stride he takes; yet, he is no fool, and the clichés and euphemisms and daily exchanges which he brings to language as well as receives from it do not turn him into

49. *Being and Time* (section 27), pp. 165–166 (English pagination).

a mediocrity. If he is dull and if his language sags, it is not common sense which should be denigrated. The individual may or may not "believe in" the language he utilizes. And to whom should he look for what is exemplary in, say, English speech? Our prose, having fallen upon hard times, has broken every bone in its body. The ordinary individual is on his own.

"I know that I shall die and I fear to die" constitute the "fundamental anxiety," so Schutz holds, in terms of the "working" world. Within the natural attitude, I know that I must "get on" with my projects if I wish to accomplish what I have set out to do—to achieve my goals. This "fear" in its typicality—not in its existential force—is enough to "move" the individual in the everyday world and also "move" him from one finite province to another. That is to say that the fundamental anxiety is at the ultimate foundation of changing emphases in the accent of reality. But the fundamental anxiety does not operate in unstructured circumstances. The "life-plan" of the individual has an obverse (if immanent) side: the "death-plan." Schutz did not use the last phrase in his writing but he did say to me that the idea had been suggested to him by a friend or friends who had read the manuscript of his essay "Some Structures of the Life-World"[50] and that he thought the suggestion had merit. Yet Schutz was deeply acquainted with the existential tradition in general and with its conception of death in particular. Despite everything, does his notion of the "fundamental anxiety" reveal a camouflaged Heideggerian? I think not; if anything, it should be said that both Heidegger and Schutz were indebted to Kierkegaard's thinking. Anxiety is Kierkegaard's theme. Something of a conflict in interpretation arises: Schutz, in his theory of multiple realities, is not concerned with fear or anxiety as existential issues, yet the "fundamental anxiety" owes something to the most precious of the existential thinkers. I think that there *is* a paradox involved, but its elements have less to do with particular "existentialists" than with Schutz as a *philosopher*, as distinguished from Schutz as a methodologist and theorist of the social sciences or even Schutz as a phenomenologist. The consideration of this paradox we must reserve for our discussion of Transcendence.

We are now in a position to appreciate Schutz's claim that it is not the ontological character but the meaning-structure of finite provinces with which his analysis is concerned. Schutz writes:

50. Included in CPIII.

The finite provinces of meaning are not separated states of mental life
in the sense that passing from one to another would require a trans-
migration of the soul and a complete extinction of memory and consciousness by death, as the doctrine of metempsychosis assumes. They
are merely names for different tensions of one and the same consciousness, and it is the same life, the mundane life, unbroken from
birth to death, which is attended to in different modifications.[51]

For Schutz, there is *one* reality; "realities" are functions of different
tensions of consciousness. What are disclosed in the different provinces of meaning are "realities" whose force is powerful and consequential for the "subjective interpretation" of the actor in mundane
existence. The accent of reality is placed not only on the phenomena
of a finite province but upon the history of that province as well
Memory has an urgent mission: the present is sedimented with its
historical becoming, some of its elements alarmingly vivid, others
quiescent. In discussing the theme of death with me, Schutz recalled
his service in the Austrian Army during the First World War. He had
seen action on the Italian front (and been decorated for bravery).
More disturbing than the corpses of soldiers, he remembered, were
the carcasses of cavalry horses. That memory of himself as a young
man which Schutz reported can hardly be filed away under "Recollections from the Front." The pathos of an innocent creature fallen
in the damage of human disputes is not "balanced" or "overbal-
anced"—and here I alone am speaking my mind—by the violent death
of human beings; there is no "balance" to be struck, no way of avoiding
the interminable sadness of death's indifference.

It might be thought that at least the body escapes what the mind
cannot evade. But it is not possible to speak without qualification of
the anonymity of the body, so profound the ambivalence it expresses.
Merleau-Ponty writes: "What enables us to center our existence is also
what prevents us from centering it completely, and the anonymity of
our body is inseparably both freedom and servitude. Thus . . . the
ambiguity of being in the world is translated by that of the body, and
this is understood through that of time."[52] The "anonymous" body
may also be the bearer of a history which continues to generate the

51. CPI, p. 258.
52. *Phenomenology of Perception*, p. 85. Merleau-Ponty also speaks in a different context
of an "anonymous corporeality" (*The Prose of the World* [edited with a preface by Claude
Lefort and trans. with an introduction by John O'Neill], Evanston: Northwestern University Press, 1973, p. 140).

past. A survivor of the First World War, eighty-four years old at the time of this report, says:

> You hear old men say that their bodies have become a burden to them. My body became a burden to me when I was twenty-four, but I wouldn't say that I found it a burden now. It is very far from being a burden. Because it hampered me so much when it should not have done—when I was young—I hardly think of it at all now. Of course, there are days when you find you can't do as much, and you notice the stiffness or tiredness which is part of old age, and you can't help but see that certain disabilities are increasing, so that you feel annoyed, but someone like myself doesn't experience that awful "break-up" feeling, because one was all broken up sixty or more years ago, I suppose! Now I'm being philosophical. But I'm an old schoolmaster and I have a right to be. The Western Front proved many things for me—including the fact that I inherited a very good constitution! "Blown to hell, sergeant major," I'd said when they found me and rolled me onto that waterproof sheet—"blown to hell." But it wasn't true, was it?
>
> The War clings to me. The other day, while driving my car with my leg bent up, I felt a small, hard, rough scrap of something between my knee and my trousers. Another bit of shrapnel had worked its way out.[53]

The question has shifted, perhaps, from "Is there one reality or many?" to "Is there one anonymity or many?" But the answer has not changed: "There is but one reality with many alterations of accent which attend it" and "There is but one anonymity with a multitude of sedimentations of meaning which exhibit it." For in each movement from province to province, I think that it is possible to recognize the display of another facet of anonymity. An arresting illustration of the departure from the course of ordinary experience is presented in Schutz's account of the social scientist as theoretician who willfully "liberates" himself from mundane life in order to enter the finite province of his science. Schutz:

> ... the theoretical social scientist has to refer to his stock of pre-experiences of the existence of Others, of their acting and working, and the meaning they bestow upon their acts and works. He has acquired these pre-experiences while living as a human being with Others in the everyday world of the natural attitude, the same attitude which he had to bracket in order to leap into the province of theoretical contemplation. We have to face the difficulty involved here in full earnestness. Only then will we understand that the theoretical thinker

53. Ronald Blythe, *The View in Winter: Reflections on Old Age*, New York: Harcourt Brace Jovanovich, 1979, p. 152.

while remaining in the theoretical attitude cannot experience originarily and grasp in immediacy the world of everyday life within which I and you, Peter and Paul, anyone and everyone have confused and ineffable perceptions, act, work, plan, worry, hope, are born, grow up and will die—in a word, live their life as unbroken selves in their full humanity.[54]

How is it possible for the theoretician who must, *qua* scientist, be disinterested with regard to the phenomena he seeks to describe and to understand, also be able to locate the sources of concrete existence? How, Schutz asks, can the theoretician ". . . find an approach to the world of everyday life in which men work among their fellow-men within the natural attitude, the very natural attitude which the theoretician is compelled to abandon?"[55] The essence of Schutz's answer to these questions is already in the reader's possession.

In sum: the scientist constructs a model of the social world. The typifications which form that model are the result of a highly selective process of abstraction, methodologically indebted to phenomenological procedures, in which actors, action, motives, goals, and relevances constitute a fictive life-world. The "second-order" constructs of the theorist give us a purely anonymous reality through which we are able to comprehend the correspondingly anonymous "first-order" constructs of human beings in daily life. The vast qualification which must be made in this account is that the anonymous world which is brought into being by common-sense actors and their first-order constructs is an *abstract* world, a world abstracted from existential specificity. But there is another qualification which should be introduced in order to understand Schutz properly. When he speaks of the theoretician being compelled "to abandon" the natural attitude in order to gain access to the world of everyday life, it must be remembered that such "abandonment" has only a methodological life; it is the "abstention" which the phenomenologist enacts in performing *epoché*. The common-sense world can never be literally "abandoned"; even pathological transformations of mental life presuppose connections with *some* aspects of the life-world. The "leap" which the theoretician makes in order to enter the finite province of science does not divest him of his humanity; instead, "disinterestedness" means that the theorist keeps a rigorous patrol to guard against representatives of his "private" life or even his "common-sense" life entering his professional

54. CPI, pp. 254–255.
55. CPI, p. 254.

territory. Whether such phenomenological security is indeed enforce-
able is not the present issue. What presses upon us now is the task of
comprehending a delicately sophisticated feature of phenomenological reduction: the manner in which the "phenomenological observer"
holds before him the movement of the natural attitude at the same
time that he *sees through* that movement to its essential character. In
reduction, I *know* that I am Maurice Natanson, born in the lost city
of New York, who once saw Jim Londos wrestle in Coney Island, and
who, as many Saturdays as I could, used to wander up and down
Fourth Avenue's Book Row. The trick lies in how I know and remember all that at the moment of "fixing" identity and events as "being
or having-been-experienced"—of seeing them in seeing-through-
them.

Schutz's own account of phenomenological reduction is critically
important for the appreciation of the relationship between what is
experienced within the natural attitude and the retention of the
noetic-noematic correlate of that experience within the transcenden-
tally reduced sphere. Schutz writes:

> In order to uncover [the] sphere of the transcendental subjectivity at
> all, the philosopher, beginning his meditation within the natural atti-
> tude, must undertake that change in attitude which Husserl calls phe-
> nomenological epoché or transcendental phenomenological reduction.
> That is to say, he must deprive the world which formerly, within the
> natural attitude, was simply posited as being, of just this posited being,
> and he must return to the living stream of his experiences of the world.
> In this stream, however, the experienced world is kept exactly with the
> contents which actually belong to it. With the execution of the epoché,
> the world in no way vanishes from the field of experience of the philo-
> sophically reflecting ego. On the contrary, what is grasped in the epoché
> is the pure life of consciousness in which and through which the whole
> objective world exists for me, by virtue of the fact that I experience it,
> perceive it, remember it, etc. In the epoché, however, I abstain from
> belief in the being of this world, and I direct my view exclusively to
> my consciousness of the world.[56]

If it be thought that this statement stops short of considering the
intersubjectivity which is so central to the life-world or that Schutz is
only restating the relationship between *epoché* and what Husserl calls
the "general thesis," the continuation of what Schutz has been saying
deserves close attention:

56. CPI, p. 123.

In this universe of the experiencing life of the transcendental subjectivity I find my entire cogitations of the life-world which surrounds me, a life-world to which also belong my life with others and its pertinent community-forming processes, which actively and passively shape this life-world into a social world. In principle all of these experiences found in my conscious life, if they are not themselves originarily living and primally founding experiences of this life-world, can be examined concerning the history of their sedimentation. In this way, I can return fundamentally to the originary experience of the life-world in which the facts themselves can be grasped directly.[57]

Of course, we have attributed to the theoretician's "leap" into the finite province of science a strong phenomenological interpretation. Schutz led the way toward such a view by his use of the concept of "epoché," but he would not—nor would I—claim that every time a social scientist becomes a disinterested observer, it is as a result of phenomenological reduction. The point at issue is not what the social scientist *does* but what is philosophically presupposed in what he does. Social scientists who are transcendental phenomenologists must be as hard to come by as genuine Vermeers which are on the market: not an empty class, perhaps, but certainly a lonely one. What is valuable in Schutz's account of the scientist's leap into disinterestedness is the fresh view of anonymity which it provides. The "abandonment" by the theoretician of his place in the natural attitude of daily life is marked—quite apart from phenomenology—by the homuncular reality of the model of society which he creates. "Personal types" and "course of action types" replace individuals and their action in the "model." Common-sense life as a contexture of typifications carries pragmatic force precisely because its anonymity assures, *for all practical purposes* (a cousin of "by and large"), intended, anticipated, and acceptable results. "How," Schutz asks, "can man in his full humanity and the social relationships in which he stands with Others be grasped by theoretical thought?"[58] But, to this question, the reply "By constructing a model of society" will not do. The model includes a variable for "spontaneity"! The model does not know who I am. The idea of a model of Father Abraham is revolting. Each lunatic writes his own novel. What recourse, then, does the social scientist have? Odd as it might be, the theoretician must take a Kierkegaardian tack. His model of society is achieved by way of "indirect communication."

57. CPI, p. 123.
58. CPI, p. 254.

The instrumentality of communication which mediates between the scientific and common-sense worlds is, according to Schutz, the method of the social sciences. The model of society which the theoretician builds is energized by a fictive life-world. Schutz writes:

> This model . . . is not peopled with human beings in their full humanity, but with puppets, with *types*; they are constructed as though they could perform working actions and reactions. Of course, these working actions and reactions are merely fictitious, since they do not originate in a living consciousness as manifestations of its spontaneity; they are only assigned to the puppets by the grace of the scientist. But if . . . these types are constructed in such a way that their fictitious working acts and performances remain not only consistent in themselves but compatible with all the pre-experiences of the world of daily life which the observer acquired within the natural attitude before he leaped into the theoretical province—then, and only then, does this model of the social world become a theoretical object, an object of an actual positing of being. It receives an accent of reality although not that of the natural attitude.[59]

The anonymity of both finite provinces is communicated by the abstractive power of language; but the bestowal of the accent of reality differs qualitatively in the two spheres. The theoretician self-consciously imposes his *epoché*; the individual non-self-consciously, believingly accepts daily life. That acceptance is the core of the General Thesis of the natural attitude. Husserl maintains that "the General Thesis according to which the real world about me is at all times known not merely in a general way as something apprehended, but as a fact-world *that has its being out there*, does *not* consist of course *in an act proper*, in an articulated judgment *about* existence. It is and remains something all the time the standpoint is adopted, that is, it endures persistently during the whole course of our life of natural endeavour."[60]

The different provinces of meaning reveal different aspects of anonymity. It should be noted that prior to both first- and second-order constructs, there is the naiveté of man in the natural attitude, immersed in the General Thesis. Let us leave Schutz for a while. I would suggest that the "believingness" in which the individual lives in common-sense reality already presents, in phenomenological terms, a primordial mode of anonymity. Pre-predicative experience is not

59. CPI, p. 255.
60. *Ideas* (Boyce Gibson translation), section 31, p. 107.

egologically determinate; the passive and active syntheses which comprise the immediacy of "actual" life are not indexed according to individual human beings. If I am correct in locating a basal anonymity in the realm of pre-predicative experience, then the "taken-for-granted" elements of common sense not only point to an anonymous realm but presuppose anonymity as well. The individual in day-to-day existence cannot utter the lived reality of concrete being. That being simply *is*. First-order constructs enable the individual to have a "public" world in which action is, practically speaking, efficacious. The anonymity of the world of first-order constructs consists of the typifications and the "because" and "in-order-to" motives; the logic of the entire model of the social world is an anatomy of its anonymous order. We have, then, three aspects of anonymity; we do not have three anonymities. The question remains: Why is it that the individual moves from straightforward acceptance of experience to a mastery, relatively speaking, of how the common-sense world "works" to the possibility at least of a theoretical comprehension of the whole: a science of society. At this point we return to Schutz:

> . . . a special motivation is needed in order to induce the naive person even to pose the question concerning the meaningful structure of his life-world, even *within the general thesis*. This motivation can be very heterogeneous; for example, a newly appearing phenomenon of meaning resists being organized within the store of experience, or a special condition of interest demands a transition from a naive attitude to a reflection of a higher order. . . . If such a motivation for leaving the natural attitude is given, then by a process of reflection the question concerning the structure of meaning can always be raised.[61]

In these terms, a phenomenology of the social world may be carried out *within* the natural attitude. "All these phenomena of meaning," Schutz writes, "which obtain quite simply for the naive person, might be in principle exactly described and analyzed even *within the general thesis*."[62] This is the Archimedean point for understanding what Schutz means by a "constitutive phenomenology of the natural attitude."[63] There is what I would call a methodological parallelism between the intentional structure of phenomena described at the level of transcendental phenomenology and phenomena of the natural attitude.

61. CPI, p. 136.
62. Ibid.
63. CPI, p. 137. Note: See Aron Gurwitsch, *The Field of Consciousness*, pp. 399 ff., in particular.

"In essence," Schutz holds, "all analyses carried out in phenomenological reduction must retain their validation in the correlates of the
phenomena investigated within the natural sphere."[64] Thus, Schutz's
reservations regarding Husserl's transcendental analysis of intersubjectivity and Schutz's belief ". . . that intersubjectivity is not a problem
of constitution which can be solved within the transcendental sphere,
but is rather a datum (*Gegebenheit*) of the life-world"[65] should not be
taken to mean that he renounced transcendental phenomenology. A
constitutive phenomenology of the natural attitude—even one carried
out *within* the natural attitude—is an interpretive demarcation of the
estate of phenomenology, not a repudiation of the results of transcendental reduction. How Schutz views the transcendental as a philosophical problem still remains to be considered. Later!

How far have we strayed from William James's *Principles*? What was
it in James's chapter "The Perception of Reality" which Schutz found
so resonant with the essay "On Multiple Realities"? One answer lies
in James's treatment of "the self"—something we have chosen to leave
unexamined; another answer involves the concept of "social role"—
again, something we have set aside. It cannot be said that "self" and
"role" are unproductive themes for a meditation on anonymity. To
say that I have written about them elsewhere is true but hardly a
reason to exclude them here. Nor do I have anything to hide: I have
confessed my sins in the Bibliography. The reason I have turned to
other features of anonymity is that the psychological and sociological
dimensions of my theme have been subordinated to the philosophical
character of Schutz's thought in the hope that what is distinctively
phenomenological in his account of anonymity will come to as much
clarity and fullness as I can give it by the end of this essay. It should
be recognized that, for Schutz, a "constitutive phenomenology of the
natural attitude" may, terminologically, be called "Intentional Psychology or, better, General Sociology."[66] There is more put at risk
than may be gained by the facile use of these terms. Perhaps avoiding
them would be the most beneficial thing to do. Instead of invoking
Husserl's respect for *The Principles* or speaking of an affinity of the
later James's "radical empiricism" with certain phenomenological ten-

64. CPI, p. 139.
65. CPIII, p. 82.
66. CPI, p. 137.

ets, I prefer to be satisfied with pointing to the insistence of both James and Schutz on the primacy of abstraction in the life of consciousness. James says it best: "That we can at any moment think of the same thing which at any former moment we thought of is the ultimate law of our intellectual constitution."[67]

---

67. *Principles of Psychology*, Vol. II, p. 290.

V

ENCLAVES

One February morning about fifty years ago, I walked into my elementary school classroom and found a substitute teacher who had a brown spot in the middle of her forehead. As a reader of Jack London's South Sea Tales, I was aware of the significance of exotic phenomena. Two things were immediately certain: that the teacher was in the early stages of leprosy and that I alone was aware of her condition. Since she had announced at the beginning of the class that our regular teacher would be back the next day, I knew that I had only a short time to tell the substitute the grim news. But I couldn't. When the final bell for the day sounded, I dawdled, helplessly caught between the awful knowledge that only I could warn her in time and a paralyzing embarrassment over doing so. Paralysis won the day, and I left the classroom carrying with me a vision of the poor woman destined now to be one of those who forever "walk alone."

In what finite province of meaning did that experience in childhood take place? I was certainly in the paramount reality of everyday life; I was certainly not just "imagining" what that malignant spot meant— I *knew* what it meant. Yet I said nothing to anyone about what I had discovered. To the question at home: "What happened at school?" I said nothing about the substitute teacher. Nor did I share my diagnosis with anyone my own age. Did I somehow sense or "realize" that I was dreaming the whole thing up out of some stories in a book? It never occurred to me to leave an unsigned note on the teacher's desk, saying "The substitute has leprosy." Had I done so, I can envision the relentless proceedings that would have followed: "I want the person who left a note on my desk to stand up"; "This looks like your handwriting"—all the apparatus of prison, as experienced in childhood, brought to bear on "getting to the bottom of this." As I see it now, what chance did Jack London or leprosy have in the Great Depression? The time was out of joint.

What I've just recounted really happened to me. So I was *there*, in the world, thumping along in the paramount reality, yet swiftly imagining what I had read of tropical life, with its perils of little fingers turning black with disease, foreboding spots on the skin, paradise invaded by infection, romance corrupted by exile. The finite province of meaning which I inhabited also included the realm of imagination— at least parts of both domains overlapped. More than that, the entire experience was mine alone; secrecy gave what I "knew" not only a spine to make it real but a deliciousness to make the solitude of my knowledge unshareable.[1] The overlapping of parts or aspects of provinces Schutz calls "enclaves" of meaning. Although he devotes little attention to this concept, it is enormously significant not only for the theory of multiple realities but for the understanding of "familiarity" and of anonymity. What Schutz does say about the subject in direct terms follows his caution that finite provinces of meaning should not be interpreted in static form, as though a choice of one province ruled out movement through others. "There is, furthermore," Schutz writes, "the problem of 'enclaves,' that is, of regions belonging to one province of meaning enclosed by another. . . . To give an example of this disregarded group of problems: any projecting within the world of working is itself . . . a phantasying, and involves in addition a kind of theoretical contemplation, although not necessarily that of the scientific attitude."[2]

Enclaves, then, are not "places" as much as "othernesses"—my language, not Schutz's—which impinge on placement in one "world" or another. While doing my job in the world of working, I may reflect not only on the job which I am doing but on what someone with my talents should really be doing; and phantasy may replace reflection or, in the stream of consciousness, swim along in tandem with scheming. *Projecting* a course of action, in Schutz's sense, always entails the potential admixture of meaning which has its source in alternative worlds. Even the phenomenologist must be cautious: Can the quartets of Haydn be heard by a transcendental listener? Are the acoustics good within the reduced sphere? Was Schutz, through whose mind Haydn frequently raced (so he told me), able to keep pace with that magic traveler without *ever* musing on the subtleties of inner-time? Not after or before but *during* the hearing? Is this something like

1. Cf. Sissela Bok, *Secrets: On the Ethics of Concealment and Revelation*, New York: Pantheon Books, 1982.
2. CPI, footnote, p. 233. Also see Ibid., p. 307 and cf. SLW, footnote, p. 24.

those remarkable translators who are able to do immediate, expert translations while playing a strong game of chess? Such a comparison is not only wide of the mark but has no conception of what the mark is. The problem with which we are concerned is not that of how to account for simultaneous attention being given to multiple and quite different tasks; rather, the problem is whether meaning, when it arises in a particular province of meaning, is not really enclaved from the outset, by its own disposition. We can leave aside the question of transcendental reduction; our assignment is far simpler: what are we to make of enclaves of meaning within the natural attitude?

Within the course of daily life, enclaves are more often than not "inhabited" by Others; enclaves are phenomena of intersubjectivity. You and I share some region of work, family relationship, avocation, past history which is our intersection in the world, not only unshared by but unknown to Others. The temptation here is to concentrate on intimacies, on private features of the individual's life: hidden religious or sexual activity, for example. But in the matter of enclaves, these examples would lead us away from a more vital, a more nearly structural aspect of the social world: that, as Schutz holds, provinces of meaning overlap, that meaning in the paramount reality may be infiltrated by meaning-elements which are derivative from the world of dreams, that phantasy and imagination as well as "sheer madness and vagary" may affect our action in the mundane world. Again, it would be a profound miscalculation either to agree or to disagree with what has just been said on the assumption that a causal process was being described. Within the enclave, my working self is not altered by what I imagine in the sense that something from one province strikes something in another, however subtly. The enclave of work already "includes" features of other regions which the paramount reality overlaps—includes those features as co-present, not as causal agents. But a substantial illustration is needed to advance the discussion. This time a fictive flight will not do.

The talk will be in egological terms, that is, approached from the standpoint of a self glimpsed purposely without the infringement of Others. A mild reduction of sorts is being invoked. As I write this sentence, I am striking the keys of my typewriter so as to make the necessary impression of the letters on the paper before me. My concern, thematically speaking, is with elucidating Schutz's concept of "enclave." Yet I "know" that unless there is a properly functioning

ribbon in my typewriter, nothing readable will result. Until this moment, my "knowing" about the typewriter ribbon was a tacit affair. If
there was anything reflectively present in my mind apart from the
conceptual work of presenting my ideas, it was *some* very slight awareness that my pounding at an old manual Olivetti was a way of ex-
pressing a completely unfounded but passionately held grievance
against word-processing machines. Atrocity stories are fresh in my
mind. Where *are* those pages, chapters, entire manuscripts which have
vanished from retrieval's reach? To be sure, nothing of that sort has
ever happened to me, but I have reliable knowledge of cases, which
I am not at liberty to divulge. In my breviary, the word processor is
a sin against the Holy Ghost.

Far more important in my writing is the project in which I am
engaged: anonymity in Schutz. That project is not a piece of the paramount reality; rather, I "live" its presence in the intention of every
segment of my writing as it moves toward its completion. In discussing
enclaves I am exemplifying, in immanent fashion, the illustration presently unfolding. Without deliberate plans, outlines, or even a general
notion of exactly how the sentence I am now composing is going to
lead to the end of this chapter, I am aware that I am to keep a rendezvous, a reunion. For the moment, my straightforward effort to
offer an account of what is meant by enclaves is colored by a mode
of reflection which is thematically oriented but also memorially informed. I *know* very well that writers, in certain contexts not unlike
mine, resort to beginning with where they are. Schutz starts the first
chapter of *Reflections on the Problem of Relevance* in this way: "Having
decided to jot down some thoughts on the matter of relevance, I have
arranged my writing materials on a table in the garden of my summer
house. Starting the first strokes of my pen, I have in my visual field
this white sheet of paper, my writing hand, the ink marks forming
one line of characters after the other on the white background."[3]

My knowing that writers often make use of the "here I am" device
in getting started and that such a choice ceased to be original long
ago does not *enter* into my account, for I have not so much utilized it
as "noticed" that it was present from the outset. On this particular
occasion I am not after originality but content to describe what I find
in my egological adventure. That I realize that there is a reflective
"moment" possible as I proceed to write about enclaves and that that

3. RPR, p. 1.

"moment" is part of the enclave of my projecting—such recognition displays the prong of intentionality. There is a choice presented in my writing of whether to pursue, without interruption, my goal of clarifying the status of enclaves or whether to attend to the turning of consciousness toward imagination—that cohabiter from another province—within the sensed limit of what is relevant to my project. Nor is language without its own evil genius. I am tempted to say more about the enclave than "by and large" can accommodate; I want all of it—root and branch; lock, stock, and barrel. I suffer from the phenomenologist's sin of pride: that encrusted language must be relinquished. Here "familiarity" exacts its price. Within the reduced sphere—however loosely the *epoché* has been performed or attempted—linguistic choices are also possible: when words bite, they should not adhere to language like plaque.

Not familiarity but anonymity comes to my attention now. My enclave within the worlds of working and imagination presents an "otherness" which reflection can fix upon as a subject but which the very "fact" of the enclave anticipates. "It could be otherwise" is known to me in the natural attitude, where "it" refers to any state of affairs. Within my tentative reduction, however, "it" points to what there is, not to some particular state of affairs "within" what there is. The "it" may be bizarre to ordinary experience but no mystery is involved. "What there is" amounts to mundane experience altogether, to whatever may be grasped as the "totality" of that experience. Perhaps, if challenged, I must confess that whenever I experience something, it is just that: "experience" is an intentional term. The "sum" of experience may be thought of; it hardly seems to be intentionally negotiable as a noematic unity. Yet the "otherness" does present itself as the "nameless." In existential terms the "nameless" takes the form of anguish or dread. I suggest—and take sole responsibility now—that the world of working, the paramount reality of common sense, carries with it another "side" or aspect which may be understood in phenomenological rather than existential form, in a neutral way. The "otherness" at issue is not an "otherwise." It would not do to reduce what I am suggesting to this: In the enclave of work-imagination, I perceive the state of affairs which might simply be called "having a spat" and that I can readily imagine an alternative state of affairs "being cozy together." The translation is not wrong because its result is banal; the translation is simply irrelevant because in substituting an "otherwise" for "otherness," "what there is" has been replaced by a particular state of affairs. I am concerned with a negative mode of what Husserl called "appresentation."[4]

Although Husserl recognizes a more general form of appresentation ("An appresentation occurs even in external experience, since the strictly seen front of a physical thing always and necessarily appresents a rear aspect and prescribes for it a more or less determinate content"[5]), the core of his theory has to do with appresentation of the Other and is grounded in an analysis of intersubjectivity. What I have called a negative mode of appresentation has no place in *Cartesian Meditations* and is purely, even fancifully, derivative; but parasites have their rights too! Since "otherness" has to do with the presentation of negation, it might be more helpful to turn to Husserl's *Ideas,* in particular to his discussion of reflection with regard to the purely intended object, the object as "meant"—the noema. He points out that even for someone who has become familiar with the doctrine of the intentionality of consciousness, "there is still a great temptation to apprehend noematic characters . . . *as mere 'determinations of reflexion.' "* and he goes on to say:

> Thus the negated, the affirmed, and the like, are to be reached in this way, that the object of the "judgment" in reflexion is characterized as negated when the reflexion bears on the negating, as affirmed when it bears on the affirming, as probable when it bears on the presuming, and so everywhere. But this view is a mere subjective construction, which already proclaims its perversity through the fact that if these predicates were really no more than relating predicates of reflexion, they could be *given* only in the actual reflecting upon the act-aspect and in relation to it. But they are evidently *not* given through such reflexion. We grasp what concerns the correlate as such through the glance being turned directly on the correlate itself. We grasp the negated, the affirmed, the possible, the questionable, and so forth, as directly qualifying the appearing object as such. In no wise do we here glance back upon the act. Conversely, the noetic predicates which emerge through such reflexion are far from having the same meaning as the noematic predicates in question. Connected with this is the fact that even from the standpoint of *truth*, "not-being" is clearly only equivalent to and not identical with "being validly negated"; similarly "being

4. See *Cartesian Meditations*, pp. 108 ff. (section 50ff.).
5. Ibid., p. 109 (section 50).

possible" is not identical with "being held possible in a valid way, and the like."[6]

In the context of the experience of the Other, Husserl speaks of appresentation as "analogical." When I refer to "negative appresentation," however, I am attempting to avoid the analogical in favor of an otherwise—a "being possible" which, as we see in *Ideas*, is not identical with a judgment such as "I deem it possible." The more primordial, "protojudgmental" awareness that "it could be otherwise" appresents an opaque aspect of "what there is." The "it" of "it could be otherwise" is my experience of everyday life, my acquaintance with common sense. To speak of a negative mode of appresentation, then, is to question the necessity of the paramount reality. What gives common sense dominion in my everyday world? What assurance is there that the paramount *is* paramount? "For most men," James writes, "the 'things of sense' . . . are the absolutely real world's nucleus."[7] And Schutz cautions us that "it is characteristic of the natural attitude that it takes the world and its objects for granted until counterproof imposes itself."[8] Yet "otherness" remains fugitive to common sense. The "things of sense" are apprehended differently, at least in some ways, in pathology. Still the enclaves between "normalcy" and "aberration" do not habitually disturb the ordinary person; it is the extraordinary person who sees in the clinical universal the astonishing particular.[9] Something is amiss. Perhaps the difficulty at the moment is not so much the precise meaning of "otherness" as the precise meaning of "common sense." We may appeal to Clifford Geertz for an advance in the discussion. He writes:

> . . . common sense remains more an assumed phenomenon than an analyzed one. Husserl, and following him Schutz, have dealt with the conceptual foundations of "everyday" experience, how we construe the world we biographically inhabit, but without much recognition of the distinction between that and what Dr. Johnson was doing when he kicked the stone to confute Berkeley, or Sherlock Holmes was doing when he reflected on the silent dog in the night; and Ryle has at least remarked in passing that one does not "exhibit common sense or the

6. *Ideas* (Boyce Gibson translation), p. 305 (section 108). Note: I have not altogether followed the difference between single and double quotation marks. Cf. Kersten's translation of *Ideas*, p. 257, which is closer in this respect to the original.
7. *The Principles of Psychology*, Vol. II, p. 294.
8. CPI, p. 228.
9. See Oliver Sacks, "The Autist Artist," *The New York Review of Books*, Vol. XXXII, April 25, 1985, pp. 17–21.

lack of it in using a knife and fork. [One does] in dealing with a plausible beggar or a mechanical breakdown when [one has] not got the proper tools." But generally, the notion of common sense has been rather commonsensical: what anyone with common sense knows.[10]

Common sense for Dr. Johnson and Sherlock Holmes, I would take it, involves an activity of mind rather than a description of everyday experience. If common sense is not a faculty of mind, it is at least an exercise in problem solving. But the two worthies were engaged in different pursuits. What Dr. Johnson demonstrated with respect to Berkeley was an advance in civility: from throwing stones to kicking them. Sherlock Holmes, however, pursued his own methods:

> I had grasped the significance of the silence of the dog, for one true inference invariably suggests others . . . a dog was kept in the stables, and yet, though someone had been in and had fetched out a horse, he had not barked enough to arouse the two lads in the loft. Obviously the midnight visitor was someone whom the dog knew well.[11]

That one true inference does not invariably suggest others, is of little account compared to the importance of the distinction which is being made between common sense as structure and common sense as activity in the statement by Professor Geertz. "Use your common sense!" is not the declaration of someone appealing to the phenomenology of the natural attitude. To be sure, there is a valuable way in which "problem solving" can be managed by mother wit rather than by special or technical training or the presumption of a scholarly fund of information or knowledge. And that such problem solving is an activity is noteworthy. So, too, Ryle's distinction between "common sense" mistaken for habituality and the "real thing" is worth mentioning. I find it difficult to believe that Schutz would not have agreed with me in this. At the same time, both the brute givenness of actuality and the activity of common sense at work are integral parts of Schutz's conception of common sense. It is when things go wrong that common sense stirs. Schutz writes:

> It is characteristic of the natural attitude that it takes the world and its objects for granted until counterproof imposes itself. As long as the once established scheme of reference, the system of our and other people's warranted experiences works, as long as the actions and op-

10. Clifford Geertz, *Local Knowledge: Further Essays in Interpretive Anthropology*, New York: Basic Books, 1983, p. 77.
11. Sir Arthur Conan Doyle, "Silver Blaze," in *The Complete Sherlock Holmes* (with a preface by Christopher Morley), Garden City: Doubleday, 1930, p. 349.

erations performed under its guidance yield the desired results, we trust these experiences. We are not interested in finding out whether this world really does exist or whether it is merely a coherent system of consistent appearances. We have no reason to cast any doubt upon our warranted experiences which, so we believe, give us things as they really are. It needs a special motivation, such as the irruption of a "strange" experience not subsumable under the stock of knowledge at hand or inconsistent with it, to make us revise our former beliefs.[12]

If we can puzzle things out within the framework of an established scheme of reference, then common sense proves to be an activity which utilizes what our stock of knowledge provides in order to take a step beyond what has previously been taken for granted. The puzzle may be relatively simple or elusive; *using* one's common sense is framework-bound. The system of typifications and relevances provides the materials which common sense needs to work upon if its activity is to be consequential in daily life. I do not think that Dr. Johnson or Sherlock Holmes or Gilbert Ryle believed in or advanced the claim that there is a special faculty of common sense. What there *is* shows itself, by its presence or absence, in these examples:

Some years ago, an oversized truck which was carrying government material was stopped on the highway by the presence of an overhead bridge. The special route which the truck had followed had been carefully worked out by military authorities. It was essential to get the material to its destination within a certain time; no other means of transportation was possible. What stopped the truck was that it was a fraction of an inch too high to get under the bridge. Nothing could be done. Army engineers were called in for consultation. The situation was at a stalemate when a child in the crowd of onlookers called out: "Let some air out of the tires." That was done and the truck proceeded on its way.

I was not present when the tires were deflated—I read about it in the newspapers—but I was on hand when my next example occurred. At some national election which was held a long time ago, it was announced as a local requirement that every voter had to bring to the polling place proof of graduation from high school. The man ahead of me in line presented his college diploma. "That won't do," he was told; "you have to show a high school diploma." It took consultation with higher authorities to permit the man to exercise the franchise.

12. CPI, p. 228.

Schutz's intentions are quite clear. To be sure, he is concerned with a phenomenology of the natural attitude—a conceptual affair if there ever was one—but his starting point is that common sense which is not unknown to sociologists and anthropologists. In his essay "The Stranger," Schutz writes:

> . . . we shall investigate how the cultural pattern of group life presents itself to the common sense of a man who lives his everyday life within the group among his fellow-men. Following the customary terminology, we use the term "cultural pattern of group life" for designating all the peculiar valuations, institutions, and systems of orientation and guidance (such as the folkways, mores, laws, habits, customs, etiquette, fashions) which, in the common opinion of sociologists of our time, characterize—if not constitute—any social group at a given moment in its history.[13]

But "The Stranger" has been called one of Schutz's "applied" essays. Perhaps there is less concern in this essay with "the conceptual foundations of 'everyday' experience" than in his more theoretical work. It is unclear to me what "applied" means in this context; more important, it is unclear to me what Geertz means by the distinction between "how we construe the world we biographically inhabit" and what Johnson and Holmes were doing (or Ryle mulling over). Something other than a distinction between conception and activity is at issue in Geertz's formulation. Indeed, we have approached Geertz's essay "Common Sense as a Cultural System" from the back door. A substantial paragraph preceding the one we quoted sets forth his theme if not his thesis:

> . . . common sense, or some kindred conception, has become a central category, almost *the* central category, in a wide range of modern philosophical systems. It has always been an important category in such systems from the Platonic Socrates (where its function was to demonstrate its own inadequacy) forward. Both the Cartesian and Lockean traditions depended, in their different ways—indeed, their culturally different ways—upon doctrines about what was and what was not self-evident, if not exactly to the vernacular mind at least to the unencumbered one. But in this century the notion of (as it tends to be put) "untutored" common sense—what the plain man thinks when sheltered from the vain sophistications of schoolmen—has, with so much else disappearing into science and poetry, grown into almost the thematic subject of philosophy. The focus on ordinary language in Wittgenstein, Austin, Ryle; the development of the so-called phenomenology of ev-

13. CPII, p. 92.

eryday life by Husserl, Schutz, Merleau-Ponty; the glorification of personal, in-the-midst-of-life decision in continental existentialism; the
taking of garden-variety problem solving as the paradigm of reason in
American pragmatism—all reflect this tendency to look toward the
structure of down-to-earth, humdrum, *brave type* thought for clues to
the deeper mysteries of existence. G. E. Moore, proving the reality of
the external world by holding up one hand and saying here is a physical
object and then holding up the other and saying here is another, is,
doctrinal details aside, the epitomizing image of a very large part of
recent philosophy in the West.[14]

Before setting out to consider this passage, I will hawk sharply in
order to rid myself of some vituperative phlegm: "doctrinal details
aside . . ." is a *bit*—and that is enough—like saying, "biological details
aside, beetles and bears are brothers." But I am not concerned with
whether conflation for the sake of an interesting point—let us subsume
it under the doctrine of Noble Conflation—is warranted in Geertz's
swift history of philosophy. Nor will I give way to temptation and say
that Moore's great advance had less to do with "*brave type* thought"
than with a shift from furniture and toothache to hands. It may at
least be asked whether Moore's efforts to explain his ideas were always
examples of "*brave type* thought."[15] What *is* telling in Geertz's statement
is not what appears to be his display of "the epitomizing image" but

14. *Local Knowledge*, pp. 76–77.
15. In responding to essays on his thought by, in this instance, two very able colleagues, Moore writes: "Mr. [Arthur E.] Murphy . . . , in the concluding pages of his
essay . . . —pages which puzzled me very much when I first read them—is advocating,
if I understand him rightly, a view very similar to Mr. [O. K.] Bouwsma's in both
respects. He also, so far as I can see, must have misunderstood how I was using the
term 'sense-datum,' since he thinks, apparently, that I was mistaken in holding that
when, for instance, looking at my right hand and the sheet of paper on which I am
writing, as I now do, I say to myself 'This hand is touching this sheet of paper' (a
proposition which I know for certain to be true), I am making an assertion, if I say
this to myself, about at least two objects which I *see directly*, and therefore about at least
two 'sense-data,' in my sense of the term. Or does Mr. Murphy mean to deny that, in
such a case, I am making any assertion at all about anything which I *see directly*—see,
that is, in the same sense in which, when I have an after-image with my eyes closed, I
see that after-image? I can hardly think that he can mean to deny this, and therefore
I am driven to suppose that he did not understand that I was using 'sense-datum' in
such a sense that *anything whatever* which is 'directly seen' must be a sense-datum. I
think he must have supposed that I was using 'sense-datum' in such a sense that the
part of the surface of my hand and the part of the surface of this sheet of paper, which
I am seeing, *cannot* be sense-data, and therefore was mistakenly attributing to me the
view that, in making the assertion 'This hand is touching this sheet of paper,' I was
making an assertion about two objects which are *not* identical with any physical reality.
His own view, then, I suppose, must be that I was making an assertion about my hand
and about this sheet of paper, and about that part of the surface of each which I was
seeing, and (since he can hardly deny that I was making an assertion about at least two

rather the thesis he is advancing in his essay as a whole—an essay which we have merely picked at randomly so far and to which we cannot do justice. That thesis consists in a distinction between what have been taken to be the immediate "givens" of common sense— that, to use Geertz's examples, "rain wets" and "fire burns"—as reality-presenters (as I would express it) and the "analysis of common sense," which does not reduce it to stray contingencies but instead shows common sense to be what I would call a hermeneutical lalapalooza. Professor Geertz is more judicious:

> This analytical dissolution of the unspoken premise from which common sense draws its authority—that it presents reality neat—is not intended to undermine that authority but to relocate it. If common sense is as much an interpretation of the immediacies of experience, a gloss on them, as are myth, painting, epistemology, or whatever, then it is, like them, historically constructed and, like them, subjected to historically defined standards of judgment. It can be questioned, disputed, affirmed, developed, formalized, contemplated, even taught, and it can vary dramatically from one people to the next. It is, in short, a cultural system, though not usually a very tightly integrated one, and it rests on the same basis that any other such system rests; the conviction by those whose possession it is of its value and validity. Here, as elsewhere, things are what you make of them.[16]

---

things which I was 'seeing directly') that the two latter 'objects' (the two surfaces mentioned) were 'directly seen': which is exactly what, I gather, Mr. Bouwsma also would hold. But *this* view is in no way inconsistent with my view that I was making an assertion about at least two sense-data: on the contrary, once my use of 'sense-datum' is understood, it is evident that this view of mine *follows* from Mr. Murphy's own view! But it is true that I also have *another* view—namely that there is good reason to suppose that, when I made that assertion, I was *not* seeing *directly* any part of the surface of my hand or of this sheet of paper, and that, therefore, since I certainly was making an assertion about *some* pair of objects which I was directly seeing, I must have been making an assertion not only about my hand and this sheet of paper, and about the parts of the surface of each which I was seeing, but *also* about a pair of directly seen objects *not* identical with any of these four. And I think it is very likely that Mr. Murphy is objecting, as Mr. Bouwsma was, to *this* view of mine. *This* view of mine is, of course, not inconsistent with Mr. Murphy's and Mr. Bouwsma's view (if this *is* their view) that, when I made that assertion, I *was* seeing *directly* both the part of the surface of my hand and the part of the surface of this sheet of paper which I was certainly *seeing*: it only says that there is a good reason for doubting whether that view of theirs is true. But nevertheless I think it it quite likely that Mr. Murphy is objecting to it; and, if so, I have given an answer to that objection.—I think, however, that it is very likely that I have failed to catch Mr. Murphy's point here, or at least part of it; but I have done my best to state what I think he means, and how I should answer it, if he does mean that" (G. E. Moore, "A Reply to My Critics," in *The Philosophy of G. E. Moore* (edited by Paul Arthur Schilpp) [The Library of Living Philosophers], Evanston: Northwestern University, 1942, pp. 648–649). And so *that* matter was set to rest.

16. *Local Knowledge*, p. 76.

It is evident that the thesis which Geertz is advancing (as I have expressed it) is only part—though a most significant part—of a larger and longer story, one having to do with the variegation of everyday experience, the intricacy of the mundane, the deep relevance of anthropology for the life-world. We should say of Geertz what Geertz should have said about Moore: that his analysis of common sense is troublingly complex in a most productive sense, for what Moore and Geertz have to say about common sense is most suggestive the less certain it is what is being said. In the case of Moore, I believe that the "less certain" has to do with questions of how one goes about or ought to go about thinking of "method" in philosophy; in the case of Geertz, I would guess that the "less certain" has to do with still not fully imagined ways in which the density of experience in its widest reach may be illuminated as well as systematized. Toward the end of his life, Schutz discovered Moore's essay "A Defence of Common Sense" and thought that he could use it to buttress phenomenological findings. I disagreed; it seemed to me that what appeared to be similar results represented conflicting standpoints, that the results were not really similar. This discussion of Geertz leads me to believe that he has reached some results which are similar to those arrived at by Schutz; it may be that Geertz will say of me what I said to Schutz about Moore. And there *are* differences: common sense does not remain "more an assumed phenomenon than an analyzed one" in the work of Schutz. The analysis which Schutz provides shows common sense to be richly textured, well traveled, and thoroughly experienced in the business of human being. Still, without having received any encouragement, I welcome Professor Geertz to these pages. For all (perhaps because of) his acumen, Moore would have found phenomenology baffling; perhaps a resonance with what is primal serves Geertz well—early on, he was one of the few social scientists who showed themselves to be discerning readers of Schutz. Now a final word of tribute is owing to G. E. Moore. Certainly, there is much dispute about which philosopher had the greatest mind, but there can surely be little doubt about which philosopher had the most distinguished hands; they belonged to Professor Moore.

What aspect of our discussion was Geertz supposed to advance? I had been talking about "otherness" and remarking, in a passing way, about the manner in which a problem that upsets the applecart of everyday experience may nevertheless linger in enclaves shared by the mundane and the strange. More, for the moment, than "otherness," common sense appeared to need further examination. Geertz, I thought, might help with such an examination. And I believe he has. But Geertz is not a phenomenologist, not a Husserlian and not a Schutzian. Nor is there any good reason why he should be. We are left to our own devices in getting on with the clarification of the meaning of what I have termed "otherness." Before returning to the consideration of enclaves, it might be useful to give a preliminary answer to the related questions which I have raised: What is otherness and what is the relationship of otherness to common sense? Tentatively: Otherness is common sense stripped not only of the possibility of being "otherwise," but negated in what it is. Is it possible to think of social reality without common sense being part of that reality? For immediate purposes, let us take a broad view of common sense, one which embraces both Schutz and Geertz as its students. If common sense were to flee, would reality still be "social"? Stop the individual who replies, "That depends on what you mean by. . . ." Nothing will come of that. I do not know whether there was in antiquity a god or goddess of fencing; perhaps the father of Romulus and Remus will be the closest we can come to the ancient sire we need. In mythology, then, Mars in his old age fathered two belligerents, Thrust and Parry, who, after many adventures, escaped from the underworld to enter the life of philosophy, where they have ever since thrived. When they are in good form, their act is well received. "Un sot trouve toujours un plus sot qui l'admire"—which might, with extravagance, be rendered: As long as there are imbeciles there will always be idiots to applaud them.

What would it mean to dump common sense? Before we rid ourselves of it, let us insult it. In Kierkegaardian spirit, let us address an animadversion against common sense. In the first place, why does it so often give itself airs, as though what it knows is worth knowing simply because such knowledge is so widespread? In the second place, where is the proof of its indispensability? Who has come forward to testify persuasively: "I tried to do without it but failed." And there is much more to be said against common sense: it *is* common, it is not a "pearl of great price," it is like a handkerchief into which a hundred noses have trumpeted their best. Besides, common sense repeats itself, repeats itself, repeats itself until one longs to be released from all sanity. That and language as well: sodden, corrupt, at once obsequious to tradition and dithery about trends, one word fixed to what is standard and the next unhinged by the latest cry. And who bequeathed common sense to us, anyway? Is it not a legacy which we are free to

relinquish? Whose almighty hand carved out this life of tedium? What
ultimate power demands the servitude of boredom? Are we not free
at last to blot out common sense, to dismember it, to devastate it
altogether, and finally—once and for all—to blow it to kingdom come?

If common sense be not a native capacity of mind, still are we all
matriculated in its faculty. It is a school from which we can never
graduate, an academy from which no examination will ever release
us. Vilify it as we may, common sense inescapably sustains us in our
protestations and generates the very invective we would urge against
it. In fine, we are stuck not only with it but in it. Matters of pathology
demand attention in any qualification of the inevitability of common
sense; gone awry, however, common sense still maintains its own *Lebenswelt*, its own architecture of chaos. Consider the story of one of
Esquirol's patients:

> M. N., aged 51 years, of a bilious sanguine temperament, having a large
> head, short neck and flushed face, was, in 1812, prefect of a large city
> of Germany, the inhabitants of which rose upon the rear-guard of the
> French army, in its retreat. The disorder which resulted from these
> events, and the responsibility which rested upon the prefect, deprived
> him of the use of his reason. He considered himself accused of high
> treason, and consequently disgraced. In this state of mind he cut his
> throat with a razor. As soon as he had recovered his senses, he hears
> voices that accuse him. Cured of his wound, he hears the same voices,
> and persuades himself that he is surrounded with spies.[17]

In the course of one of Esquirol's visits, M. N. says to him: "I need
neither a physician nor a spy."[18] Yet, we are told, aside from being
convinced of the evils of his enemies, ". . . he reasons with perfect
propriety, and all his intellectual faculties preserve their wonted integrity. He participated in conversation with the same degree of spirit,
intelligence and readiness, as before his sickness."[19] Nor is the case

17. E. Esquirol, *Mental Maladies: Treatise on Insanity* (trans. with additions, by E. K.
Hunt), Philadelphia: Lea and Blanchard, 1845, pp. 93–94.
18. Ibid., p. 94.
19. Ibid. Note: For those who want to know what happened to M.N., we continue
with Esquirol's account: "Towards the end of March, 1814, after a long conversation,
I invite M.N. to pay me a visit, in order to satisfy himself by examining my library,
whether I was a physician. He declines; but three days after, thinking that he had taken
me at unawares, he proposes to visit my study immediately. I accept the proposal. After
having examined the books for a considerable time, he says; 'If these books were not
placed here expressly for me, this library is that of a physician.' Some days afterwards,
the siege of Paris takes place, but the patient remains convinced that it is not a battle,
but merely an exercise with fire-arms. The king is proclaimed, and I send him the
journals with the arms of France; he reads and returns them, adding; 'these journals
were printed expressly for me.' I reply, that this would not only be very expensive, but
very dangerous also. This argument does not change his mind. I propose, in order to

different with more modern patients. "Except for . . ." continues to be part of the formula of explanation given by relatives or friends of many who are deranged. It is the "for" which cannot be ignored, because it has occasioned pain and upheaval and loss. Pathology, we must conclude, offers no essential escape from the matrix of common sense. But if common sense has so few exits—death, severe cases of organic mental disorder (Pick's disease or Alzheimer's disease—and even there we are cautioned: "Physicians must not make the error of concluding that a patient is untreatable because the disease from which he or she suffers is untreatable"[20]), its intersections are many; it is replete with enclaves.

The overlapping of provinces of meaning, as Schutz presents the matter, is not a chance affair. To the contrary, we may say, such overlapping is a constitutive feature of the social world. In his conversation and occasionally in his lectures, Schutz used to refer to "interrupted activities." It is seldom the case that an activity in daily life can be carried out without other activities impinging upon it. Indeed, interruptions are interrupted. But to take a commonplace example: I am talking on the telephone; the cat leaps to and is parading on my desk. Infuriated, I interrupt the phone conversation to yell, "Ariel, get the hell off my proofs!" Whereupon, Ariel sits down on my papers and proceeds to lick herself. Resigned, I pick up the telephone and resume the conversation. One might dismiss such events as distractions, but they are signals of more fundamental discontinuities. The larger projects and themes of my daily activity have indwelling limitations on time-duration or are affected by external circumstances. Illustration is not a problem here. A more decisive consideration pre-

---

convince him, to walk with him about the city, but he declines. On the 15th of April, 'Let us go abroad,' said he to me promptly, and without any suggestion on my part. In a moment we directed our steps to the Garden of Plants, where we found a large body of soldiers wearing the uniform of all nations. We had scarcely walked a hundred steps, when M.N. presses my arm violently, saying; Let us return, I have seen enough, you have not deceived me; I was sick, but am now cured. From that moment the *babblers* [M.N.'s voices] were silent, or were heard only in the morning, immediately after rising. My convalescent turned his attention from them, with the aid of the shortest conversation, by the perusal of a book for a few moments, or by a walk. At this time also, he regarded this symptom as I did myself. He looked upon it as a nervous phenomenon, and expressed his surprise at having so long been the dupe of it. He permitted the application of some leeches, employed the foot-bath, and drank some tumblers of purgative mineral water" (Ibid., p. 95). Our M.N. thus leeched, bathed, and purged, I take my leave of my pseudo-initial-namesake, for "M.N." is an abbreviation for "Monsieur N."

20. Charles E. Wells, "Organic Mental Disorders" (Ch. 19) in *Comprehensive Textbook of Psychiatry/IV*, 4th edition (edited by Harold I. Kaplan and Benjamin J. Sadock), Baltimore: Williams and Wilkins, 1985, p. 867.

sents itself when the actor in the everyday world realizes that along with the inescapability of "interrupted activities" there comes the recognition that "interrupter" and "interrupted" coincide in fragmentary ways on uncertain occasions to form an enclave. One is tempted to think of interrupted activities as bearing their own form of *epoché*. Beyond coincidence, however, there is what might be termed the "stabilization" of the enclave: a habitation of sorts, which in its most sophisticated form becomes a sharing between persons of "another reality."[21]

It might be thought that formal alliances—marriage, friendship, business partnership—might automatically establish enclaves; they do not. What is intimately shared in such relationships may be held secret from the rest of the world, and yet the secret may not cross the boundaries of the finite province in which it is held. The moment the privacies of different provinces are conjoined, an enclave is entered. Its destiny is convoluted. But we must be fair to the more common aspects of associations. It might, for instance, be thought that academic departments are seething enclaves; they do not qualify. In fact, we must reorient our thinking, for when it comes to academic departments, Tolstoi's line needs to be revised: "Every happy department is happy in its own way; unhappy departments are all alike." Empedocles was pushed. A more substantial question remains: What have enclaves to do with anonymity? We have already begun an answer to this question by referring to "interrupted activities." We must now return to that theme!

Once we have left behind us the obvious disturbances which regularly interrupt our projects of action, we are free to consider the more subtle agitations which arise from within a finite province of meaning. As Schutz notices: ". . . even with the sub-universe of Don Quixote's private world there is the possibility of dream and imagination, a world of phantasy within the world of phantasy; even in this sub-universe the frontiers of reality are gliding, even here are enclaves mirrored into it from other sub-universes."[22] Interruptions, then, may be gen-

---

21. What Robert Musil calls in *The Man Without Qualities* the "other condition" (*der andere Zustand*), a problem discussed by Peter L. Berger in two essays: "The Problem of Multiple Realities: Alfred Schutz and Robert Musil," in *Phenomenology and Social Reality: Essays in Memory of Alfred Schutz* (edited by Maurice Natanson), The Hague: Martinus Nijhoff, 1970, pp. 213–233 and "Robert Musil and the Salvage of the Self," *Partisan Review*, Vol. LI, 1984, pp. 638–650.

22. CPII, p. 148.

erated within the same intentionality which guides our projecting.
Husserl's idealization of "and so forth and so on," I would suggest, is
immanently accompanied by the caution (expressed in Schutz's words)
"until further notice."[23] If "and so forth and so on" is an idealization—
an *a priori* of our experience of the world—so is "until further notice"
an idealization. Schutz never claimed this; I do. "Until further notice,"
I expect the events of daily life to be "ordinary," that is, subsumable
under the appropriate typification which describes them. But within
the sub-universe of my phantasy there is, "until further notice," the
expectation of fictive continuity. The two cases may be illustrated:

Putting down my Husserl and Schutz, I pick up some casual reading
for relaxation, something to coast on. After smooth sailing, I come
upon the following passage:

> A person intending to remove a body out of England must obtain the
> coroner's sanction. This affects removal to Scotland, Northern Ireland,
> The Isle of Man and the Channel Islands but not to Wales.[24]

Why not to Wales? How irksome to have an exception of this sort.
No doubt, further research would clarify the reason for this restric-
tion, but I shall never enter into that research. I am left dissatisfied;
why not to Wales?

The second illustration: In my dream, a Dynamite Blonde is plead-
ing with me to run off with her. "Before that can be done," I tell her,
"I must work up a bibliography on the subject." Still in the dream,
Regina Olsen enters and asks, "Where is S. K.?" I remain silent. "Did
he leave any message?" Regina asks. "Yes," I reply, "he said: Ich bin
ein Berliner."[25]

What lies within the enclave, from an egological standpoint, includes
an intensity of experience concerning several provinces of meaning,
a remembered, anticipated, imagined, or phantasied state of affairs
in which only the aspect of experience relevant to the enclave is attended to while the rest—an immense remainder—is not only set at
distance but is apperceived as anonymous. "Anonymous" in what

23. CPI, p. 7.
24. G. Thurston, revised by J. C. Burton, "Deaths," in *Taylor's Principles and Practice
of Medical Jurisprudence* (edited by A. Keith Mant), 13th edition, Edinburgh: Churchill
Livingstone, 1984, p. 31.
25. For those who may think that my dream requires psychoanalytic interpretation,
one of Schutz's observations is apropos: "We may consider the whole psychoanalytic
technique of dream interpretation as an attempt to refer the contents of the dream to
the originary experiences in the world of awakeness in which and by which they were
constituted" (CPI, p. 242).

sense? Interest in the "remainder" is, in effect, bracketed; *whatever* it may be, the "remainder" is set off from consideration. A glimpse of "otherness" is provided within such a conception of the enclave. But this instance is to be distinguished from the more familiar state of affairs in which the individual knows Others only through the enclaves formed by the taking of social roles. Setting the remainder off is not synonymous with ignoring, nor is "bracketing" here being used in a strict Husserlian sense. Rather, I am suggesting that holding the remainder at distance is a way of blocking off its possibilities, not merely its contents. The glimpse of otherness begins, in this manner, with what might be called a cauterization of the subjunctive: the life of the remainder is divested of its "and so forth and so on." Within the enclave, the ego's horizon is expanded to include several states of affairs known at once, that is, comprehended in the domain of their compossibility; at the same time, what is distanced from the enclave intimates an altogether different realm, one in which the truncation of possibility signifies the recognition of anonymity no longer as a mode of abstraction but as otherness.

We have started our consideration of enclaves from the egological standpoint. Even before a "we" is encountered, it should be noted that what "occurs" in enclaves may be chosen or imposed. Don Quixote. I may decide to attend only to that enclave of coincidence between my professional and my religious life. Anselm's is, to my taste, by far the most interesting argument for the existence of God. That argument is a frame through which Perfection may be viewed, or at least approached. St. Anselm helps me to see why an ontological argument "in reverse" cannot work: I have an idea of a being than which nothing more evil can be conceived; therefore the Devil exists. That won't do. But the ontological argument does not give me God in my religious life; no argument does. The "God of the philosophers" exists for "Intro." courses. The final "triangle" Franz Rosenzweig left us with points out the way, delivering me beyond the printed page.[26] Within the enclave which includes the ability to recite the ontological argument and the tremor of faith, I discover the odd relationship between the illumination which Anselm provides in an argument which transcends itself and the secure abandonment of Rosenzweig's *Star*. The relationship is this: "proof" is an uneasy burden to bear; although it

26. Franz Rosenzweig, *The Star of Redemption* (trans. by William W. Hallo), Notre Dame: Notre Dame Press, 1985, p. 424.

is not enough, it cannot be abandoned. In fine, the enclave issues demands which neither philosophy nor religion on its own orders. It becomes more and more difficult to distinguish between what is chosen and what is imposed in the life of the enclave.

Whatever interrupted activities may tell us about anonymity, they say a good deal about the life-world. A most striking paradox excites Schutz's theory of the "meaning-construction" of the social world. Daily life is both an orderly, patterned, comprehensible field of action and a maze of disjointed, unoriented, arcane events. In common-sense terms the actor employs a variety of course-of-action types in order to secure typical results. Yet misunderstanding, misinterpretation, and failure in communication are also familiar features of daily life. Schutz appears to be concerned primarily with the question: How is a rational world constructed? That question may be met at qualitatively different levels: rationality for the theorist and rationality for common sense. The latter leads to the paradox. Schutz writes:

> . . . "rational action" on the common-sense level is always action within an unquestioned and undetermined frame of constructs of typicalities of the setting, the motives, the means and ends, the courses of action and personalities involved and taken for granted. They are, however, not merely taken for granted by the actor but also supposed as being taken for granted by the fellow-man. From this frame of constructs, forming their undetermined horizon, merely particular sets of elements stand out which are clearly and distinctly determinable. To these elements refers the common-sense concept of rationality. Thus we may say that on this level actions are at best partially rational and that rationality has many degrees.[27]

And this is a way of saying that the more "purified" typification becomes, the less it can encompass the primacy of everydayness in its babble of violence, confusion, distortion, and suffering. Schutz formulates the paradox with precision:

> To be sure, the more standardized the prevailing action pattern is, the more anonymous it is, the greater is the subjective chance of conformity and, therewith, of the success of intersubjective behavior. Yet—and this is the paradox of rationality on the common-sense level—the more standardized the pattern is, the less the underlying elements become analyzable for common-sense thought in terms of rational insight.[28]

The paradox of rationality at the level of common sense has nothing

27. CPI, p. 33.
28. Ibid.

to do with the question of whether rational models of irrational conduct can be formulated. That question has already been answered at
the theoretical level: any textbook of psychiatry is loaded with such
models. The paradox emerges in the common-sense domain because
it is there that the "underlying elements" are resident, those powers
of ordinary experience which are wayward, intransigent, and embattled. The paradox of rationality is not a paradox of common sense
but in common sense: the greater the clarity we achieve about the
mundane the more anonymous it becomes. What we find at the end
of this dialectic of common sense is the beginning of that more primordial meaning of anonymity which we have called "otherness." It
is at this point that we take leave of Schutz—with his blessing, we
hope—to explore the transcendencies of otherness. What we are leaving, at least, should be clear: Schutz has used the word "anonymous"
to signify both the abstraction and the abstractive act (through the
variant "anonymization") which replace the time-bound, circum-
stance-determined, *situated* particulars of individual existence. The
"primes" of life have been suppressed to yield the purity of the type—
more or less. Thus: the greater the purity, the greater the anonymity.
In this way, typification generates sameness. At last, for Schutz:

> *The typical and only the typical is homogeneous*, and it is always so. In the
> typifying synthesis of recognition I perform an act of anonymization
> in which I abstract the lived experience from its setting within the
> stream of consciousness and thereby render it impersonal.[29]

"Anonymous," "anonymity," "anonymization"—these are the words
employed by Schutz to display the structure of the "impersonal." Others have attempted to enrich the vocabulary. So, for example, "anonymosity" has been put forth.[30] Now, a "seriousing"[31] of our language
is necessary. What is called for is not a neologism but a recovery of
"anonymity" as a distinctively philosophical rather than methodological term. Although Schutz devoted most of his work regarding anonymity to its fundamental methodology, I believe that he had the

29. PSW, p. 186.
30. Donald Barthelme, *Guilty Pleasures*, New York: Farrar, Straus and Giroux, 1974,
p. 86. Note: It is curious that so exacting a craftsman as Barthelme should, before
entering the house of poststructuralism, peer at the lintel of "anonymosity" only to miss
the threshold of "anonimosity."
31. This "word" is not of Heideggerian coinage; it comes from numismatics, or at
least a report from that realm: see Russ Mackendrick, "Numismatics," *The New York
Times*, July 23, 1978, p. D 33.

deepest concern for the philosophical implications of his subject. Schutz has already been set off from Heidegger, but the treatment of *das Man* has not been given a thorough examination. Other issues than death are involved in understanding the "They." The movement from a subjective process of the constitution of meaning to "objective meaning" presents us with a philosophical set of problems, apart from the difficult questions of structure at issue in such a movement. The displacement of subjective processes in favor of achieving objective "products" signifies a new placement of meaning in the relationship of ego to alter ego. Beyond the suppression of primes, there is a suppression of the Other—Schutz refers to the "Thou"—in gaining a truly "objective" world, a world whose "products" may be understood without reinvoking the subjective conditions of their constitution. Schutz writes:

> The objective meaning of a product that we have before us is . . . by no means interpreted as evidence for the particular lived experience of a particular Thou. Rather, it is interpreted as already constituted and established, abstracted from every subjective flow of experience and every subjective meaning-context that could exist in such a flow. It is grasped as an objectification endowed with "universal meaning." Even though we implicitly refer to its author when we call it a "product," still we leave this author and everything personal about him out of account when we are interpreting objective meaning. He is hidden behind the impersonal "one" (someone, someone or other). This anonymous "one" is merely the linguistic term for the fact that a Thou exists, or has once existed, of whose particularity we take no account.[32]

The "Thou," his biographical situation decimated, may be the *das Man* of the paramount reality, but he is first intimated by his passion in the enclave which anonymity provides. His origin and passion taken from him, the anonymized Other continues to be a human "otherwise"; his possibilities cast off, the Other becomes a fugitive "Thou,"

32. PSW. p. 135. Note: The passage continues: "I myself or you or some ideal type or Everyman could step into its shoes without in any way altering the subjective meaning of the product. We can say nothing about the subjective processes of this anonymous 'one,' for the latter has no duration, and the temporal dimension we ascribe to it, being a logical fiction, is in principle incapable of being experienced. But precisely for this reason the objective meaning remains, from the point of view of the interpreter, invariant for all possible creators of the meaningful object. Insofar as that object contains within its very meaning the ideality of the 'and so forth' and of the 'I can do it again,' to that extent is that meaning independent of its maker and the circumstances of its origination. The product is abstracted from every consciousness as such. Objective meaning is merely the interpreter's ordering of his experiences of a product into the total context of his experience" (Ibid.).

an otherness. There being enclaves of social reality means that the limit of everything which can be otherwise has been reached, that otherness is a negativity implicit in human being. Why should the disclosure of so primordial a negativity manifest itself in enclaves rather than in common sense? Because finite provinces of meaning cannot stand as independent, autonomous states; they are of necessity floating boundaries which invade and cross each other. Action within the paramount reality, the world of working, bears its reflective moment. I may "live in my acts," but I can also reflect upon my acts, and reflection once exercised leads me to the enclave in which working recognizes itself: my work is my project.

Finite provinces of meaning cannot stand as autonomous states; these provinces generate enclaves; enclaves reveal individuals who in turning to each other make it possible to "negate" Others. The negativity which is implicit in human being and which I have identified with "otherness" may be traced in its intersubjective character to the ontology of looking and being looked at. Schutz has considered some of those problems in the context of his essay "Sartre's Theory of the Alter Ego."[33] In exposing Sartre's theory of the Other, Schutz, at one point, illuminates the intersubjective dimension of the fundamental negativity to which I have turned in trying to explain what I mean by "otherness." For the moment, Schutz is exposing Sartre, but the result goes beyond reportage:

> Sartre formulates the following criteria for a valid theory of the Other's existence. 1. Such a theory need not *prove* the Other's existence, the affirmation of which is rooted in a "pre-ontological" understanding. 2. The Cartesian *cogito* is the only possible point of departure in order to find (not reasons for my belief in the Other's existence, but) the Other himself as being-not-me. 3. The Other does not have to be grasped as an object of our cogitations, but in his existence "for us" as affecting our actual concrete being. 4. The Other has to be conceived as being "not me" but this negation is not an external spatial one; it is an internal negation, defined by Sartre as a synthetic and active connection between two terms, either of which constitutes itself by negating the other.[34]

Although it is not clear which encounters qualify as constitutive in establishing enclaves, it does seem in the encounter with the Other that, in being "looked at," in finding myself as an "object" for the subjectivity of the Other—as Sartre contends—a central moment in

33. Included in CPI, pp. 180–203.
34. Ibid., pp. 187–188.

the becoming of the enclave is revealed: negativity is occasioned by the "look" of the Other but experienced in me, the "looked-at," as a "nothing" which is already the herald of otherness. This proto-reflective process of consciousness in which an internal negativity arises is, I believe, an aperture of the enclave through which the protection or fortification of the enclave is made possible. Others are permitted access to the enclave in abused form; their unity negated, their possibilities denied, the work of the enclave accomplished, *Others* have become, at last, anonymous. And this anonymity holds good for fictive as well as "real" persons. A grand census of the enclaves would have to include those who are imagined as well as those who possess actuality—who have "papers" to establish their identity. It is time for the credentials of those who have fictive being to be examined. Such a scrutiny might be accomplished by moving from finite provinces of meaning to enclaves. It is time for a reunion of our "characters"—at least for a gathering of the enclaves.

"We're in graduate school Mrs. Ehrlich."
"So exact you look."
"We're twins."
"And what do twins study in graduate school?"
"We're involved in a project on incest."
"*Gevalt!*"

"I found myself in this line of children and someone put a tag on my jacket. Then we took off. The group was called 'Friends of the Snail Darter' and we landed in Los Angeles and were put on a special bus to this retreat. It's a long story but about fifteen years later, a college recruiter told me that I could get a full scholarship ('Descendants of Veterans of the Spanish-American War'), eight points of credit for 'life experience,' and that I had already fulfilled the foreign language requirement because at the retreat I had talked in unknown tongues."
"What did you major in?"
"Computer Science."

"It was a joke, wasn't it, Ceil?"
"I was laughing with tears in my eyes."

"That's a song; I'm talking about what happened."
"What does that mean?—what happened."
"Don't give me epistemology!"
"No wonder they called the manager."

"*Stimmung* is everything."
"Yes, a completely new *Gestalt*."
"A different *Weltanschauung*."
"A sign of the *Zeitgeist*."
"*Dasein*."
"The *Lebenswelt*."
"It's Happy Hour; let's have a spritzer."

"Did your grandfather leave you with any of his recollections of the War, Mr. Trentstaven?"
"Mr. Trentstaven keeps his own council."
"Are you related to him?"
"In a way. I work in the Post Office. What do you do?"
"I work with problem juveniles."
"How did you get into that?"
"Fact is, I once was one myself—history."

"Slidemoor, I don't have a peace pipe, but to celebrate our reconciliation, smoke one of my Brazilians."
"Why did they quit making Henry Clay?"
"You know, one Clay was too much even for a connoisseur like Thomas Mann."
"The real story of Henry Clay has never been told."
"Here, let me light you up. But there's more to life than a good cigar. Ever hear of 'Old Mock'?"[35]
"I'm willing to listen."
"Well, this Brazilian is to Henry Clay as Jack Daniels is to Old Mock."
"Consider the hatchet buried."

35. "Old Mock"—a legend which burns in a galaxy of spirits which are its fit company: ". . . corn liquor, white lightning, sugar whiskey, skull cracker, popskull, bush whiskey, stump, stumphole, 'splo, ruckus juice, radiator whiskey, rotgut, sugarhead, block and tackle, wildcat, panther's breath, tiger's sweat, sweet spirits of cats a-fighting, alley bourbon, city gin, cool water, happy Sally, deep shaft, jump steady, old horsy, stingo, blue John, red-eye, pine top, buckeye bark whiskey, and see seven stars" (Alec Wilkinson, *Moonshine: A Life in Pursuit of White Liquor*, New York: Alfred A. Knopf, 1985, p. 28).

"He kept calling for years. Left messages. Sightings in Santa Fe, Orlando, Memphis, Vancouver. Nothing checked out. Finally, he went mad; used to call me collect from state asylums, said the boy was right in my own home! Had I looked?"

"The stomach is essentially vengeful."
"Transportation and medical costs keep going up."
"Ungrateful organ!"
"Soon they'll charge you to walk, professor."
"Reality is treacherous."

VI

TRANSCENDENCE

Toward the end of his essay "Some Leading Concepts of Phenomenology," after having elucidated and explored a number of central phenomenological themes, Schutz writes:

> And now I am afraid I have to disappoint the reader. A trained phenomenologist would not regard the foregoing as an account of phenomenological *philosophy*. He would perhaps admit that one or two questions of what Husserl called phenomenological *psychology* have been touched on. Phenomenological philosophy deals with the activities of the transcendental ego, with the constitution of space and time, with the constitution of intersubjectivity, with the problems of monads; indeed it is an approach to the questions hitherto called metaphysical.[1]

Schutz regarded his own work—and this is exactly what he told me—as a constitutive phenomenology of the natural attitude, done at the level of phenomenological psychology. It might appear that what Schutz said about Husserl could be said of my account of Schutz. Perhaps I have moved to a more superficial level than that of phenomenological psychology in presenting Schutz's views. Let us say instead that I have endeavored to simplify some of Schutz's ideas on occasion—not to substitute the spirit for the letter but to appropriate the letter for the sake of the letter. The problem with the Husserl-Schutz analogy, however, lies elsewhere. Husserl did not confine his writings to transcendental phenomenology; much of what he wrote consisted of phenomenological psychology; and a good deal of his work moved—not always clearly or consistently—from level to level. Almost fifty years after his death, the "philosophy" of Edmund Husserl is still emerging in the series of volumes being edited from his vast manuscript estate and published as "Husserliana."[2]

1. CPI, pp. 115–116.
2. The Hague: Martinus Nijhoff.

Any attempt to clarify the meaning of Husserl's phenomenological philosophy—the metaphysical horizon of phenomenology—for whatever good it might do here, would be a suicidal venture.[3] Instead, it might be wiser to settle for what I once heard Professor Dorion Cairns say: "By 'phenomenology' Husserl meant whatever he was doing at the time." I would add, in the same spirit, that by "phenomenological philosophy" Husserl meant the metaphysical implications of whatever he was doing at the time. Although philosophy appears in great force in Husserl's work, philosophy is more elusive in the writings of Schutz. It would be quite misleading to say that because Schutz is not a transcendental phenomenologist, philosophy is absent from his work. Deeper and stronger: It would be a violent error to conclude from the fact that Schutz did not accept Husserl's transcendental argument respecting intersubjectivity and that Schutz had grave reservations about the possibility of *any* transcendental proof for the existence of the Other that he rejected the legitimacy of phenomenological philosophy. To the contrary, there is good reason to believe that Schutz regarded phenomenological philosophy as a propaedeutic ". . . to the discovery of the general principles which govern all human knowledge."[4] Still, it is arguable even within Husserl's phenomenology whether all of his fundamental terms of discourse are equally clear, that is, whether phenomenological method has succeeded in generating a completely satisfactory conceptual framework. Schutz writes:

> In a brilliant paper presented to the "Colloque international de phénoménologie à Royaumont 1957" Professor Eugen Fink deals with what he calls the operative concepts in Husserl's phenomenology. He distinguishes in the world of any major philosopher between thematic and operative notions. Whereas the former aim at the fixation and preservation of the fundamental concepts, the latter are used in a vague manner as tools in forming the thematic notions; they are models of thought or intellectual schemata which are not brought to objectifying fixation, but remain opaque and thematically unclarified. According to Fink, the notions of "phenomenon," of "constitution," and "performances" (*Leistungen*), and even those of "epoché" and of "transcendental logic" are used by Husserl as operative concepts. They are not

3. The reader who wishes me long life but who is still curious about the furthest reaches of Husserl's thought might do well to consult Ludwig Landgrebe, "Phenomenology and Metaphysics," *Philosophy and Phenomenological Research*, Vol. X, 1949, pp. 197–205.
4. CPI, p. 66.

thematically clarified or remain at least operatively adumbrated, and are merely headings for groups of problems open to and requiring further analysis.[5]

As examples of thematic concepts in the history of philosophy, Fink cites (among some others) the concept of "idea" in Plato, of "substance" (*ousia*) in Aristotle, of "monad" in Leibniz, of "transcendental" in Kant, of spirit (*Geist*) in Hegel, and of "transcendental subjectivity" in Husserl. Fink cautions: "Of course such thematic concepts of a philosophy are never univocal, free of problems; rather they contain the whole tension of an understanding which is aimed towards the ineradicable enigmatic character of being as such."[6] The difference between thematic and operative concepts should not be reduced to the distinction between the permanent and the transitory, the received and the developing, the arrival and the journey. The function of operative concepts surpasses that of heuristic devices, for operative concepts retain their efficacy after thematic concepts have been established. Fink writes:

> But in the formation of thematic concepts, creative thinkers *use* other concepts and patterns of thought, they *operate* with intellectual schemata which they do not fix objectively. They think *through* certain cognitive presentations toward the basic concepts which are essentially their themes. Their understanding moves in a *conceptual field*, in a *conceptual medium* that they are not at all able to see. They expend intermediate lines of thought to set up that which they are thinking about. We call that which in this way is readily *expended* and *thought through* in philosophical thinking, but not *considered* in its own right, operative concepts. They form, metaphorically speaking, the shadow of a philosophy.[7]

"Phenomenological reduction" was a concept which continued to trouble Husserl throughout his mature career. It is to be wondered, then, how so operative a concept could find philosophical rest in what Fink considers the thematic concept of "transcendental subjectivity"

5. CPIII, p. 92. The paper to which Schutz refers is Eugen Fink, "Les Concepts opératoires dans la phénoménologie de Husserl," in *Husserl* (with an avant-propos by M.-A. Bera), Cahiers de Royaumont, Philosophie, No. III, Paris: Les Éditions de Minuit, 1959, pp. 214–230. Note: For an English version of Fink's paper, see "Operative Concepts in Husserl's Phenomenology" (trans. from the German by William McKenna), in *Apriori and World: European Contributions to Husserlian Phenomenology* (edited and trans. by William McKenna, Robert M. Harlan, and Laurence E. Winters with an introduction by J. N. Mohanty), The Hague: Martinus Nijhoff, 1981, pp. 56–70.

6. Fink, "Operative Concepts in Husserl's Phenomenology" (McKenna translation), p. 59.

7. Ibid.

in Husserl. And even if "phenomenological reduction" finds no rest, what assures thematic status to "transcendental subjectivity"? Fink's essay is subtle and illuminating. My questions are not meant to challenge his findings as much as to anticipate the next step in our deliberations regarding Schutz. For after citing Fink's report, Schutz goes on to assert that ". . . the notion of typicality, which according to Husserl's later philosophy, characterizes our experiencing of the life-world in the natural attitude on both the predicative and the prepredicative level, and even the notion of ideation . . . are also widely used by him as mere operative schemata of a highly equivocal character and are in need of further clarification."[8]

If "typicality" and "ideation" are added to the list of operative concepts in Husserl, it must be the supportive genius of the operative which sustains what appears to be a philosophy so thematically diminished. More immediately, for our purposes, if "typicality" is, as Schutz indicates, an operative concept in Husserl, how, we must inquire, does it fare in Schutz's own work? Surely, "type," "typicality," and "typification" would appear to be thematic concepts in Schutz's philosophy. Perhaps they are, but we are not in a position to confirm, deny, or doubt their status. The fact is that Schutz has not given us his *philosophy*; at most, he has made penetrating but fragmentary advances beyond phenomenological psychology; he has left us with gorgeous intimations of what a phenomenological metaphysics might be. No confusion need exist here: Schutz never set out to present his philosophy; he never promised a metaphysics; he rigorously restricted himself to the task he set: a phenomenology of the natural attitude. Husserl said that "he could almost hope, were Methuselah's span of days allotted him, to be still able to become a philosopher."[9] This has another resonance: One might well imagine Kierkegaard saying, "Were Methuselah's span of days allotted to me, I could almost hope still to become a Christian." Perhaps the intimacy—the transcendental contrivance—between the operative and the thematic is that becoming is the shadow of the become, that setting forth a philosophy is setting forth in search of philosophy.

The difference between Husserl and Schutz as far as the distinction between thematic and operative concepts is concerned is that Husserl presents us primarily with a philosophy whose thematic core is tor-

8. CPIII, p. 92.
9. *Ideas* (Boyce Gibson translation), p. 29 ("Author's Preface to the English Edition").

mented by operative concepts, whereas Schutz developed a phenomenology of the natural attitude whose philosophical status
remains uncertain. If there are operative concepts in Schutz's work,
they are in search of their thematic entelechy. It may still be the case
that such a central term of Schutz's discourse as "typification" is unclear in the way in which Fink's "operative concepts" are said to be
vague. But the scene has changed. Schutz has not adopted Husserl's
method as a mountain climber selects his gear; Schutz, like every
superior phenomenologist, is influenced but not dominated by Husserl. Briefly: I do not think that it is appropriate to apply Fink's clas-
sification—suggestive as it is for understanding Husserl—to Schutz's
thought. Yet if there is any concept which qualifies as being "thematic"
in Schutz's work, I would say that it is "transcendence." This choice
ought to be dismaying, for in Schutz's writings "transcendence" does
not occupy a central role, does not take up many of his pages. Nevertheless, "transcendence" is, in my judgment, not only the most distinctively philosophical of Schutz's concepts but the one which points
most directly to his unwritten "philosophy." Although the result will
be a quotation which is rather long, I will condense some pages of
Schutz's essay "Symbol, Reality and Society," which are of the first
importance for appreciating Schutz's "philosophy." He writes (and
here I repeat, in part, a statement I have already presented):

> I find myself in my everyday life within a world not of my own making.
> I know this fact, and this knowledge itself belongs to my biographical
> situation. . . . I know furthermore, that in a similar way the social world
> transcends the reality of my everyday life. I was born into a preorgan-
> ized social world which will survive me, a world shared from the outset
> with fellow-men who are organized in groups, a world which has its
> particular open horizons in time, in space, and also in what sociologists
> call social distance. . . . I experience both of these transcendences, that
> of Nature and that of society, as being imposed upon me in a double
> sense: on the one hand, I find myself at any moment of my existence
> as being within nature and within society; both are permanently co-
> constitutive elements of my biographical situation and are, therefore,
> experienced as inescapably belonging to it. On the other hand, they
> constitute the framework within which alone I have the freedom of my
> potentialities, and this means they prescribe the scope of all possibilities
> for defining my situation. In this sense, they are not elements of my
> situation, but determinations of it. In the first sense, I may—even more,
> I have to—take them for granted. In the second sense, I have to come
> to terms with them. But in either sense, I have to understand the natural

and the social world in spite of their transcendences, in terms of an order of things and events. . . . But in the common-sense thinking of everyday life we simply know that Nature and society represent some kind of order; yet the essence of this order as such is unknowable to us. It reveals itself merely in images by analogical apprehending. But the images, once constituted, are taken for granted, and so are the transcendences to which they refer.

How is this possible? "The miracle of all miracles is that the genuine miracles become to us an everyday occurrence," says Lessing's Nathan. This is so because we find in our sociocultural environment itself socially approved systems offering answers for our quest for the unknowable transcendences.[10]

To know, in common-sense terms, that "Nature and Society represent some kind of order" but also to recognize that "the essence of this order . . . is unknowable to us" is to experience the kind of "transcendence" which is no longer a methodological consideration but a philosophical moment in human being. *Within* common sense, I am confronted or at least touched by a philosophical "given": that my world has a coherence which I can never comprehend. The acceptance of that ultimate limitation of a "world-never-to-be-comprehended" is, as Schutz maintains, an inescapable feature of common sense. Yet that inescapable "moment" of existence is a prime subject for philosophical inquiry. Nor is it the case that such inquiry is restricted to privileged transcendentalists. It is the experience of the transcendental which is the condition for our achieving human being.[11] The experience of the transcendental occurs within common sense; the thematization of the transcendental is the beginning of philosophy. So, Schutz ends his essay "Don Quixote and the Problem of Reality": " 'We have only to commend ourselves to God and let fortune take what course it will,' says Sancho, who, in spite of all temptations of the transcendental, remains deeply rooted in the heritage of common sense."[12]

Transcendence, then, in my view, would have been a thematic concept in Schutz's philosophy, if he had formulated that philosophy. As it stands, "transcendence" is not an operative concept but the ragged nucleus of thought which has gone beyond methodology but not

10. CPI, pp. 329–331.
11. "I am not among those who believe that Science is the only or the best or even merely a privileged way to master the experience of the transcendental—which . . . alone makes us into humans" (from a letter by Schutz to Kurt H. Wolff, quoted by Helmut R. Wagner, *Alfred Schutz*, p. 245).
12. CPII, p. 158.

reached metaphysics. This is not a criticism but merely an attempt to clarify the place of philosophy in Schutz's writings. In Professor Thomas Luckmann's reconstruction of Schutz's *The Structures of the Life-World*, especially in Vol. II, the theme of transcendence is taken up in a more nearly philosophical sense. In the second volume, the limits (or boundaries) of experience in the life-world are contrasted with the experience of limits (or boundaries) of the life-world in terms of various transcendences.[13] Schutz and Luckmann also go on to distinguish between different orders (or degrees) of transcendence from "kleinen" to "grossen," including the movement from daily life to sleep and dreams.[14] In my judgment, Luckmann's unfolding, enlargement, and extension of Schutz's detailed outlines for his last work are admirably responsible. Although I have made a few references to *The Structures of the Life-World*, I have not gone beyond pointing to the two volumes. Paradoxically, my own reconstruction of Schutz cannot build upon another reconstruction of Schutz.[15] I choose to be left on my own. My own task, of course, is quite different from Luckmann's— different in scope, different in its relationship to Schutz's outlined intentions, different even in its differences, for I am trying to move with and through Schutz to the location of a fugitive thematic concept, to a hidden philosophy of anonymity which I think affirms Schutz's qualified but integral bond with transcendental phenomenology. It is not that I alone can assume the burden of such a task; but I am convinced that, indebted as I am to other students of Schutz, I must proceed alone.

Transcendence, then, is the concept which haunts daily life. Yet our experience of that concept is fragmentary—fragmentary not merely in the sense of being partial or incomplete but fragmentary in a more forceful, fundamental way: every one of us is, as Simmel has shown, doubly fragmented in being but a part of the world and also a part of our own possibilities. This insight of Simmel's was taken by Schutz most seriously. Each of us is at the same time part of Man

13. Alfred Schütz and Thomas Luckman, *Strukturen der Lebenswelt*, Vol. II (Ch. VI: "Grenzen der Erfahrung und Grenzüberschreitungen: Verständigung in der Lebenswelt"), Frankfurt am Main: Suhrkamp, 1984, pp. 139ff.

14. Ibid., pp. 142ff.

15. I might have made use of Schutz's own outlines, which are included in *Strukturen der Lebenswelt*, Vol. II, but I have decided to limit myself almost entirely to what Schutz completed. His unpublished papers do not provide me with the philosophy which I am trying to probe here. My reflections on anonymity are too idiosyncratic to utilize, in good faith, the support of others.

and the partial realization of what we might be. In his lectures, Schutz often referred to Simmel's statement:

> All of us are fragments, not only of general man, but also of ourselves. We are outlines not only of the types "man," "good," "bad," and the like but also of the individuality and uniqueness of ourselves.[16]

We transcend ourselves by virtue of our fragmentation; at the same time, the recognition by the individual that he is a fragmented being may move toward self-knowledge or fade into bad faith. Am I indispensable to myself? Not if I do not want someone indispensable about me. By chance, Simmel tells the perfect story in this regard:

> . . . when it was suggested to an outstanding German official that he transfer to another branch of the government, the ruling prince is supposed to have asked his minister: "Is the man indispensable to us?" "Entirely so, Your Highness." "Then we shall let him go. I cannot use indispensable servants."[17]

The root-situation of the social world, as Schutz presents it, is that the individual is able to "gear into" society by mastering, more or less, the typifications of daily life. Even if I do not fully understand social reality, I can, as a "wide-awake" individual, utilize these constructions which will grant me an effective place in its objective order. The perplexing message of human existence, I would say, is that individuality can express itself in common-sense terms by negating or suppressing its uniqueness in favor of anonymous dispositions. Whether this "message" is heard faintly or in booming tones, a species of fragmentation enters into view: Transcendence not only is grasped in fragmentary form but fragments the individual. For Schutz, the issue central to human being in the world is that of "coming to terms" with what I have called the fragmented and fragmenting power of transcendence. Common sense is not only the terrain on which such resolution may occur; common sense is the means by which it may occur. The most profound prime suppressed, in Schutz's account of abstraction—so I think—is that of the individual. Let us capitalize the word to avoid

16. Georg Simmel, *On Individuality and Social Forms: Selected Writings* (edited with an introduction by Donald N. Levine), Chicago: University of Chicago Press, 1971, p. 10. Note: The essay from which this quotation is drawn is "How Is Society Possible?" and was translated by Kurt H. Wolff and originally published in *Georg Simmel, 1858–1918: A Collection of Essays, with Translations and a Bibliography* (edited by Kurt H. Wolff), Columbus: Ohio State University Press, 1959, pp. 337–356.
17. *The Sociology of Georg Simmel* (translated, edited, and with an introduction by Kurt H. Wolff), Glencoe: The Free Press, 1950, p. 199.

misunderstanding: the Individual. Anonymity replaces inwardness. By the same token, the displacement of inwardness—the loss of the Individual even (and perhaps especially) momentarily—may reveal anonymity in the slightest gesture, the most singular act.[18]

If I am correct in thinking that transcendence comes closest to what would be a thematic concept in Schutz's "philosophy," then I am encouraged to suggest that anonymity is the most pressing term in Schutz's phenomenology of the natural attitude—pressing because its clear and restricted use so consistently avoids the question of whether it is philosophically permissible (methodologically warranted as it might be) to avoid the consideration of the transcendental status of "anonymity." For Schutz, "I was born, I grow older, and I have to die are three expressions for a single metaphysical fact determining the experience of our existence within this world."[19] So too, I say, is it a metaphysical fact that birth, aging, and death take place necessarily in a mundane reality which can be "entered" by man and fellow-man

18. John Vinocur, "At Long Nazi Trial, the Sense of Horror is Vanishing in a Murmur of Legalisms," *The New York Times*, November 10, 1978, p. A3: "Dusseldorf, West Germany, Nov. 6—On many days the horror of the Maidanek concentration camp stops at the courtroom door.

"Inside, where 14 men and women are on trial in connection with the torture and murder of 250,000 Jews in Maidanek, at Lublin, in Nazi-occupied Poland, the old members of the S.S., the Elite Guard, read the soccer results and smooth their hair . . . the trial, which was billed before it began as West Germany's last major war-crimes prosecution, wanders into a fourth year this month. . . . On a recent Friday Chief Judge Günther Bogen came to court 15 minutes late. He joined a panel of judges under a white enamel cross and called to order the defendants and lawyers who sit in front of him on long benches that give the chamber the look of a classroom.

"The defendants put aside their newspapers—the headlines were about great soccer victories—and slumped in their seats. They are all charged with murder, but there is no outward sign of this, no manacles, no armed attendants, nothing in their dress or looks to distinguish them from anyone else. . . .

"At 9:31 A.M., 16 minutes after the session started, the judge called a recess until 10 . . . the judge came back at 10:16, went into his chambers at 10:21 to mull over a defense motion concerning whether a document would be officially or unofficially excluded from evidence and came back at 10:26 to hear another police officer.

"Again there was a question of the validity of a deposition. There was a vague reference to what the deposition was about—the recruiting of S.S. personnel at Maidanek with offers of brandy and cigarettes for a special detail on Nov. 3, 1943, called 'the harvest festival,' in which 17,000 Jews were machine-gunned to death. However, it seemed barely a detail in relation to the interest in the circumstances under which the statement was made.

"At 11:05 A.M., after hearing Siegfried Kindler, another police officer, the judge stopped the trial again, saying he would be back at 11:30. In the central hall a defense lawyer practiced a controlled run-skid on the marble floor." The last line is the most brilliant single reportorial sentence which I have ever read in *The New York Times*. It might have been written in Prague around the time of the First World War.

19. RPR, p. 179.

only through the constructs of anonymity. The constitution of the constructs (at the level of the natural attitude) is methodological business; that there *is* anonymity, inescapable anonymity, as the "objective" order in which common-sense life is lived is transcendental business. Schutz is fully within his authorial rights in limiting his research to the methodology of anonymity, but he is far too sophisticated a phenomenologist not to know that the "problems of monads" include the metaphysical station of anonymity. A central feature of the metaphysical problem of anonymity is that of the career of the *Individual* in the "objective" realm of common sense. Must the Individual retreat to an existential enclave in order to survive with honor—to retain his inwardness in the multiple realities of daily life? How is such a retreat possible? Can the Knight of Faith transcend mundane existence? For Schutz, who has referred to Kierkegaard in order to advance distinctions in the essay "On Multiple Realities," is the individual *possible* in the life of typification? What is the place of inwardness in a phenomenology of the natural attitude?

A divergence is met as soon as we try to respond to these questions. Either we must say that Schutz's notion of anonymity, even if carried to its philosophical limits, remains essentially methodological or else— and this is what I believe—the extension of Schutz's concept of anonymity leads ultimately to a desolation of common sense, to a dread which I have called "otherness." There is no need to try to "existentialize" Schutz; he is "existential" enough without my assistance or interference. It is Schutz who wrote of "the fundamental anxiety";[20] it is Schutz who forebodingly wrote ". . . that we are born into a world and a situation not of our making, that we inescapably grow older together, that within the essentially undetermined fact of our future one simple certainty stands out, namely that we have to die, uncertain when and how. . . ."[21] At the same time that we may confidently say that it is absurd to call Schutz an "existentialist," we may say with equal confidence that "existential" problems are integral to all philosophers who seek to uncover "originary" ground. I cannot in good conscience say that if Schutz had developed his conception of anonymity beyond its methodological frontiers, he would have ended up with something like the notion of "otherness" which I have suggested. My guess is that had Schutz had, say, another ten years of work given him, he

20. CPI, p. 249.
21. RPR, p. 181.

would have found—under optimum circumstances—that his own *Structures of the Life-World* would have turned into a four-volume deepening as well as extension of the outlines he originally made for that book. I cannot believe that the development or statement of Schutz's "philosophy" would have included the assertion that "anonymity leads ultimately to a desolation of common sense." That view is mine, not Schutz's. Still, I find it just as hard to believe that Schutz would not have grasped and appreciated—whatever his criticisms might be—the meaning of the claim that being born into the world is the commencement of a struggle to penetrate the abstract character of everydayness and decode its concealment. Merleau-Ponty said it well: "One day, once and for all, something was set in motion which, even during sleep, can no longer cease to see or not to see, to feel or not to feel, to suffer or be happy, to think or rest from thinking, in a word to 'have it out' with the world."[22]

We must leave unsettled the question of what Schutz's position on a philosophy of anonymity might have been. It seems much more likely that we could predict how that position would have been presented in his writing. No essential change in style is envisioned. But "style" and "manner" in philosophy are, as Schutz recognized, intimately related and infinitely problematic. It is Schutz's reference to "indirect communication" in Kierkegaard which draws us immediately to the matter of "style." A dialectical problem arises for Schutz in his examination of "multiple realities":

> Are we sure that the awakened person really can tell his dreams, he who no longer dreams? It will probably make an important difference whether he recollects his dream in vivid retention or whether he has to reproduce it. Whatever the case may be, we encounter the eminent dialectical difficulty that there exists for the dreamer no possibility of direct communication which would not transcend the sphere to which it refers. We can, therefore, approach the provinces of dreams and imageries merely by way of "indirect communication," to borrow this term from Kierkegaard, who has analyzed the phenomena it suggests in an unsurpassable way. The poet and the artist are much closer to an adequate interpretation of the worlds of dreams and phantasms than the scientist and the philosopher, because their categories of communication themselves refer to the realm of imagery. They can, if not overcome, at least make transparent the underlying dialectical conflict.[23]

22. Maurice Merleau-Ponty, *Phenomenology of Perception*, pp. 406–407.
23. CPI, p. 244.

Is the direct communication of the scientist and the philosopher sufficient to account for as well as to report truly the states of affairs which comprise the paramount reality of everyday life? Remember that both science and philosophy have spoken their stories in quite different voices. In addition to the treatise and the essay, we have poems, dialogues, question-and-answer procedures, and—one way or another—fragments. And of course, scientists and philosophers do not always stick to their last. How many philosophers or scientists today who, without looking to the title page of the book, opened to the following beginning paragraph would continue reading after the following sentence:

> When Manasses set up a carved image in the house of the Lord, and built altars in the two courts of the house, to all the host of heaven, and us'd inchantments and witchcraft, and familiar spirits, and for his great wickedness was invaded by the army of Asserhadon King of Assyria, and carried captive to Babylon; the book of the Law was lost till the eighteenth year of his grandson Josiah.[24]

Ah, but that's different! Different? Who says it's different? That "different" has the unction of the chronic patronizer. Alas, his voice is legion. Although the voice may be heard in many ways, I hear it as a whine: "Stick to your last!" means "Watch your language!" The warning may come—self-directed—from the most eminent of thinkers. W. V. Quine writes:

> Occasionally in my writing I find myself groping unduly for fanciful figures and analogies. I have learned to recognize this as a sign that I am not clear in my mind about the theory I am trying to expound. It is a signal to go walking or canoeing and ponder the ideas without benefit or malefit of pen and paper.[25]

I asked whether direct communication is enough to report the paramount reality. Without entering the alehouse of qualifications, let us say that the poet and the artist are much closer to an adequate interpretation of common sense than Schutz allows for in his statement about "indirect communication." Elsewhere in Schutz's writings (in his essays "Making Music Together" and "Mozart and the Philosophers"[26]), he expands upon the boundaries of "indirect com-

24. Sir Isaac Newton, *Observations Upon the Prophecies of Daniel, and the Apocalypse of St. John: In Two Parts*, London: J. Darby and T. Browne, 1733, p. 1.
25. W. V. Quine, *The Time of My Life: An Autobiography*, Cambridge: MIT Press (A Bradford Book), 1985, p. 477.
26. Both essays are included in CPII.

munication" and approaches, I believe, the inner station of Kierkegaard's island. Schutz:

> I submit that Mozart's main topic is . . . the metaphysical mystery of
> the existence of a human universe of pure sociality, the exploration of
> the manifold forms in which man meets his fellow-man and acquires
> knowledge of him. The encounter of man with man within the human
> world is Mozart's main concern. This explains the perfect humanity of
> his art. His world remains the human world even if the transcendental
> irrupts into it.[27]

The danger in this discussion is to say too much. Although Schutz
(like Husserl) was deeply impressed with Kierkegaard's brilliance,
Schutz was not dazzled by it. An influence is not an alliance. Despite
the fact that almost all of Schutz's work is in the realm of direct communication, that work, in my judgment, is not impersonal, for I believe
that Schutz would have agreed with Kierkegaard's contention that
"the highest triumph of all errors is to acquire an impersonal means
of communication. . . ."[28] The problem of "style" in philosophy cannot
be severed from either direct or indirect communication: "acceptable"
language in professional discourse is a contradiction in terms when
it comes to philosophy. "Acceptable to whom?" is not the first question
to be asked. Rather, we are thickly embattled in a problem by now
old in these pages: is acceptable language to be understood as the
amanuensis of proof or is style a dialectical concept? How does proof
stand to conviction? I shall, arbitrarily of course, give the final say to
Trollope's judge, Baron Maltby:

> "A man with what is called a logical turn of mind may prove anything
> or disprove anything; but he never convinces anybody. On any matter
> that is near to a man's heart, he is convinced by the tremour of his own
> thoughts as he goes on living, not by the arguments of a logician, or
> even by the eloquence of an orator. Talkers are apt to think that if
> their listener cannot answer them they are bound to give way; but non-
> talkers generally take a very different view of the subject."[29]

27. CPII, p. 199.

28. *Søren Kierkegaard's Journals and Papers* (edited and trans. by Howard V. Hong
and Edna H. Hong, assisted by Gregor Malantschuk), Vol. II, F–K, Bloomington:
Indiana University Press, 1970, p. 480 (entry No. 2152). Note: I have cut off Kierkegaard's statement. The full sentence: "The highest triumph of all errors is to acquire
an impersonal means of communication and then anonymity." But the last part is not
to my purpose; Kierkegaard had other things in mind here by "anonymity." My snipped
quotation stands on its own and does its author no violence.

29. Anthony Trollope, *Orley Farm*, New York: Dover Publications, 1981, p. 229 (Vol.
II, Ch. XXIX: "The Two Judges").

The problem of style in philosophy today is the erosion of language. I am well aware that in the last generation, philosophers have written in manifold ways, that it is only fair to name the philosophers I have in mind when I speak of the "erosion" of language. I have no intention of complying with reasonable expectations. Instead, I shall dismiss the entire subject—like a desperate cavalier—with a

NEWS CONFERENCE

"Ladies and Gentlemen, I have been asked to make the following announcement:

> Language passed away today at 3:52 P.M. Greenwich time. Further details will not be released until the immediate family has been notified. Funeral plans are pending.

"That's it. I'll take questions now."
"You mean it's dead?"
"As a doornail."
"How do you know it's dead?"
"Dead is dead."
"What did it die of?"
"Aggravation."
"Did it suffer greatly?"
"Toward the end, the pain was exquisite."
"Were there any early warning signs?"
"The first thing to go was the colon."
"What were its last words?"
"There were none: it just combusted. I have time for one more question."
"Were the authorities prepared for this?"
"Well, language *was* quite old. I guess it just stressed out."

Besides its travails and tantrums, language has its triumphs. Mundane life has its own cries and chants which lend themselves to the improvisatory genius of the streets: verbal graffiti. And if language is sinking into the primordial sea, it has some ripe words to utter as it goes down. I am less concerned with the way in which common sense expresses itself than with the manner in which its theorists have their say. Although I have no privileged place on which to stand, I insist on shaking my fist. In philosophy, an old problem returns to trouble us: the relationship between thought and life. "But how is it possible," Schutz asks, "for the solitary thinker, with his theoretical attitude of disinterestedness and his aloofness from all social relationships to find an approach to the world of everyday life in which men work among their fellow-men within the natural attitude which the theoretician is compelled to abandon? . . . How . . . can man in his full humanity and the social relationships in which he stands with Others be grasped by theoretical thought?"[30] He can't! Schutz's theoretician is compelled to build models of society, to form constructions of the world which eludes his "immediate grasp."[31] I am not pointing out a limitation in Schutz's conception of the social scientist; I am reporting Schutz's own view of the matter. Theory cannot capture life. But that statement needs to be amended: Theory cannot capture life directly. The social scientist makes use, whether he realizes it or not, of a philosophical procedure in order to overcome his inability to seize mundane reality in its immediacy. That procedure is Kierkegaard's. The theoretical social scientist, according to Schutz,

> . . . has to build up an artificial device, comparable to . . . "indirect communication," in order to bring the intersubjective life-world in view— or better, not this world itself, but merely a likeness of it, a likeness in which the human world recurs, but deprived of its liveliness, and in which man recurs, but deprived of his unbroken humanity. This artificial device—called the method of the social sciences—overcomes the . . . dialectical difficulty by substituting for the intersubjective life-world a model of this life-world.[32]

Kierkegaardian indirection is an effort to arouse in the Other what direct discourse can never touch, to bring the Other by his own insight—the clamor of his being—to recognize what he always "knew" but succeeded in avoiding: that truth can never be the possession of the crowd, that inwardness can never recognize Authority, that one is not born but must become an Individual. The self that has never "known" the meaning of subjectivity cannot be told or informed or lectured into knowledge. Nettled or spurred by Kierkegaardian in-

30. CPI, p. 254.
31. Ibid., p. 255.
32. Ibid.

direction, the individual seeking to become an Individual must, in the words of a glorious misadventure in printing, "follow in the foolsteps of Socrates."[33] Schutz's use of Kierkegaard's notion of "indirect communication" is wayward in its results. The theoretical social scientist can, at best, create a model which is "a likeness" of the life-world "in which the human world recurs." Schutz has used (and we have followed him) a number of related terms: social scientist, theoretical social scientist, scientist, scientific observer, philosopher. It is patent that there is a qualitative distance, for Schutz, between the disciplinary responsibilities of the social scientist and the philosopher. It is also evident—to me, at least—that the theorist and the philosopher, in Schutz's view, share a professional enclave. An aspect of the philosopher's task proves to be the exercise of phenomenological psychology; what remains unclarified is the further reach of the relationship between phenomenological philosophy and the social world. The second chapter of *The Phenomenology of the Social World*, "The Constitution of Meaningful Lived Experience in the Constitutor's Own Stream of Consciousness," reveals Schutz self-consciously at work in the region of transcendental phenomenology. His stricture regarding his temporary "stay" within the sphere of "phenomenological reduction" is sharply indicated.[34] This chapter is an exception to Schutz's way of proceeding in his writing; for the most part, the "psychology" of "phenomenological psychology" is examined closely, whereas the "philosophy" of "phenomenological philosophy" is left waiting. Taken together as a unity, "phenomenological philosophy" is given a searching examination with respect to Husserl's theory of intersubjectivity in one of Schutz's late and most remarkable essays, "The Problem of Transcendental Intersubjectivity in Husserl."[35] But philosophy as philosophy remains marginal.

33. Robert Watson Winston, *Horace Williams: Gadfly of Chapel Hill*, Chapel Hill: University of North Carolina Press, 1942, p. 65.

34. PSW, p. 43: "In order to be clear about the status of the following investigations from the point of view of phenomenology, it should be stated that:

"Our studies of the constituting process in internal time-consciousness will be carried out within the 'phenomenological reduction.' Therefore they presuppose the bracketing (disconnection) of the natural world and therewith the carrying into effect of a complete change of attitude (the *epoché*) toward the thesis of the 'world given-to-me-as-being there *(als daseiende gibt)*'. . . . However, our analysis will be carried out within the phenomenological reduction only so far as this is necessary for acquiring a clear understanding of the internal time-consciousness."

35. In CPIII, pp. 51–91 (including discussion).

Whose problem, then, is the "unbroken humanity" of the life-world? Must we settle for a model of what seems to be beyond the conceptual reach of the theorist? Is a philosophy of the life-world to be the life-world with its "life" drained out? It may be that the poet, as Schutz has said, is closer to the realm of imagery than the philosopher, but it may be that the contrast between literature and philosophy hides part of what it should reveal: that the "models" of the imagination and the "models" of the theorist have enclaves within which literature and philosophy illuminate each other. The individual may stand to the abstract model of society which the theorist has described and analyzed in a way which is similar to the writer's relationship to the fictive microcosm which he has created. And—to beat everything—the writer's stance may enter his fiction. In Saul Bellow's novel *Humboldt's Gift*, Charles Citrine the protagonist is bound in love and fury to his friend—sometime "blood brother"—Von Humboldt Fleisher, poet, essayist, poetry editor, reviewer, occasional university instructor (in extremis), and harassed hero of letters, whose belligerent madness has finally landed that talented *tummler* of intellectuals in New York's Bellevue—the name, for New Yorkers, of the quintessential loony bin. In desperation, Humboldt telephones Citrine:

> From Bellevue he phoned me at the Belasco Theatre. I heard his voice shaking, raging but rapid. He yelled, "Charlie, you know where I am, don't you? All right, Charlie, this isn't literature. This is life."[36]

But it *is* literature.[37] Finally, language invades itself: the cry of the life-world reverberates in the world of the novel. We are no longer in the realm of representation or portrayal but of immediacy—the prose of immediacy.[38] And, of course, we are already beyond the range of fiction but still concerned with the fictive. Problems of evidence return to jostle us. Is philosophy a story? Is it made up? Is daily life the only entertainment the homeless can afford? Perhaps I have been on too "familiar" grounds with my subject and have ended by

36. Saul Bellow, *Humboldt's Gift*, New York: Viking Press, 1975, p. 156.
37. That Citrine "is" Bellow and that Humboldt "is" Delmore Schwartz (see James Atlas, *Delmore Schwartz: The Life of an American Poet*, New York: Farrar, Straus and Giroux, 1977) does not complicate matters: matters are beyond complication. What does "is" mean in this boiler room of reality? I can only say that the words "metaphysics" and "metaphysical" are used more times in *Humboldt's Gift* than in any novel I can name.
38. A prose with diverse representatives: James Agee, Grace Paley, Larry Woiwode, and Susan Sheehan, for example.

making a carnival of anonymity. Although I am completely serious in undertaking a study of the place of anonymity in the philosophy of Alfred Schutz, I am aware of the ontological dangers of what Sartre calls the "*spirit of seriousness.*"[39] "Seriousness," in this sense, is related to Bad Faith: it is an immanent but "chosen" activity of a nihilating consciousness to quash anguish by providing values with an origin and residence in the world; freedom comes from the world, not from man.[40] For Sartre:

> The spirit of seriousness has two characteristics: it considers values as transcendent givens independent of human subjectivity, and it transfers the quality of "desirable" from the ontological structure of things to their simple material constitution. For the spirit of seriousness, for example, *bread* is *desirable* because it is *necessary* to live (a value written in an intelligible heaven) and because bread *is* nourishing. The result of the serious attitude, which as we know rules the world, is to cause the symbolic values of things to be drunk in by their empirical idiosyncrasy as ink by a blotter; it puts forward the opacity of the desired object and posits it in itself as a desirable irreducible. Thus we are already on the moral plane but concurrently on that of bad faith, for it is an ethics which is ashamed of itself and does not dare speak its name. It has obscured all its goals in order to free itself from anguish.[41]

The "serious man," as Sartre calls him,[42] is always looking over his ethical shoulder, keeping in line—a "line" taken to be incised by Nature itself—and upholding the received wisdom whenever possible, free of any antic mood. As an "ideal type," we might say, the serious man returns the embrace of the language which hugs him. What is wanted by Others—colleagues, editors, publishers—is provided; stylistic admixtures are shunned. It is writing in philosophy to which I refer. Wittgenstein might have gotten away with dark aphorisms in the *Tractatus*, but there were truth tables to compensate for them. After the Second World War, the influence of Oxford was shown stylistically by the epigones of the masters of "ordinary language" analysis. I recall hearing and reading papers which were modeled, I thought, after "This is the house that Jack built." And the influence

39. Jean-Paul Sartre, *Being and Nothingness: An Essay on Phenomenological Ontology* (trans. with an introduction by Hazel E. Barnes), New York: Philosophical Library, 1956, p. 626.
40. Ibid., pp. 39–40.
41. Ibid., p. 626.
42. Ibid., p. 39.

of the Continent has had its pernicious side: artificial insemination (taken as language) was violent and flagrant—verbs raped nouns. The linguistic energies of the post-Heideggerian period in philosophy are unremitting: we now have Derridasein. There appears, then, to be a motley of recent method and style. Perhaps. The "serious man," however, tends to take few risks; he wants a stability in his life which he thinks is already assured by the patronomy of tradition. It is the world and not man in whose vault security is assured. In the confines of Bad Faith, style suffocates. I have proceeded somewhat erratically in this book because, in part at least, I am wary of the "serious man." He is the heartworm of language. Fairly or unfairly, he puts me in mind of the Snopeses. "Mr. Faulkner," the author was once asked, "why are you so fond of the Compsons and the Snopses?" And he replied, "Well, I feel sorry for the Compsons. That was blood which was good and brave once, but has thinned and faded all the way out. Of the Snopes, I'm terrified."[43]

I will not elaborate on the positive function—at least as I intend it—of the fictive interludes and the few quotations from literature which are scattered in these pages. If nothing positive is gained by the reader, why go into it? The reader who understands me needs no explanation. But it is to the reader who might be a little puzzled or even baffled by why I would choose to introduce these "scenes"— the reader who might by faintly amused now and again by a line or two in these fictions—that I owe something more than I have given. I am not concerned with agreement but I would like to be understood. Let me present my addenda in the form of admonitions: The fictions should not be taken as illustrations of philosophical concepts; the fictions are not thrown into the text to lend it spice; the fictions should not be understood as interruptions of a discussion but as parts of a discussion; the fictions should not be thought of as "devices" to accomplish what direct argumentation somehow cannot achieve; finally, the fictions cannot be shunted to one side in reading these pages— for those in philosophy who would reduce style to ornamentation, despair is a neurological frailty and Gregor Samsa someone with a periodontal problem.

In sight of the end of this essay, we arrive at a final vantage point

43. Frederick L. Gwynn and Joseph L. Blottner (editors), *Faulkner in the University: Class Conferences at the University of Virginia, 1957–1958*, New York: Vintage Books, p. 197.

from which to view our project: to take anonymity as a transcendental clue to the meaning of the philosophy of Alfred Schutz. That philosophy is the largely silent presence in Schutz's writing; in turn, the philosophical status of anonymity remains speculative. I do not consider these results negative. Rather, "philosophy" and "anonymity" illuminate Schutz's thought as transcendental beacons. To repeat: "The ideal of everyday knowledge," Schutz writes, "is not certainty, nor even probability in a mathematical sense, but just likelihood."[44] The certitude—the apodictic—which Husserl sought seems to be shipwrecked by "likelihood." But it would not seem so either to Husserl or to Schutz, for phenomenology is an effort to recover and to elucidate the *sense* of that "likelihood." The recovery and the elucidation are not elements of "likelihood" but features of transcendental thought. Schutz writes:

> . . . psychology and even phenomenological psychology (both in its empirical and eidetic disciplines) is a "positive" science promoted in the "natural attitude" with the world before it as the basis for all its themes. For the purposes of such a psychology, therefore, the phenomenological reduction is a pure methodological device for analyzing the life of consciousness. But phenomenological reduction is also of basic importance for the foundation of *transcendental phenomenological philosophy*. . . .
>
> By performing the phenomenological reduction, the psychological subjectivity on its part loses just that which makes it something real in the world that lies before us, namely its meaning as a "soul," as a human ego in the universal, existentially posited world. . . .
>
> But transcendental subjectivity means far more for Husserl: the pure transcendental "*Ego cogito*" is no longer . . . a mind belonging to a body that exists in an objective spatiotemporal Nature being interested in the world, but exclusively the self-identical subject of all its cogitations, their identical focus. That means: All the "intentional objects" of its cogitations are objects only for the ego and by the ego; they are intentional objects for the stream of its cognitive life or, to use Husserl's technical term, they are constituted by its synthetic activities. To explore this transcendental realm, to explain its existential meaning, and to describe its constitution is the great task of phenomenological philosophy.[45]

The "likelihood" of everyday knowledge belongs to no *one*; it is the possession of anyone in daily life. The root of "anyone" rests in tran-

44. CPII, p. 73
45. CPIII, pp. 7–8.

scendental subjectivity.[46] In phenomenological terms, the "genesis" of *our* world—the world of daily life—has as its transcendental ground an originary, anonymous ego. That anonymous transcendental ego constitutes the anonymity of the life-world. The "history" of such constitution is the story of the sedimentation of meaning in the life of consciousness. For Husserl, the transcendental ego has the power of *origin*— a central word in the vocabulary of phenomenology—and is not called "anonymous." Whether or not Husserl's egology "apparently condemns us to a solipsism, albeit a transcendental solipsism,"[47] is open not so much to dispute as to interpretation. "As a matter of fact," Husserl writes, "we shall see that, in a certain manner, a transcendental solipsism is only a subordinate stage philosophically; though, as such, it must first be delimited for purposes of method, in order that the problems of transcendental intersubjectivity, as problems belonging to a higher level, may be correctly stated and attacked."[48] Is transcendental phenomenology ultimately to be understood in Santayana's terms: "The solipsist . . . becomes an incredulous spectator of his own romance, thinks his own adventures fictions, and accepts a solipsism of the present moment"?[49] Schutz's

46. It is no longer the ontological foundation of *"das Man"* which interests us but the transcendental ground of anonymity. A still different interpretation is offered by Sartre: "To go from the subway station at 'Trocadéro' to 'Sèvres-Babylon,' 'They' change at 'La Motte-Picquet.' This change is forseen, indicated on maps, etc.; if I change routes at La Motte-Picquet, I am the 'They' who change. To be sure, I differentiate myself by each use of the subway as much by the individual upsurge of my being as by the distant ends which I pursue. But these final ends are only on the horizon of my act. My immediate ends are the ends of the 'They,' and I apprehend myself as interchangeable with any one of my neighbors. In this sense we lose our real individuality, for the project which we are is precisely the project which others are. In this subway corridor there is only one and the same project, inscribed a long time ago in matter, where a living and undifferentiated transcendence comes to be absorbed. To the extent that I realize myself in solitude as any transcendence, I have only the experience of undifferentiated-being (e.g., if alone in my room I open a bottle of preserves with the proper bottle opener). But if this undifferentiated transcendence projects its projects, whatever they are, in connection with other transcendences experienced as real presences similarly absorbed in projects identical with my projects, then I realized my project as one among thousands of identical projects projected by one and the same undifferentiated transcendence. Then I have the experience of a common transcendence directed toward a unique end of which I am only an ephemeral particularization; I insert myself into the great human stream which from the time that the subway first existed has flowed incessantly into the corridors of the station 'La Motte-Picquet-Grenelle' " (*Being and Nothingness*, p. 424). Note: In the French, Sartre uses *"on"* (with quotation marks) for what is translated in the first sentence we have quoted as "They" (*L'Être et le néant: essai d'ontologie phénoménologique*, Paris: Gallimard, 1943, p. 496).

47. *Cartesian Meditations*, p. 30 (section 13).

48. Ibid., pp. 30–31 (section 13).

49. *Scepticism and Animal Faith*, p. 15.

position on the matter of solipsism in phenomenology seems to me to be self-divided. In discussing intersubjectivity in the context of Husserl's *Formal and Transcendental Logic*, Schutz writes:

> On the one hand, the transcendental subjectivity of consciousness, by whose operations the world as accepted by me is constituted with all its contents—things, my own self, Others—is first of all, I, that is, my own self. On the other hand, the world is the objective world common to all of us and as such it has the categorial form of a world truly existing once and forever not only for me but for everyone. World-experience is not my private, but shared experience. But the world as the "world for all of us" is primarily "my" world.
>
> This primal fact, Husserl says, must be faced by the philosopher, and he must not shut his eyes to it for one moment. "For philosophical children this may be the dark corner haunted by the ghosts of solipsism, psychologism, or relativism. The true philosopher, rather than avoiding it, will throw light on it." (Par. 95)[50]

What Schutz cannot resolve in Husserl's terms is the essential question of "how another psychophysical ego comes to be constituted in my ego. . . ."[51] The sticking point is the constitution of the Other. It would appear that here the position of Schutz is virtually indistinguishable from that of his friend Eric Voegelin, who writes:

> The relation to the transcendence of the others, it seems to me, cannot be dealt with by the methods which Husserl, in his *Méditations Cartésiennes* has pushed to an extreme. Husserl's great question—How is the Thou constituted in the I as an *alter ego*?—takes care of itself in that the Thou is not constituted in the I at all. The problem of the Thou seems to me to resemble that of all other classes of transcendence. The fact that consciousness has an experience at all of the other, as a consciousness of the other, is not *a problem* but a given of experience from which one may start out but behind which one may not retreat.[52]

Although Schutz has, in effect, allied himself with this position in his own writings, I am not convinced that the reasons which lie at the formative grounds of Professor Voegelin's assertion are identical with Schutz's reasons for not accepting Husserl on transcendental intersubjectivity. For one thing, Voegelin has, in other works, elaborated a theory of transcendence which goes beyond Schutz's statements and which, in my opinion, cannot be ignored in reading the words of

50. CPIII, pp. 53–54. Note: The quotation from Husserl will be found in Dorion Cairns's translation of *Formal and Transcendental Logic* on p. 237.
51. CPIII, p. 54.
52. Eric Voegelin, *Anamnesis* (translated and edited by Gerhart Niemeyer), Notre Dame: University of Notre Dame Press, 1978, p. 23.

Voegelin which we have cited. Furthermore, Voegelin had, I think, not only an extraordinary but an extravagant reading of Husserl. So, for example, Voegelin maintains with respect to Husserl's *The Crisis of European Sciences and Transcendental Phenomenology* that "Husserl's apocalyptic construct had the purpose of abolishing history and thereby to justify the exclusion of the historical dimension from the constitution of man's consciousness."[53] Schutz's criticisms of Husserl are strong but they remain immanent criticisms. Schutz is a phenomenologist; Voegelin is not a phenomenologist. To the end of Schutz's life, Husserl was "the old magician."[54]

A fundamental criticism—even a repudiation—of Husserl's theory of transcendental intersubjectivity does not carry with it the charge: Phenomenology won't work; look elsewhere! Husserl himself was highly dissatisfied with the results of his Fifth Meditation. Even if it were the case that the ontological givenness of the Thou precedes any attempt to constitute the Other by way of the transcendental ego or through transcendental subjectivity, the constitution of "my" world persists as the irrevocable task of phenomenological philosophy. The history of the becoming of the transcendental ego, approached in terms of anonymity rather than "a solipsism of the present moment," may be understood as sedimented in its unfolding with "possibilities"—possibilities of meaning which intend Others. Gigantic (for our purposes) among the possibilities is the constitution of an everyday world, a world of daily life which is not only shared by fellow-men but taken-for-granted as shareable by Others. The identity of the transcendental ego, then, is an "everyone" each of us is or may become. We are no longer in the vicinity of *das Man*, no longer lost in the "They," but in the midst of a "We" whose meaning each of us is called upon to decipher. If anonymity is indeed trustworthy as a "transcendental clue" to sociality, its value is to be found in the way in which it *leads back* to transcendental grounds. The place of "essence" in Husserl's thought is secure; the "trouble" with essences, for those interested in phenomenology, is that they appear to be "collectable" and like precious gems are wondrously discrete.

53. Ibid., p. 10. Note: Schutz and Voegelin carried on an intensive correspondence about Husserl's *Crisis*. See the German edition of *Anamnesis* for details (Munich: R. Piper, 1966). See Helmut R. Wagner, *Alfred Schutz* and Helmut R. Wagner, "Agreement in Discord: Alfred Schutz and Eric Voegelin," in *The Philosophy of Order: Essays on History, Consciousness, and Politics* (edited by Peter J. Opitz and Gregor Sebba), Stuttgart: Klett-Cotta, 1981, pp. 74–90.

54. After having flawed my pages with so many "as Schutz once said to me" 's, I am driven—too late—to resort to the same formula in footnotes.

However worthy they may be, "essences" are remote from ordinary life; talk about them in the everyday world is sometimes viewed with suspicion. "Essence"—the word itself—sounds foreign! But the person in daily life is no foreigner; he's me! We are back in the neighborhood! "It's me!" I call up, ungrammatical but steady, as I make my way up the stairs to my apartment. "I'm home!" I call out, as I push the apartment door open with my foot, my hands occupied with the key and a bag of groceries. It is that "me," that "I" which a phenomenology of the natural attitude seeks to understand. Transcendental philosophy seems irrelevant to the "homecomer"; but at the moment the "me" or the "I" sings out, says "Here I am in-the-world," the force of the transcendental is at its strongest. The "me" and the "I" are *in* the world as beings whose possibility it is to trace back their history, their "becoming"; and that possibility, I suggest, is the tension, the fist of phenomenology. If I have an "essence" it is that I am a being who can trace back the history of my becoming in the world I share with everybody else. Emmanuel Levinas has stated the case exceptionally well:

> ... there is the possibility *sich zu besinnen*, of grasping oneself, or of getting back to oneself, of posing with distinctness the question: "Where are we?", of taking one's bearings. Perhaps this is phenomenology in the largest sense of the term, beyond the vision of essences, the *Wesen-schau* which made such a fuss. A radical reflection, obstinate about itself, a *cogito* which constitutes the world and the object, but whose objectivity in reality occludes and encumbers the look that fixes it. From this objectivity one must always trace thoughts and intentions back to the whole horizon at which they aim, which objectivity obscures and makes one forget. Phenomenology is the recall of these forgotten thoughts, of these intentions; full consciousness, return to the misunderstood implied intentions of thought in the world.[55]

Finding our way back, returning, recovering what is hidden in our human careers—these movements of the self become translated in phenomenology into an egology whose source we have tried to indicate, if not clarify. Paradoxically, egology is the individual's means of recovering what is distinctively social, just as anonymity is the way of locating what is decisively individual. For Schutz, *we* typify the world, *we* generate the meaning-construction of social reality, *we* grow older together and die. Yet the paradox of the individual within the

55. Emmanuel Levinas, *Ethics and Infinity: Conservations with Philippe Nemo* (trans. with an introduction by Richard A. Cohen), Pittsburgh: Duquesne University Press, 1985, p. 30.

social remains as a "metaphysical constant" of mundane existence, and Schutz states the paradox most simply: "Graves and reminiscences can neither be transferred nor conquered."[56]

When, in 1953, my formal study with Alfred Schutz was completed, I had an evening's conversation with him at his home. He asked me what I planned to go on with in philosophical work. I told him that there were two themes which especially interested me: anonymity and death. I was then almost thirty; Schutz advised me to leave aside work on the philosophy of death until I was in my fifties. But he added: "Perhaps you will find in the end that anonymity and death are the same." I must leave the reader with those words, with that impression. It is not only too late but inappropriate to turn to conclusions, for in all transcendental work there remains at last a figure of indefinite reference, imperfectly formed, not an occult presence but—and despite everything this should be taken as a sanction—a term of stubborn indeterminacy: recognition without identification, the music of awareness.

56. CPII, p. 97.

A RATHER WAYWARD PROLOGUE
TO A SOMEWHAT ERRATIC
BIBLIOGRAPHY

A comprehensive list of the books and monographs and articles which have aided and accompanied the writing of this book cannot be provided here: such a list would trace not only the career of my book but the life of its author—far too much for the occasion. Besides, it is not my intention to provide a comprehensive (let alone exhaustive) bibliography for anything. Enough clues will be given the reader about more extensive compilations. Two kinds of listings might be expected from me; neither will be offered. First, a most thorough account of the literature by and about Alfred Schutz; second, a bibliography of "anonymity." This is not the place for a long listing of titles by and about Schutz. There are already several bibliographies available: Maurice Natanson (editor), *Phenomenology and Social Reality* (cited later); Richard Grathoff, "Alfred Schutz," in *Klassiker des soziologischen Denkens*, Vol. II (cited later); Burke C. Thomason, *Making Sense of Reification* (cited later); (Alfred Schutz) *Alfred Schutz on Phenomenology and Social Relations* (edited by Helmut R. Wagner and cited later); Thomas S. Eberle, *Sinnkonstitution in Alltag und Wissenschaft* (cited later). What is relevant to my concerns in this book has been listed. It should be noted that whereas Schutz's major works have been included, only a sampling of the literature about him has been offered. I have included titles which I admire, titles which I think are sound, and titles of which I am wary. Some of Schutz's critics have written on strong grounds, some on conventional grounds, and some on coffee grounds. The reader will have to judge for himself, but I do not think that it will be too difficult to distinguish between those who are expert on Schutz, those who are reasonable and sober critics, those who are not altogether sure of themselves or their author, and those who are, when it comes to phenomenology, conceptually disadvantaged. The reader may find it odd that the author, who has been miserly when it comes to citing the secondary literature on Schutz, should prove to be so expansive when he lists his own writings. I wish

to record what I have done regarding Schutz and concerning anonymity. This is my summing up. The reader is then free to determine
whether I have been, over a period of many years, consistent and
enterprising. As to a bibliography on "anonymity": I do not understand what such a project would mean.

What is included in the Bibliography falls largely under these headings: A listing of all titles which are referred to in the text or footnotes;
Titles which are not referred to but which are related to the thought
of Schutz and the theme of anonymity; Titles which are not referred
to but which have directly or indirectly proved to be suggestive to me
in writing this book; A scattering of reference works which I have
consulted.

I have listed all authors in alphabetical order because I believe in
(or aspire to) a metaphysics of chance. Let the occasional reader wonder why I include in the same Bibliography—whatever may be referred to in the text and notes—both Husserl's *The Crisis of European
Sciences and Transcendental Phenomenology* and the obituary for Albert
Tanner. It would seem that the mouse has labored and brought forth
a mite. Husserl will not languish; I'm for Mr. Tanner! So, too, the
most sympathetic reader may wonder how McPhee's *The Survival of
the Bark Canoe* is even remotely related to my subject. A simple answer
will have to do: McPhee is an extraordinary descriptivist; he creates
a "tensed" sentence; he has written something valuable about "seeing."
There are some other "strange" cases in my Bibliography, but I will
not comment on them. Rather, I will point to several hidden themes
which are important to my book and in that way indicate a reason for
including titles which might seem to be unconnected with Schutz or
anonymity. The order of consideration will be random.

1. Aesthetic configurations: taken up chiefly (but not exclusively)
with photography. Here perceptual immediacy is presented—but immanently "analyzed"—through the work of such artists as Walker Evans (see the entry for Agee and Evans), Doris Ulmann (see the entry
for Featherstone), and André Kertész.

2. Psychiatric pathology: but not in the ordinary sense of "mental
illness." I think of pathology in mundane life as it is to be encountered
by all of us—not by psychiatrists alone—*in mundane life*, in the lunatics
who loaf on the street corners of daily life or roar through its thor-
oughfares. And so, in addition to the psychiatrists from whom I
quote, I list such authors as Blondel, Minkowski, and Straus.

3. Experiential physiognomy: "physiognomy" in the eighteenth-
and nineteenth-century sense (the oblique insight of Lavater, for example, if the reader can manage—and that is difficult—to set aside
surface absurdities and distractions: A way of viewing Others-in-the-
world in the quietude as well as fury of their expressive being). I list
in this category Gratiolet, Bell, and Picard.

4. Human anatomy: inwoven in physiognomy and pathology. In
place of titles, I offer this bit of autobiography: In many ways, the
most important academic course of study which I ever pursued was
one postgraduate year, devoted largely to Gross Anatomy—a year of
lectures and the laboratory discipline of the complete dissection of a
human cadaver. This led to some practical benefits: James Joyce was
freshly accessible to me and I was able to find my way about that great
London emporium Foramen Magnum. While pursuing my anatom-
ical research, I was permitted also to observe a number of autopsies,
including one carried out by the distinguished pathologist, Dr. Har-
rison S. Martland, once Chief Medical Examiner for Essex County
(Newark), New Jersey, and late Professor of Forensic Medicine, New
York University College of Medicine. Although I witnessed that au-
topsy about thirty-eight years ago, I have a lively impression of Dr.
Martland—a very large apron tied around a large person, who re-
sembled, I thought, a fiercely jovial English butcher, casually tossing
organs on a hanging scale, marveling still again, it seemed, at the
immense ignorance of his fascinated audience, and—my final but
quick image—cutting slices (steaks, they seemed to be) of the liver and
leaning toward me with a grin, as if to say, "That'll be 3 and 6, Mr.
Hornaday." My study of anatomy gave me a special view of the general
and the particular, the familiar and the anonymous. None of these
categories emerged cleanly; they came with, in the antiquarian book-
seller's terminology, "marginal worming." The worming has persisted.

At last: Some titles and references have been suggested or provided,
copies of papers have been made accessible, and certain information
as well as courtesy has been given by these people: Judith Malamut,
Principal Reference Librarian, Reference Department, Yale University Library, swiftly searched out a page reference when it was important to me to have that information at once; Professor Kazuhiko
Okuda of the International University of Japan located, at my request,
an article which I otherwise would have been unable to obtain; Professor Kah Kyung Cho provided a reprint of one of his articles; Mrs.

Ilse Schutz told me about Eberle's book and lent me her copy; Mrs. Janet Rabinowitch, the Editor of this press, showed understanding patience; Louise H. Martin skillfully prepared the manuscript for the printer. Nicholas Natanson perspicaciously assisted me. Finally, Professor Ernst M. Manasse suggested the right book at the right time: *Greek Foundations of Traditional Logic* by Ernst Kapp (cited later), which also is noted here just in time to draw our attention to a quotation which Dr. Kapp gives from Aristotle's *Topics* (a work to which, on occasion, Schutz alluded—always appreciatively), which may be taken as a "post-motto" for my book and a "pre-motto" for its Bibliography:

> . . . in the case of all discoveries the results of previous labors that have been handed down from others have been advanced bit by bit by those who have taken them on, whereas the original discoveries generally make an advance that is small at first though much more useful than the development which later springs out of them. (183b)

BIBLIOGRAPHY

Adloff, Jean Gabriel. *Sartre: Index du corpus philosophique*, I, *L'Être et le néant, Critique de la raison dialectique*. Paris: Klincksieck, 1981.

Agee, James, and Walker Evans. *Let us Now Praise Famous Men: Three Tenant Families*. Boston: Houghton Mifflin, 1941.

The Annals of Phenomenological Sociology. I, 1976. Note: This issue includes several articles relating to Schutz.

Aristotle. *Topics* (translated by W. A. Pickard-Cambridge), in *The Complete Works of Aristotle: The Revised Oxford Translation* (edited with a preface by Jonathan Barnes), Vol. I. Princeton: Princeton University Press, 1984.

Armstrong, Edward G. "On Phenomenology and Sociological Theory." *British Journal of Sociology* XXVII (1976), pp. 251–254.

Atlas, James. *Delmore Schwartz: The Life of an American Poet*. New York: Farrar, Straus and Giroux, 1977.

Auden, W. H. "Musée des Beaux Arts," in *The Collected Poetry of W. H. Auden*. New York: Random House, 1945.

Bachelard, Suzanne. *A Study of Husserl's "Formal and Transcendental Logic"* (translated by Lester E. Embree). Evanston: Northwestern University Press, 1968.

Barber, Michael David. *The Place of Sociology of Knowledge in Alfred Schutz's Phenomenology* (unpublished Ph.D. dissertation, Department of Philosophy, Yale University, 1985).

Barthelme, Donald. *Guilty Pleasures*. New York: Farrar, Straus and Giroux, 1974.

Bastion, Felix. *The Enclaves*. Garden City: Doubleday, 1965.

Bauman, Zygmunt. *Hermeneutics and Social Science*. New York: Columbia University Press, 1978.

Baumann, Bedřich. "George H. Mead and Luigi Pirandello: Some Parallels between the Theoretical and Artistic Presentation of the Social Role Concept." *Social Research* XXXIV (1967), pp. 563–607.

Bell, Sir Charles. *The Anatomy and Philosophy of Expression: As Connected with the Fine Arts*, 7th ed., revised. London: George Bell, 1877.

Bell, Sir Charles. *The Hand: Its Mechanism and Vital Endowments, as Evincing Design*, 6th ed., revised (preceded by an Account of the Author's Discoveries in the Nervous System by Alexander Shaw). London: John Murray, 1860.

Bellow, Saul. *Humboldt's Gift*. New York: Viking Press, 1975.

Berger, Peter L. *Invitation to Sociology: A Humanistic Perspective*. Garden City: Doubleday (Anchor Books), 1963.

Berger, Peter L. "The Problem of Multiple Realities: Alfred Schutz and Robert Musil," in *Phenomenology and Social Reality: Essays in Memory of Alfred Schutz* (edited by Maurice Natanson). The Hague: Martinus Nijhoff, 1970, pp. 213–233. Note: This essay has been reprinted in *Phenomenology and Sociology: Selected Readings* (edited by Thomas Luckmann). New York: Penguin Books, 1978, pp. 343–367.

Berger, Peter L. "Robert Musil and the Salvage of the Self." *Partisan Review* LI (1984), pp. 638–650.

Berger, Peter L., and Hansfried Kellner. *Sociology Reinterpreted: An Essay on Method and Vocation.* Garden City: Anchor Books/Doubleday, 1981.

Berger, Peter L., and Thomas Luckmann. *The Social Construction of Reality: A Treatise in the Sociology of Knowledge.* Garden City: Doubleday, 1966.

Bergson, Henri. *Essai sur les données de la conscience.* Paris: Félix Alcan, 1889. Note: *Time and Free Will: An Essay on the Immediate Data of Consciousness* (translated by F. L. Pogson). London: George Allen and Unwin, 1921.

Bergson, Henri. *Matière et mémoire: essai sur la relation du corps à l'esprit.* Paris: Félix Alcan, 1997. Note: *Matter and Memory* (translated by Nancy Margaret Paul and W. Scott Palmer). London: George Allen and Unwin, 1950.

Bernstein, Richard J. *The Restructuring of Social and Political Theory.* Oxford: Basil Blackwell, 1976. Note: See Part III in particular.

Best, R. E. "New Directions in Sociological Theory? A Critical Note on Phenomenological Sociology and its Antecedents." *British Journal of Sociology* XXVI (1975), pp. 133–143. Note: Cf. Armstrong, "On Phenomenology and Sociological Theory."

Bierstedt, Robert. "The Common Sense World of Alfred Schutz." *Social Research* XXX (1963), pp. 116–121.

Binswanger, Ludwig. *Über Ideenflucht.* Zürich: Art. Institut Orell Füssli, 1933. Note: Reprinted by Garland Publishing, New York, 1980.

Blanshard, Brand. *On Philosophical Style.* Bloomington: Indiana University Press, 1967.

Blondel, Charles. *La Conscience morbide: essai de psychopathologie général,* 2nd. ed. Paris: Félix Alcan, 1928.

Blythe, Ronald. *The View in Winter: Reflections on Old Age.* New York: Harcourt Brace Jovanovich, 1979.

Bok, Sissela. *Secrets: On the Ethics of Concealment and Revelation.* New York: Pantheon Books, 1982.

Bonafoux, Pascal. *Portraits of the Artist: The Self-Portrait in Painting.* New York: Skira/Rizzoli, 1985.

Boulding, Kenneth E. *The Image: Knowledge in Life and Society.* Ann Arbor: University of Michigan Press, 1956.

Brand, Gerd. *Die Lebenswelt: Eine Philosophie des konkreten Apriori.* Berlin: Walter de Gruyter, 1971.

Brauner, Hilmar. *Die Phänomenologie Edmund Husserls und ihre Bedeutung für soziologische Theorien.* Meisenheim am Glan: Anton Hain, 1978.

Brown, Richard H. *A Poetic for Sociology: Toward a Logic of Discovery for the Human Sciences.* Cambridge: Cambridge University Press, 1977.

Buber, Martin. *Pointing the Way: Collected Essays* (edited and translated by Maurice S. Friedman). New York: Schocken Books, 1957.

Bubner, Rüdiger. *Modern German Philosophy* (translated by Eric Matthews). Cambridge: Cambridge University Press, 1981.

Cairns, Dorion. *Guide for Translating Husserl.* The Hague: Martinus Nijhoff, 1973.

Cairns, Dorion. "Phenomenology," in *A History of Philosophical Systems* (edited by Vergelius Ferm). New York: Philosophical Library, 1950, pp. 353–364.

Cairns, Dorion. *The Philosophy of Edmund Husserl* (unpublished Ph.D. dissertation, Department of Philosophy, Harvard University, 1933).

Campbell, Tom. *Seven Theories of Human Society*. Oxford: Clarendon Press, 1981.

Canetti, Elias. *Crowds and Power* (translated by Carol Stewart). New York: Viking Press, 1962.

Cassirer, Ernst. " 'Spirit' and 'Life' in Contemporary Philosophy" (translated by Robert Walter Bretall and Paul Arthur Schilpp), in *The Philosophy of Ernst Cassirer* (edited by Paul Arthur Schilpp). Evanston: The Library of Living Philosophers, 1949, pp. 857–880.

Castro, Américo, *The Spaniards: An Introduction to Their History* (translated by Willard F. King and Selma Margaretten). Berkeley: University of California Press, 1971.

Cervantes Saavedra, Miguel de. *The Adventures of Don Quixote* (translated with an introduction by J. M. Cohen). Harmondsworth: Penguin Books, 1952.

Cervantes Saavedra, Miguel de. *Don Quijote de la Mancha* (texto y notas de Martín de Riquer), Vol. II, Part Two. Barcelona: Editorial Juventud, 1979.

Cervantes Saavedra, Miguel de. *The Portable Cervantes* (translated, edited, and with an introduction and notes by Samuel Putnam). New York: Viking Press, 1958.

Chastaing, Maxime. *L'Existence d'autrui*. Paris: Presses Universitaires de France, 1951.

Cho, Kah Kyung. "Anonymes Subjekt und phänomenologische Beschreibung." *Phänomenologische Forschungen* XII (1982), 21–56.

Cho, Kah Kyung. "Mediation and Immediacy for Husserl," in *Phenomenology and Natural Existence: Essays in Honor of Marvin Farber* (edited with an introduction by Dale Riepe). Albany: State University of New York Press, 1973, pp. 56–82.

Cicourel, Aaron V. *Method and Measurement in Sociology*. New York: The Free Press, 1964.

Clive, Geoffrey. *The Romantic Enlightenment*. New York: Meridian Books, 1960.

Cohen, Hermann. *Logik der reinen Erkenntnis*, 3rd ed. Berlin: Bruno Cassirer, 1922.

Cox, Ronald R. *Schutz's Theory of Relevance: A Phenomenological Critique*. The Hague: Martinus Nijhoff, 1978.

Curme, George O. *A Grammar of the English Language*, Vol. II: *Syntax*. Essex: Verbatim, 1977.

Dahrendorf, Rolf. *Essays in the Theory of Society*. Stanford: Stanford University Press, 1968. Note: See Ch. II: "Homo Sociologicus."

Dallmayr, Fred R. *Beyond Dogma and Despair: Toward a Critical Phenomenology of Politics*. Notre Dame: University of Notre Dame Press, 1981.

Dallmayr, Fred R. "Phenomenology and Social Science: An Overview and Appraisal," in *Explorations in Phenomenology: Papers of the Society for Phenomenology and Existential Philosophy* (edited by David Carr and Edward S. Casey). The Hague: Martinus Nijhoff, 1973, pp. 133–66.

Danto, Arthur C. "Philosophy As/And/Of Literature." *Proceedings and Addresses of the American Philosophical Association* LVIII (1984), pp. 5–20.

Dauenhauer, Bernard P. *Silence: The Phenomenon and Its Ontological Significance.* Bloomington: Indiana University Press, 1980.

de Boer, Theodore. *The Development of Husserl's Thought* (translated by Theodore Plantinga). The Hague: Martinus Nijhoff, 1978.

de Laguna, Grace A. *On Existence and the the Human World.* New Haven: Yale University Press, 1966.

Demske, James M. *Being, Man, and Death: A Key to Heidegger.* Lexington: The University Press of Kentucky, 1970.

Derrida, Jacques. *Edmund Husserl's "Origin of Geometry": An Introduction* (translated with a preface by John P. Leavey and edited by John B. Allison). New York: Nicolas Hays, 1978. Note: Husserl's "The Origin of Geometry" (translated by David Carr) is included as an Appendix.

Dickens, Charles. *Nicholas Nickleby* (edited with an introduction and notes by Michael Slater and original illustrations by Hablot K. Browne ["Phiz"]). New York: Penguin Books, 1976.

Dolci, Danilo. "What Does it Mean, to Die?" (translated by Adrienne Foulke). *Hudson Review* XVII (1964), pp. 167–186.

Douglas, Jack D. (Ed.) *Understanding Everyday Life: Toward the Reconstruction of Sociological Knowledge.* Chicago: Aldine, 1970.

Doyle, Sir Arthur Conan. "Silver Blaze," in *The Complete Sherlock Holmes* (with a preface by Christopher Morley). Garden City: Doubleday, 1930.

Dreitzel, Hans Peter. *Die gesellschaftlichen Leiden und das Leiden an der Gesellschaft: Vorstudien zu einer Pathologie des Rollenverhaltens.* Stuttgart: Ferdinand Enke, 1968.

Dupré, Ernest. *Pathologie de l'imagination et de l'émotivité* (with a preface by Paul Bourget and a short biographical statement by Dr. Achalme). Paris: Payot, 1925.

Eberle, Thomas S. *Sinnkonstitution in Alltag und Wissenschaft: Der Beitrag der Phänomenologie and die Methodologie der Sozialwissenschaften.* Bern und Stuttgart: Verlag Paul Haupt, 1984. Note: Here is the sole exception to what I have said about the Bibliography. I did not learn about this book until after my manuscript was completed. However, I have decided to include it for the reader's benefit.

Edie, James M. "Expression and Metaphor." *Philosophy and Phenomenological Research* XXIII (1963), pp. 538–561.

Edie, James M. (Ed. with an introduction) *Phenomenology in America: Studies in the Philosophy of Experience.* Chicago: Quadrangle Books, 1967.

Eisler, Rudolf. *Wörterbuch der philosophischen Begriffe und Ausdrücke.* Berlin: Ernst Siegfried Mittler und Sohn, 1899. Note: There are later editions; this is the one which I consulted.

Elliston, Frederick and Peter McCormick (Eds., with an introduction by the editors and a foreword by Paul Ricoeur). *Husserl: Expositions and Appraisals.* Notre Dame: University of Notre Dame Press, 1977.

Embree, Lester. "Everyday Social Relevancy in Gurwitsch and Schutz." *The Annals of Phenomenological Sociology* II (1977), pp. 45–61.

Embree, Lester (Ed. with a biographical sketch). *Life-World and Consciousness: Essays for Aron Gurwitsch.* Evanston: Northwestern University Press, 1972.

Enright, D. J. (Ed.) *Fair of Speech: The Uses of Euphemism.* New York: Oxford University Press, 1985.

Esquirol, E. *Mental Maladies: A Treatise on Insanity* (translated by E. K. Hunt). Philadelphia: Lea and Blanchard, 1845.

Ey, Henri. *Consciousness: A Phenomenological Study of Being Conscious and Becoming Conscious* (translated by John H. Flodstrom). Bloomington: Indiana University Press, 1978.

Ey, Henri, P. Bernard, and Ch. Brisset. *Manuel de psychiatrie*. Paris: Masson, 1960.

Farber, Marvin (Ed.). *Philosophical Essays in Memory of Edmund Husserl*. Cambridge: Harvard University Press, 1940. Note: Reprinted in Westport by the Greenwood Press, 1968.

Featherstone, David. *Doris Ulmann, American Portraits*. Albuquerque: University of New Mexico Press, 1985.

Feick, Hildegard (Compiler). *Index zu Heideggers "Sein und Zeit,"* 3rd ed. Tübingen: Max Niemeyer, 1980.

Ferrater-Mora, José. *Diccionario de Filosofi*. Buenos Aires: Editorial Sudamericana, 1958. Note: There is a much later, more expanded version; I have cited the edition which I used.

Filmer, Paul, Michael Phillipson, David Silverman, and David Walsh. *New Directions in Sociological Theory*. London: Collier-Macmillan, 1972.

Fingarette, Herbert. "Alcoholism and Self-Deception," in *Self-Deception and Self-Understanding: New Essays in Philosophy and Psychology* (edited with an introduction by Mike W. Martin). Lawrence: University Press of Kansas, 1985, pp. 52–67. Note: To be read in conjunction with Fingarette's *Self-Deception. Self-Deception and Self-Understanding* has a useful bibliography.

Fingarette, Herbert. *Self-Deception*. London: Routledge and Kegan Paul, 1969.

Fink, Eugen. "Operative Concepts in Husserl's Phenomenology" (translated from the German version by William McKenna), in *Apriori and World: European Contributions to Husserlian Phenomenology* (edited and translated by William McKenna, Robert M. Harlan, and Lawrence E. Winters with an introduction by J. N. Mohanty). The Hague: Martinus Nijhoff, 1981, pp. 56–70.

Foucault, Michel. *This Is Not a Pipe: With Illustrations and Letters* by René Magritte (translated and edited by James Harkness). Berkeley: University of California Press (Quantum Books), 1983.

Friedländer, Saul. *Reflections of Nazism: An Essay on Kitsch and Death* (translated by Thomas Weyr). New York: Harper and Row, 1984.

Friedrichs, Robert W. *A Sociology of Sociology*. New York: The Free Press, 1970.

Gabel, Joseph. *False Consciousness: An Essay on Reification* (translated by Margaret A. Thompson with the assistance of Kenneth A. Thompson, with an introduction by Kenneth A. Thompson). Oxford: Basil Blackwell, 1975.

García-Gómez, Jorge. "Of Bearings in the Lifeworld," in *Essays in Memory of Aron Gurwitsch* (edited by Lester Embree). Washington, D.C.: Center for Advanced Research in Phenomenology and University Press of America, 1984, pp. 169–193.

Garfinkel, Harold. *The Perception of the Other: A Study in Social Order* (unpublished Ph.D. dissertation, Department of Sociology, Harvard University, 1952).

Gay, William C. "Probability in the Social Sciences: A Critique of Weber and Schutz." *Human Studies* I (1978), pp. 16–37.

Geertz, Clifford. *The Interpretation of Cultures: Selected Essays*. New York: Basic Books, 1973.

Geertz, Clifford. *Local Knowledge: Further Essays in Interpretive Anthropology*. New York: Basic Books, 1983. Note: See Ch. 4: "Common Sense as a Cultural System."

Giddens, Anthony. *Central Problems in Social Theory: Action, Structure and Contradiction in Social Analysis*. Berkeley: University of California Press, 1979.

Giddens, Anthony. *New Rules of Sociological Method: A Positive Critique of Interpretive Sociologies*. New York: Basic Books, 1976.

Giddens, Anthony. *Profiles and Critiques in Social Theory* (Ch. 2 contributed by Fred Dallmayr). Berkeley: University of California Press, 1982. Note: See Ch. 6: "Schutz and Parsons: Problems of Meaning and Subjectivity."

Gonzalez-Crussi, F. *Notes of an Anatomist*. New York: Harcourt Brace Javanovich, 1985.

Gorman, Robert A. *The Dual Vision: Alfred Schutz and the Myth of Phenomenological Social Science*. London: Routledge and Kegan Paul, 1977.

Grassi, Ernesto. *Rhetoric as Philosophy: The Humanist Tradition*. University Park: Pennsylvania State University Press, 1980.

Grathoff, Richard. "Alfred Schutz," in *Klassiker des soziologischen Denkens*, Vol. II: *von Weber bis Mannheim* (edited by Dirk Käsler). Munich: C. H. Beck, 1978, pp. 388–416. Note: See Bibliography, pp. 497–507.

Grathoff, Richard. *The Structure of Social Inconsistencies*. The Hague: Martinus Nijhoff, 1970.

Grathoff, Richard and Bernhard Waldenfels (Eds. with a foreword by Bernhard Waldenfels). *Sozialität und Intersubjektivität: Phenomenologische Perspektiven der Sozialwissenschaften im Umkreis von Aron Gurwitsch und Alfred Schutz*. Munich: Wilhelm Fink, 1983.

Gratiolet, Pierre. *Physionomie: et des mouvements d'expression* (suivi d'une notice sur sa vie et ses trauvaux, et de la nomenclature de ses ouvrages by Louis Grandeau). Paris: J. Hetzel, n.d. (c. 1865–70).

Green, F. L. *Odd Man Out*. Boston: Rowan Tree Press, 1982.

Gurwitsch, Aron. "The Common-Sense World as Social Reality—A Discourse on Alfred Schutz." *Social Research* XXIX (1962), pp. 50–72. Note: Reprinted as the introduction to Schutz's *Collected Papers*, Vol. III.

Gurwitsch, Aron. *The Field of Consciousness*. Pittsburgh: Duquesne University Press, 1964.

Gurwitsch, Aron. *Human Encounters in the Social World* (edited by Alexandre Métraux and translated by Fred Kersten). Pittsburgh: Duquesne University Press, 1979.

Gurwitsch, Aron. *Marginal Consciousness* (edited by Lester Embree). Athens: Ohio University Press, 1985.

Gurwitsch, Aron. *Phenomenology and the Theory of Science* (edited by Lester Embree). Evanston: Northwestern University Press, 1974.

Gurwitsch, Aron. *Studies in Phenomenology and Psychology*. Evanston: Northwestern University Press, 1966.

Gustafsson, Lars. *The Death of a Beekeeper* (translated by Janet K. Swaffar and Guntram H. Weber with an afterword by Janet K. Swaffar). New York: New Directions, 1981.

Gwynn, Frederick, and Joseph L. Blottner (Eds.). *Faulkner in the University: Class Conferences at the University of Virginia 1957–1958*. New York: Vintage Books, 1965.

Habermas, Jürgen. *Zur Logik der Sozialwissenschaften*. Tübingen: Mohr, 1967.

Habermas, Jürgen. *The Theory of Communicative Action*, Vol. I: *Reason and the Rationalization of Society* (translated with an introduction by Thomas McCarthy). Boston: Beacon Press, 1984. .

Hamilton, Peter. *Knowledge and Social Structure: An Introduction to the Classical Argument in the Sociology of Knowledge*. London: Routledge and Kegan Paul, 1974.

Hannay, Alastair. *Kierkegaard*. London: Routledge and Kegan Paul, 1982.

Heap, James L., and Philip A. Roth. "On Phenomenological Sociology," in *Contemporary Sociological Theory*. (Edited by Alan Wells). Santa Monica: Goodyear, 1978, pp. 279–293.

Heidegger, Martin. *Being and Time* (translated by John Macquarrie and Edward Robinson). New York: Harper, 1962.

Heilbroner, Robert (Ed. with an introduction). *Economic Means and Social Ends: Essays in Political Economics*. Englewood Cliffs: Prentice-Hall, 1969.

Hickman, Hannah. *Robert Musil and the Culture of Vienna*. La Salle: Open Court, 1984. Note: See Ch. 1: "Development of the Analytical Eye: Early Notebooks and Influences."

Hindess, Barry, "The 'Phenomenological' Sociology of Alfred Schutz." *Economy and Society* I (1972), pp. 1–27.

Homans, George C. *The Nature of Social Science*. New York: Harcourt, Brace and World (Harbinger Book), 1967.

Honigsheim, Paul. *On Max Weber* (translated by Joan Rytina with a foreword by J. Allan Beegle and William H. Form). New York: The Free Press, 1968.

Husserl, Edmund. *Cartesian Meditations: An Introduction to Phenomenology* (translated by Dorion Cairns). The Hague: Martinus Nijhoff, 1960.

Husserl, Edmund. *The Crisis of European Sciences and Transcendental Phenomenology: An Introduction to Phenomenological Philosophy* (translated with an introduction by David Carr). Evanston: Northwestern University Press, 1970.

Husserl, Edmund. *Experience and Judgment: Investigations in a Genealogy of Logic* (revised and edited by Ludwig Landgrebe and translated by James S. Churchill and Karl Ameriks with an introduction by James S. Churchill and an afterword by Lothar Eley). Evanston: Northwestern University Press, 1973.

Husserl, Edmund. *Formal and Transcendental Logic* (translated by Dorion Cairns). The Hague: Martinus Nijhoff, 1969.

Husserl, Edmund. *Formale und transzendentale Logik* [*Jahrbuch für Philosophie und phänomenologische Forschung*, zehnte Band]. Halle: Max Niemeyer, 1929.

Husserl, Edmund. *Ideas: General Introduction to Pure Phenomenology* (translated by W. R. Boyce Gibson). New York: Macmillan, 1931.

Husserl, Edmund. *Ideas Pertaining to a Pure Phenomenology and to a Phenomenological Philosophy*, First Book: *General Introduction to a Pure Phenomenology* (translated by F. Kersten). The Hague: Martinus Nijhoff, 1982.

Husserl, Edmund. *Ideen zu einer reinen Phänomenologie und phänomenologischen Philosophie* [*Jahrbuch für Philosophie und phänomenologische Forschung*, erster Band, Teil 1 (zweiter unveränderter Abdruck)]. Halle: Max Niemeyer, 1922.

Husserl, Edmund. *Logical Investigations*, 2 vols. (translated with an introduction by J. N. Findlay). London: Routledge and Kegan Paul, 1970.

Husserl (with an "Avant Propos" by M.-A. Bera). Cahiers de Royaumont, Philosophie No. III. Paris: Les Éditions de Minuit, 1959.

James, William. *The Principles of Psychology*, 2 vols. New York: Henry Holt, 1893.

Jaspers, Karl. *General Psychopathology* (translated by J. Hoenig and Marian W. Hamilton). Chicago: University of Chicago Press, 1963.

Jaspers, Karl. *Three Essays: Leonardo, Descartes, Max Weber* (translated by Ralph Manheim). New York: Harcourt, Brace and World, 1964.

Jehenson, Roger. "A Phenomenological Approach to the Study of the Formal Organization," in *Phenomenological Sociology: Issues and Applications* (edited with an introduction by George Psathas). New York: John Wiley, 1973, pp. 219–247.

Jessner, Lucie. "On Becoming a Mother: Some Observations from Women in First Pregnancy," in *Conditio Humana: Erwin W. Straus on his 75th Birthday* (edited by Walter von Baeyer and Richard M. Griffith). Berlin: Springer-Verlag, 1966, pp. 102–114.

Jolivet, Régis. *Le Problème de la mort: chez M. Heidegger et J.-P. Sartre*. Abbaye Saint Wandrille: Éditions de Fontenelle, 1950.

Joyce, James. *Ulysses* (with a foreword by Morris L. Ernst and the Decision of the United States District Court Rendered by Judge John M. Woolsey). New York: The Modern Library, 1942.

Jung, Hwa Yol. *The Crisis of Political Understanding: A Phenomenological Perspective in the Conduct of Political Inquiry*. Pittsburgh: Duquesne University Press, 1979.

Kapp, Ernst. *Greek Foundations of Traditional Logic*. New York: Columbia University Press, 1942. Note: Reprinted in New York by AMS Press, 1967.

Kersten, Frederick I. "The Constancy Hypothesis in the Social Sciences," in *Life-World and Consciousness: Essays for Aron Gurwitsch* (edited with a biographical sketch by Lester Embree). Evanston: Northwestern University Press, 1972, pp. 521–563.

Kersten, Frederick I. "The Life-World Revisited." *Research in Phenomenology* I (1971), pp. 33–62.

Kersten, Frederick I., and Richard M. Zaner (Eds.). *Phenomenology: Continuation and Criticism: Essays in Memory of Dorion Cairns*. The Hague: Martinus Nijhoff, 1973.

Kertész, André. *On Reading*. New York: Penguin Books, 1982.

Kierkegaard, Søren. *Either/Or: A Fragment of Life*, Vol. 1 (translated by David F. Swenson and Lillian Marvin Swenson). Princeton: Princeton University Press, 1946. Note: See "The Rotation Method: An Essay in the Theory of Social Prudence," pp. 231–247.

Kierkegaard, Søren. *Philosophical Fragments: Or a Fragment of Philosophy* (translated with an introduction by David F. Swenson). Princeton: Princeton University Press, 1944.

Kierkegaard, Søren. *Philosophical Fragments/Johannes Climacus* (edited and translated with introduction and notes by Howard V. Hong and Edna H. Hong). Princeton: Princeton University Press, 1985.

(Kierkegaard, Søren). *Soren Kierkegaard's Journals and Papers* (edited and translated by Howard V. Hong and Edna H. Hong, assisted by Gregor Malantschuk), Vol. II F–K. Bloomington: Indiana University Press, 1970.

Klein, Jacob. "Phenomenology and the History of Science," in *Philosophical Essays in Memory of Edmund Husserl* (edited by Marvin Farber). Cambridge: Harvard University Press, 1940, pp. 143–163.

Kockelmans, Joseph J. "Deskriptive und interpretierende Phänomenologie in Schütz' Konzeption der Sozialwissenschaft" (translated by Peter Zernitz), in *Alfred Schütz und die Idee des Alltags in den Sozialwissenschaften* (edited with a foreword by Walter M. Sprondel and Richard Grathoff). Stuttgart: Ferdinand Enke, 1979, pp. 26–42.

Kockelmans, Joseph J. (Ed.). *Phenomenology: The Philosophy of Edmund Husserl and Its Interpretation*. Garden City: Doubleday (Anchor Books), 1967.

Koerner, Joseph Leo. "The Mortification of the Image; Death as a Hermeneutic in Hans Baldung Grien." *Representations*, No. 10 (Spring 1985), pp. 52–101.

Kuhn, Helmut. "The Phenomenological Concept of 'Horizon'," in *Philosophical Essays in Memory of Edmund Husserl* (edited by Marvin Farber). Cambridge: Harvard University Press, 1940, pp. 106–123.

Landgrebe, Ludwig. "Phenomenology and Metaphysics." *Philosophy and Phenomenological Research* X (1949), pp. 197–205.

Landgrebe, Ludwig. *The Phenomenology of Edmund Husserl: Six Essays* (edited with an introduction by Donn Welton). Ithaca: Cornell University Press, 1981.

Landsberg, Paul-Louis. *The Experience of Death* and *The Moral Problem of Suicide* (translated by Cynthia Rowland with a foreword by Fr. Martin Jarrett-Kerr). New York: Philosophical Library, 1953. Note: "The Experience of Death" is reprinted in *Essays in Phenomenology* (edited by Maurice Natanson). The Hague: Martinus Nijhoff, 1966.

Lang, Berel. *Philosophy and the Art of Writing: Studies in Philosophical and Literary Style*. Lewisburg: Bucknell University Press, 1983.

Lang, Berel (Ed.). *Philosophical Style: An Anthology about the Writing and Reading of Philosophy*. Chicago: Nelson-Hall, 1980.

Lavater, Johann Caspar. *Essays on Physiognomy* (translated by Henry Hunter), 5 vols. London: John Murray, 1788. Note: Engravings by Thomas Holloway.

Lefebvre, Henri. *Everyday Life in the Modern World* (translated by Sacha Rabinovitch). London: Allen Lane, The Penguin Press, 1971.

Levinas, Emmanuel. *Ethics and Infinity: Conversations with Philippe Nemo* (translated with an introduction by Richard A. Cohen). Pittsburgh: Duquesne University Press, 1985.

Levinas, Emmanuel. *Existence and Existents* (translated by Alphonso Lingis). The Hague: Martinus Nijhoff, 1978.

Löwith, Karl. *Das Individuum in der Rolle des Mitmenschen: ein Beitrag zur anthropologischen Grundlegung der ethischen Probleme*. Munich: Drei Masken Verlag, 1928. Note: Reprinted in Darmstadt: Wissenschaftliche Buchgesellschaft, 1962.

Luckmann, Benita. "Small Life Worlds of Modern Man." *Social Research* XXXVII (1970), pp. 580–596. Note: Reprinted in *Phenomenology and Sociology: Selected Readings* (edited by Thomas Luckmann). New York: Penguin Books, 1978, pp. 275–290.

Luckmann, Thomas. "The Constitution of Language in the World of Everyday Life," in *Life-World and Consciousness: Essays for Aron Gurwitsch* (edited by Lester Embree). Evanston: Northwestern University Press, 1972, pp. 469–488.

Luckmann, Thomas. *Life-World and Social Realities*. London: Heinemann Educational Books, 1983.

Luckmann, Thomas (Ed.). *Phenomenology and Sociology: Selected Readings*. New York: Penguin Books, 1978.

Lyons, J. B. *James Joyce and Medicine*. New York: Humanities Press, 1974.

Machlup, Fritz. "Homo Oeconomicus and His Class Mates," in *Phenomenology and Social Reality: Essays in Memory of Alfred Schutz* (edited by Maurice Natanson). The Hague: Martinus Nijhoff, 1970, pp. 122–139.

MacIntyre, Alastair, and Dorothy Emmet (Eds.). *Sociological Theory and Philosophical Analysis*. New York: Macmillan, 1970.

Mackendrick, Russ. "Numismatics." *The New York Times*, July 23, 1978, p. D33.

Majno, Guido. *The Healing Hand: Man and Wound in the Ancient World*. Cambridge: Harvard University Press, 1975.

Manasse, Ernst M. "The Jewish Graveyard" (translated by Judy Goldstein). *The Southern Review* XXII (1986), pp. 296–307.

Marcuse, Herbert. "On Science and Phenomenology," in *Boston Studies in the Philosophy of Science*, Vol. II: *In Honor of Philipp Frank* (edited by Robert S. Cohen and Marx W. Wartofsky). New York: Humanities Press, 1965, pp. 279–290. Note: See Aron Gurwitsch, "Comment on the Paper by H. Marcuse," Ibid., pp. 291–306 and also see Ludwig Landgrebe, *The Phenomenology of Edmund Husserl: Six Essays* (edited with an introduction by Donn Welton), Ithaca: Cornell University Press, 1981 (Ch. 6: "The Problem of a Transcendental Science of the A Priori of the Life-World").

Marx, Werner. "The Life-World and the Particular Sub-Worlds," in *Phenomenology and Social Reality: Essays in Memory of Alfred Schutz* (edited by Maurice Natanson). The Hague: Martinus Nijhoff, 1970, pp. 62–72.

Mayer, Carl. "Max Weber's Interpretation of Karl Marx" (translated by Lore Wagner). *Social Research* XLII (1975), pp. 701–719. Note: Cf. Wagner, "Marx and Weber as Seen by Carl Mayer."

McKinney, John C., and Edward A. Tiryakian (Eds.). *Theoretical Sociology: Perspectives and Developments*. New York: Appleton-Century-Crofts, 1970.

McPhee, John *The Survival of the Bark Canoe*. New York: Farrar, Straus and Giroux, 1975.

Merleau-Ponty, Maurice. "Cézanne's Doubt" (translated by Juliet Bigney). *Partisan Review* XIII (1946), pp. 464–478. And in Merleau-Ponty's *Sense and Non-Sense* (translated with a preface by Hubert L. Dreyfus and Patricia Allen Dreyfus). Evanston: Northwestern University Press, 1964, pp. 9–25.

Merleau-Ponty, Maurice. *Phenomenology of Perception* (translated by Colin Smith). London: Routledge and Kegan Paul, 1962.

Merleau-Ponty, Maurice. *The Prose of the World* (edited with a preface by Claude Lefort and translated with an introduction by John O'Neill). Evanston: Northwestern University Press, 1973.

Merleau-Ponty, Maurice. *Signs* (translated with an introduction by Richard C. McCleary). Evanston: Northwestern University Press, 1964.

Merleau-Ponty, Maurice. *Themes from the Lectures at the Collège de France 1952–1960* (translated with a preface by John O'Neill). Evanston: Northwestern University Press, 1970.

Miller, Arthur. *Death of a Salesman: Certain Private Conversations in Two Acts and a Requiem.* New York: Penguin Books, 1976. Note: Originally published in New York by Viking Press in 1949.

Minkowski, Eugène. *Lived Time: Phenomenological and Psychopathological Studies* (translated with an introduction by Nancy Metzel). Evanston: Northwestern University Press, 1970.

Minkowski, Eugène. *Traité de psychopathologie.* Paris: Presses Universitaires de France, 1966.

Mohanty, J. N. *Phenomenology and Ontology,* The Hague: Martinus Nijhoff, 1970. See Ch. XVI: "On G. E. Moore's Defence of Common Sense."

Moore, G. E. "A Reply to My Critics," in *The Philosophy of G. E. Moore* (edited by Paul Aurthur Schilpp) [The Library of Living Philosophers]. Evanston: Northwestern University, 1942.

Musil, Robert. *The Man Without Qualities* (translated with a foreword by Eithne Wilkins and Ernst Kaiser), Vol. I. London: Secker and Warburg, 1979.

Natanson, Maurice. "Alfred Schutz," in *International Encyclopedia of the Social Sciences* (edited by David L. Sills), Vol. XIV. New York: Macmillan and The Free Press, 1968, pp. 72–74.

Natanson, Maurice. "Alfred Schutz on Social Reality and Social Science." *Social Research* XXXV (1968), pp. 217–244. Note: included in Natanson's PRR.

Natanson, Maurice. "Alfred Schutz Symposium: The Pregivenness of Sociality," in *Interdisciplinary Phenomenology* (edited by Don Ihde and Richard M. Zaner). The Hague: Martinus Nijhoff, 1977, pp. 109–123.

Natanson, Maurice. "Anonymity and Recognition: Toward an Ontology of Social Roles," in *Conditio Humana: Erwin W. Straus on his 75th Birthday* (edited by Walter von Baeyer and Richard M. Griffith). Berlin and New York: Springer-Verlag, 1966, pp. 255–271. Note: Included in Natanson's PRR.

Natanson, Maurice. *Edmund Husserl: Philosopher of Infinite Tasks.* Evanston: Northwestern University Press, 1973. Note: See Ch. 6: "Phenomenology Applied."

Natanson, Maurice. "Erwin Straus and Alfred Schutz." *Philosophy and Phenomenological Research,* XLII (1982), pp. 335–342.

Natanson, Maurice. *The Journeying Self: A Study in Philosophy and Social Role.* Reading: Addison-Wesley, 1970.

Natanson, Maurice. *Literature, Philosophy, and the Social Sciences: Essays in Existentialism and Phenomenology.* The Hague: Martinus Nijhoff, 1962.

Natanson, Maurice. "Man as an Actor," in *Phenomenology of Will and Action: The Second Lexington Conference on Pure and Applied Phenomenology* (edited by Erwin W. Straus and Richard M. Griffith). Pittsburgh: Duquesne University Press, 1967, pp. 201–220. Note: See James M. Edie, "Comments on Dr. Natanson's Paper," Ibid., pp. 221–228 and further discussion by Natanson and Edie, Ibid., pp. 228–232.

Natanson, Maurice. "Phenomenology and Typification: A Study in the Philosophy of Alfred Schutz." *Social Research* XXXVII (1970), pp. 1–22. Note: Included in Natanson's PRR.

Natanson, Maurice. "Phenomenology, Anonymity, and Alienation." *New Literary History* X (1979), pp. 533–546.

Natanson, Maurice. "The Phenomenology of Alfred Schutz." *Inquiry* IX (1966), pp. 147–155. Note: Included in Natanson's PRR.

Natanson, Maurice. *Phenomenology, Role, and Reason: Essays on the Coherence and Deformation of Social Reality*, Springfield: Charles C. Thomas, 1974. Note: Abbreviated in this Bibliography as PRR.

Natanson, Maurice. "Phenomenology, Typification, and the World as Taken for Granted," in *Philomathēs: Studies and Essays in the Humanities in Memory of Philip Merlan* (edited by Robert B. Palmer and Robert Hamerton-Kelly). The Hague: Martinus Nijhoff, 1971, pp. 383–397. Note: Included in Natanson's PRR.

Natanson, Maurice. "Philosophy and Social Science: A Phenomenological Approach," in *Foundation of Political Science: Research, Methods, and Scope* (edited by Donald M. Freeman). New York: The Free Press, 1977, pp. 517–552.

Natanson, Maurice. "The Problem of Anonymity in Gurwitsch and Schutz." *Research in Phenomenology* V (1975), pp. 51–56.

Natanson, Maurice. "The Problem of Anonymity in the Thought of Alfred Schutz," in *Phenomenology and the Social Sciences: A Dialogue* (edited by Joseph Bien). The Hague: Martinus Nijhoff, 1978, pp. 60–73. Note: German version: "Das Problem der Anonymität im Denken von Alfred Schutz," in *Alfred Schutz und die Idee des Alltags in den Sozialwissenschaften* (edited by Walter M. Sprondel and Richard Grathoff). Stuttgart: Ferdinand Enke, 1979, pp. 78–88 (translated by Astrid and Bruno Hildenbrand).

Natanson, Maurice. "The World Already There: An Approach to Phenomenology." *Phenomenology and the Human Sciences* (Supplement to *Philosophical Topics*) XII (1981), pp. 101–116.

Natanson, Maurice (Ed.). *Phenomenology and Social Reality: Essays in Memory of Alfred Schutz.* The Hague: Martinus Nijhoff, 1970.

Natanson, Maurice (Ed. with introduction). *Phenomenology and the Social Sciences*, 2 vols. Evanston: Northwestern University Press, 1973.

Natanson, Maurice (Ed. with introduction). *Philosophy of the Social Sciences: A Reader.* New York: Random House, 1963.

Natorp, Paul. *Fjedor Dostojewskis Bedeutung für die gegenwärtige Kultur-Krisis: mit einem Anhang zur geistigen Krisis der Gegenwart.* Jena: Eugen Diederichs, 1923.

Newton, Sir Isaac. *Observations upon the Prophecies of Daniel, and the Apocalypse of St. John: In Two Parts.* London: J. Darby and T. Browne, 1733.

Oakeshott, Michael. *On Human Conduct.* Oxford: The Clarendon Press, 1975.

Obituary (for Albert Tanner): "Veteran of 1898 War is Dead." *The New York Times*, July 25, 1985, p. B5.

O'Connor, Flannery. *Everything That Rises Must Converge* (with an introduction by Robert Fitzgerald). New York: Farrar, Straus and Giroux, 1978.

Ogawa, Hiroshi. "Anonymity and Genesis of Society: An Analysis of Alfred Schutz's Concept of Anonymity." *Japanese Sociological Review* XXXI (1980), pp. 17–30 (in Japanese) with a summary in English on p. 114. Note: I do not read Japanese and have relied on an informal translation of this article made for my purposes by arrangement with Nobuo Kazashi.

O'Malley, John B. *Sociology of Meaning*. London: Human Context Books, 1972.

O'Neill, John. *Making Sense Together: An Introduction to Wild Sociology*. New York: Harper and Row, 1974.

O'Neill, John. "On Simmel's 'Sociological Apriorities'," in *Phenomenological Sociology: Issues and Applications* (edited with an introduction by George Psathas). New York: John Wiley, 1973, pp. 91–106.

Ortega y Gasset, José. *Man and People* (translated by Willard R. Trask). New York: Norton, 1957.

Ortega y Gasset, José. *The Revolt of the Masses* (translated, annotated, and with an introduction by Anthony Kerrigan, edited by Kenneth Moore, with a foreword by Saul Bellow). Notre Dame: University of Notre Dame Press, 1985.

Outhwaite, William. *Concept Formation in Social Science*. London: Routledge and Kegan Paul, 1983.

Outhwaite, William. *Understanding Social Life: The Method Called Verstehen*. London: Allen and Unwin, 1975.

Paley, Grace. *Later the Same Day*. New York: Farrar, Straus and Giroux, 1985.

Parsons, Arthur S. "Constitutive Phenomenology: Schutz's Theory of the We-Relation." *Journal of Phenomenological Psychology* IV (1973), pp. 331–361.

(Peirce, Charles.) *The Philosophy of Peirce: Selected Writings* (edited by Justus Buchler). New York: Harcourt, Brace, 1940.

Percy, Walker. "The Man on the Train: Three Existential Modes." *Partisan Review* XXIII (1956), pp. 478–494. Note: Reprinted in Percy's *The Message in the Bottle: How Queer Man Is: How Queer Language Is, and what One Has to Do with the Other*. New York: Farrar, Straus and Giroux, 1975, pp. 83–100.

Pettit, Philip. "The Life-World and Role-Theory," in *Phenomenology and Philosophical Understanding* (edited with an introduction by Edo Pivčević). Cambridge: Cambridge University Press, 1975, pp. 251–270.

Philipps, Lothar. *Zur Ontologie der sozialen Rolle*. Frankfurt: Vittorio Klostermann, 1963.

Piana, Giovanni. "History and Existence in Husserl's Manuscripts" (translated by Anthony Roda). *Telos*, No. 13 (1972), pp. 86–124.

Picard, Max. *The Human Face* (translated by Guy Endore). New York: Farrar and Rinehart, 1930.

Picard, Max. *The World of Silence* (translated by Stanley Godman). Chicago: Henry Regnery, 1952.

Psathas, George (Ed. with an introduction). *Phenomenological Sociology: Issues and Applications*. New York: John Wiley, 1973.

Pym, Barbara. *Crampton Hodnet* (with a note by Hazel Holt). New York: E. P. Dutton, 1985.

Quine, W. V. *The Time of My Life: An Autobiography*. Cambridge: MIT Press (A Bradford Book), 1985.

Rice, Philip Blair. "Existentialism and the Self," in *The Kenyon Critics: Studies in Modern Literature from the Kenyon Review* (edited by John Crowe Ransom). Cleveland: World Publishing Co., 1951, pp. 200–224.

Ricoeur, Paul. "Hegel et Husserl sur l'intersubjectivité," in *Phénoménologies Hégélienne et Husserlienne: Les classes sociales selon Marx* (travaux des Sessions d'Études sous la direction de G. Planty-Bonjour). Paris: Éditions du Centre National de la Recherche Scientifique, 1981, pp. 5–17.

Ricoeur, Paul. *Time and Narrative*, Vol. I (translated by Kathleen McLaughlin and David Pellauer). Chicago: University of Chicago Press, 1984.

Roche, Maurice. *Phenomenology, Language and the Social Sciences*. London: Routledge and Kegan Paul, 1973.

Rogers, Mary. *Sociology, Ethnomethodology, and Experience: A Phenomenological Critique*. Cambridge: Cambridge University Press, 1983.

Romains, Jules. *The Death of a Nobody* (translated by Desmond MacCarthy and Sidney Waterlow, with a new introduction by the author, translated by Haakon Chevalier and an afterword by Maurice Natanson). New York: New American Library (Signet Classic), 1961.

Rosenzweig, Franz. *The Star of Redemption* (translated by William W. Hallo). Notre Dame: Notre Dame Press, 1985.

Runciman, W. G. *A Critique of Max Weber's Philosophy of Social Science*. Cambridge: Cambridge University Press, 1972.

Sacks, Oliver. "The Autist Artist." *The New York Review of Books* XXXII (April 25, 1985), pp. 17–21.

Sallach, David. "Class Consciousness and the Everyday World in the Work of Marx and Schutz." *The Insurgent Sociologist* III (1973), pp. 27–37.

Salomon, Albert. "German Sociology," in *Twentieth Century Sociology* (edited with a preface by Georges Gurvitch and Wilbert E. Moore), Philosophical Library, 1945, pp. 586–614.

Santayana, George. *Scepticism and Animal Faith: Introduction to a System of Philosophy*. New York: Dover Publications, 1955.

Sarraute, Nathalie. *Portrait of a Man Unknown* (translated by Maria Jolas with a preface by Jean-Paul Sartre). New York: George Braziller, 1958.

Sartre, Jean-Paul. *Being and Nothingness: An Essay on Phenomenological Ontology* (translated with an introduction by Hazel E. Barnes). New York: Philosophical Library, 1956.

Sartre, Jean-Paul. "Consciousness of Self and Knowledge of Self" (translated by Mary Ellen and N. Lawrence), in *Readings in Existential Phenomenology* (edited by Nathaniel Lawrence and Daniel O'Connor). Englewood Cliffs: Prentice-Hall, 1967, pp. 113–142 (including discussion following the paper).

Sartre, Jean-Paul. *L'Être et le néant: essai d'ontologie phénoménologique*. Paris: Gallimard, 1943.

Sartre, Jean-Paul. *"Faces,* Preceded by *Official Portraits"* (translated by Anne P. Jones), in *Essays in Phenomenology* (edited with an introduction by Maurice Natanson). The Hague: Martinus Nijhoff, 1966, pp. 157–163.

Sartre, Jean-Paul. "Intentionality: A Fundamental Idea of Husserl's Phenomenology" (translated by Joseph P. Fell). *Journal of the British Society for Phenomenology* I (1970), pp. 4–5.

Sartre, Jean-Paul. *The Transcendence of the Ego: An Existentialist Theory of Consciousness* (translated and annotated with an introduction by Forrest

Williams and Robert Kirkpatrick). New York: Farrar, Straus and Giroux (Noonday Press), 1957.

Scheler, Max. *Problems of a Sociology of Knowledge* (translated by Manfred S. Frings and edited with an introduction by Kenneth W. Stikkers). London: Routledge and Kegan Paul, 1980.

Schelting, Alexander von. *Max Webers Wissenschaftslehre: Das logische Problem der historischen Kulturerkenntnis, Die Grenzen der Soziologie des Wissens.* Tübingen: J. C. B. Mohr (Paul Siebeck), 1934.

Schmalenbach, Herman. *On Society and Experience: Selected Papers* (edited, translated, and with an introduction by Günther Lüschen and Gregory P. Stone). Chicago: University of Chicago Press, 1977.

Scholte, Bob. "Dwelling on the Everyday World: Phenomenological Analyses and Social Reality." *American Anthropologist* LXXVI (1976), pp. 585–589.

Schrag, Calvin O. *Existence and Freedom: Towards an Ontology of Human Finitude* (with a foreword by John Wild). Evanston: Northwestern University Press, 1961.

(Schutz, Alfred.) *Alfred Schutz on Phenomenology and Social Relations: Selected Writings* (edited with an introduction and a glossary by Helmut R. Wagner). Chicago: University of Chicago Press, 1970.

Schutz, Alfred. "Choice and the Social Sciences" (edited by Lester Embree), in *Life-World and Consciousness: Essays for Aron Gurwitsch* (edited by Lester Embree). Evanston: Northwestern University Press, 1972, pp. 565–590.

Schutz, Alfred. *Collected Papers.* Vol. I: *The Problem of Social Reality* (edited with an introduction by Maurice Natanson and a preface by H. L. Van Breda). The Hague: Martinus Nijhoff, 1962. Vol. II: *Studies in Social Theory* (edited with an introduction by Arvid Brodersen). The Hague: Martinus Nijhoff, 1964. Vol. III: *Studies in Phenomenological Philosophy* (edited by I. Schutz with an introduction by Aron Gurwitsch). The Hague: Martinus Nijhoff, 1966.

Schutz, Alfred. "Fragments on the Phenomenology of Music" (edited by F. Kersten). *Music and Man* II (1976), pp. 5–71.

Schutz, Alfred. "Husserl and His Influence on Me" (edited by Lester Embree), in *Interdisciplinary Phenomenology* (edited by Don Ihde and Richard M. Zaner). The Hague: Martinus Nijhoff, 1977, pp. 124–129. Note: Includes a letter in German from Edmund Husserl to Alfred Schutz, written in 1932, in response to Schutz's *Der sinnhafte Aufbau der sozialen Welt.*

Schutz, Alfred. *Life Forms and Meaning Structure* (translated, introduced, and annotated by Helmut R. Wagner). London: Routledge and Kegan Paul, 1982.

Schutz, Alfred. *The Phenomenology of the Social World* (translated by George Walsh and Frederick Lehnert with an introduction by George Walsh). Evanston: Northwestern University Press, 1967.

Schutz, Alfred. *Reflections on the Problem of Relevance* (edited, annotated, with an introduction by Richard M. Zaner). New Haven: Yale University Press, 1970.

Schutz, Alfred. *Der sinnhafte Aufbau der sozialen Welt: Eine Einleitung in die verstehende Soziologie* (with a brief foreword to the 2nd ed. by Ilse

Schutz). Frankfurt am Main: Suhrkamp Verlag, 1974. Note: Originally
   published in Vienna by Julius Springer in 1932.
Schutz, Alfred. *Theorie der Lebensformen (Frühe Manuskripte aus der Bergson-
   Periode)*, edited and introduced by Ilja Srubar. Frankfurt am Main:
   Suhrkamp Verlag, 1981.
(Schutz, Alfred, and Talcott Parsons.) *The Theory of Social Action: The Corre-
   spondence of Alfred Schutz and Talcott Parsons* (edited with an introduction
   by Richard Grathoff and a foreword by Maurice Natanson). Bloom-
   ington: Indiana University Press, 1978.
Schutz, Alfred, and Thomas Luckmann. *Structures of the Life-World* (translated
   by Richard M. Zaner and H. Tristram Engelhardt with a preface by
   Thomas Luckmann and translators' introduction by Richard M. Zaner
   and H. Tristram Englehardt). Evanston: Northwestern University
   Press, 1973.
Schutz, Alfred, and Thomas Luckmann. *Strukturen der Lebenswelt*, Vol. I (1979)
   and Vol. II (1984). Frankfurt am Main: Suhrkamp Verlag.
Sheehan, Susan. *Is There No Place on Earth for Me?* (with a foreword by Robert
   Coles). New York: Random House (Vintage Books), 1983.
Simmel, Georg. *On Individuality and Social Forms: Selected Writings* (edited with
   an introduction by Donald N. Levine). Chicago: University of Chicago
   Press, 1971. Note: On "How is Society Possible?" compare O'Neill: "On
   Simmel's Apriorities."
Simmel, Georg. *The Philosophy of Money* (translated by Tom Bottomore and
   David Frisby with an introduction to the translation). London: Rout-
   ledge and Kegan Paul, 1978.
(Simmel, Georg.) *The Sociology of Georg Simmel* (translated, edited, and with
   an introduction by Kurt H. Wolff). Glencoe: The Free Press, 1950.
Simmel, Georg. *Soziologie: Untersuchungen über die Formen der Vergesellschaftung*.
   Leipzig: Duncker und Humbolt, 1908.
Smart, Barry. *Sociology, Phenomenology and Marxian Analysis: A Critical Discussion
   of the Theory and Practice of a Science of Society*. London: Routledge and
   Kegan Paul, 1976.
Social Research XXXVII, No. 1 (Spring 1970) (essays in commemoration of
   Alfred Schutz).
Sokolowski, Robert. *The Formation of Husserl's Concept of Constitution*. The
   Hague: Martinus Nijhoff, 1964.
Soloveitchik, Joseph B. *Halakhic Man* (translated by Lawrence Kaplan). Phila-
   delphia: Jewish Publication Society of America, 1983.
Spiegelberg, Herbert. *Doing Phenomenology: Essays on and in Phenomenology*.
   The Hague: Martinus Nijhoff, 1975. Note: See Ch. 12: " 'We': A Lin-
   guistic and Phenomenological Analysis."
Spiegelberg, Herbert. *The Phenomenological Movement: A Historical Introduction*,
   2 vols., 2nd. ed. The Hague: Martinus Nijhoff, 1965. Note: A 3rd ed.,
   with the collaboration of Karl Schuhmann, was published by Martinus
   Nijhoff in 1982.
Spitzer, Leo. "Milieu and Ambience: An Essay in Historical Semantics." *Phi-
   losophy and Phenomenological Research* III (1942), pp 1–42 and 169–218.
Sprondel, Walter M., and Richard Grathoff (Eds. with a foreword). *Alfred
   Schutz und die Idee des Alltags in den Sozialwissenschaften*. Stuttgart: Ferdinand Enke, 1979.

Sternberger, Adolf. *Der verstandene Tod: Eine Untersuchung zu Martin Heideggers Existenzialontologie.* Leipzig: S. Hirzel, 1934. Note: Reprinted in New York by Garland Publishing, 1979.

(Stevens, Wallace.) *Letters of Wallace Stevens* (selected and edited by Holly Stevens). New York: Alfred A. Knopf, 1966.

Stonier, Alfred, and Karl Bode. "A New Approach to the Methodology of the Social Sciences." *Economica*, New Series, IV (1937), pp. 406–424.

Strasser, Stephan. *Understanding and Explanation: Basic Ideas Concerning the Humanity of the Human Sciences.* Pittsburgh: Duquesne University Press, 1985.

Straus, Erwin W. "Born to See, Bound to Behold: Reflections on the Function of Upright Posture in the Esthetic Attitude." *Tijdschrift voor Philosophie* XXVII (1965), pp. 659–688.

Straus, Erwin W. *Man, Time, and World: Two Contributions to Anthropological Psychology* (translated with a preface by Donald Moss with a foreword by Walter Bräutigam), Pittsburgh: Duquesne University Press, 1982.

Straus, Erwin W. *On Obsession: A Clinical and Methodological Study.* New York: Nervous and Mental Disease Monographs, 1948.

Straus, Erwin W. *Phenomenological Psychology: Selected Papers* (translated, in part, by Erling Eng). New York: Basic Books, 1966.

Straus, Erwin W. "Psychiatry and Philosophy" (translated by Erling Eng), in *Psychiatry and Philosophy* by Erwin W. Straus, Maurice Natanson, and Henri Ey (edited by Maurice Natanson with a preface by Erwin W. Straus and Maurice Natanson). Berlin: Springer-Verlag, 1969, pp. 1–83.

Theunissen, Michael. *The Other: Studies in the Social Ontology of Husserl, Heidegger, Sartre, and Buber* (translated by Christopher Macann with an introduction by Fred R. Dallmayr). Cambridge: MIT Press, 1984.

Thomason, Burke C. (with a foreword by Tom Bottomore). *Making Sense of Reification: Alfred Schutz and Constructionist Theory.* London: Macmillan, 1982.

Thurston, G. (revised by J. C. Burton). "Deaths," in *Taylor's Principles and Practice of Medical Jurisprudence* (edited by A. Keith Mant), 13th ed. Edinburgh: Churchill Livingstone, 1984, pp. 29–38.

Timasheff, Nicholas S., and George A. Theodorson. *Sociological Theory: Its Nature and Growth*, 4th ed. New York: Random House, 1976.

Toulemont, René. *L'Essence de la société selon Husserl.* Paris: Presses Universitaires de France, 1962.

Trilling, Lionel. *Sincerity and Authenticity.* Cambridge: Harvard University Press, 1971.

Trollope, Anthony. *Orley Farm.* New York: Dover Publications, 1981.

Uexküll, J. von. *Theoretical Biology* (translated by D. L. Mackinnon). London: Kegan Paul, Trench, Trubner, 1926.

Unamuno, Miguel de. *Our Lord Don Quixote: The Life of Don Quixote and Sancho with Related Essays* (translated by Anthony Kerrigan with an introduction by Walter Starkie). Princeton: Princeton University Press, 1967.

Varet, Gilbert. *Manuel de bibliographie philosophique*, 2 vols. Paris: Presses Universitaires de France, 1956.

Varnedoe, Kirk. *Duane Hanson.* New York: Harry N. Abrams, 1985.

Vinocur, John. "At Long Nazi Trial, the Sense of Horror is Vanishing in a

Murmur of Legalisms." *The New York Times*, November 10, 1978, p. A3.

Voegelin, Eric. *Anamnesis*. Munich: R. Piper, 1966.

Voegelin, Eric. *Anamnesis* (translated and edited by Gerhart Niemeyer). Notre Dame: University of Notre Dame Press, 1978.

Voegelin, Eric. *The New Science of Politics: An Introduction*. Chicago: University of Chicago Press, 1952.

Wagner, Helmut R. "Agreement in Discord: Alfred Schutz and Eric Voegelin," in *The Philosophy of Order: Essays on History, Consciousness, and Politics* (edited by Peter J. Opitz and Gregor Sebba). Stuttgart: Klett-Cotta, 1981, pp. 74–90. Note: see part III for important material on Schutz (in English).

Wagner, Helmut R. *Alfred Schutz: An Intellectual Biography*. Chicago: University of Chicago Press, 1983.

Wagner, Helmut R. "Intersubjectivity: Transcendental Problem or Sociological Conception." *Review of Sociological Theory* IV (1977), pp. 13–31.

Wagner, Helmut R. "Marx and Weber as Seen by Carl Mayer." *Social Research* XLII (1975), pp. 720–728.

Wagner, Helmut R. "Phenomenology and Contemporary Sociological Theory: The Contribution of Alfred Schutz." *Sociological Focus* II (1969), pp. 73–86.

Wagner, Helmut R. *Phenomenology of Consciousness and Sociology of the Life-World: An Introductory Study*. Edmonton: University of Alberta Press, 1983.

Wagner, Helmut R., with Ilja Srubar. *A Bergsonian Bridge to Phenomenological Psychology*. Washington, D.C.: Center for Advanced Research in Phenomenology and University Press of America, 1984.

Waldenfels, Bernhard. "The Despised Doxa: Husserl and the Continuing Crisis of Western Reason" (translated by J. Claude Evans). *Research in Phenomenology* XII (1982), pp. 21–38. Note: Reprinted in John Sallis (Ed.), *Husserl and Contemporary Thought*. Atlantic Highlands: Humanities Press, 1983, pp. 21–38.

Ward, J. A. *American Silences: The Realism of James Agee, Walker Evans, and Edward Hopper*. Baton Rouge: Louisiana State University Press, 1985.

Webb, Rodman B. *The Presence of the Past: John Dewey and Alfred Schutz on the Genesis and Organization of Experience*. Gainesville: University Presses of Florida, 1976.

Weber, Max. *The Theory of Social and Economic Organization* (translated by A. M. Henderson and Talcott Parsons and edited with an introduction by Talcott Parsons). New York: Oxford University Press, 1947.

Wells, Charles E. "Organic Mental Disorders," (Ch. 19) in *Comprehensive Textbook of Psychiatry/IV*, 4th ed. (edited by Harold I. Kaplan and Benjamin J. Sadock). Baltimore: Williams and Wilkins, 1985, pp. 851–870.

Werkmeister, W. H. *The Basis and Structure of Knowledge*. New York: Harper, 1948. Note: See, in particular, Ch. III: "The World About Us."

Wild, John. *Existence and the World of Freedom*. Englewood Cliffs: Prentice-Hall, 1963.

Wilkinson, Alec. *Moonshine: A Life in Pursuit of White Liquor*. New York: Alfred A. Knopf, 1985.

Williame, Robert. *Les Fondemonts phénoménologiques de la sociologie compréhensive: Alfred Schutz et Max Weber.* The Hague: Martinus Nijhoff, 1973.

Winch, Peter. *The Idea of a Social Science: and Its Relation to Philosophy.* London: Routledge and Kegan Paul, 1958.

Winston, Robert Watson. *Horace Williams: Gadfly of Chapel Hill.* Chapel Hill: University of North Carolina Press, 1942.

Woiwode, Larry. "Burial." *The New Yorker* XLIX (Nov. 19, 1973), pp. 50–82. Note: Reprinted as Ch. 1 in the author's *Beyond the Bedroom Wall: A Family Album.* New York: Avon Books (Bard Book), 1979.

Wolff, Kurt H. "Phenomenology and Sociology," in *A History of Sociological Analysis* (edited by Tom Bottomore and Robert Nisbet). New York: Basic Books, 1978, pp. 499–556.

Wolff, Kurt H. (Ed.). *Alfred Schutz: Appraisals and Developments.* Dordrecht: Martinus Nijhoff, 1984. Note: Reprinted from *Human Studies* VII: 2 (1984).

Wolff, Kurt H. (Ed.). *Georg Simmel: 1858–1918: A Collection of Essays, with Translations and a Bibliography.* Columbus: Ohio State University Press, 1959.

Wyschogrod, Edith. *Spirit in Ashes: Hegel, Heidegger, and Man-Made Death.* New Haven: Yale University Press, 1985.

Zaner, Richard M. "Theory of Intersubjectivity: Alfred Schutz." *Social Research* XXVIII (1961), pp. 71–94.

Zijderveld, Anton C. *The Abstract Society: A Cultural Analysis of Our Time.* Garden City: Doubleday (Anchor Books), 1971.

Zijderveld, Anton C. *On Clichés: The Supersedure of Meaning by Function in Modernity.* London: Routledge and Kegan Paul, 1979.

Zijderveld, Anton C. "Problem of Adequacy: Reflections on Alfred Schutz's Contribution to the Methodology of the Social-Sciences." *Archives Européennes de Sociologie* XIII (1972), pp. 176–190.

Zumthor, Paul. *La Vie quotidienne en Holland au temps de Rembrandt.* Paris: Librairie Hachette, 1959.

Final Note: The manuscripts and papers of Alfred Schutz are in The Beinecke Rare Book and Manuscript Library, Yale University.

INDEX

Note: With one exception, I have not in-
    cluded any reference to the Prologue to
    the Bibliography in the Index.

MAURICE NATANSON is Professor of Philosophy, Yale University. His *Edmund Husserl: Philosopher of Infinite Tasks* won the National Book Award in 1974. Mr. Natanson studied with Alfred Schutz from 1951–53.